UNITED NATIONS
DECADE FOR
HUMAN RIGHTS EDUCATION

UNITED NATIONS
DECADE FOR
HUMAN RIGHTS EDUCATION

Editor

Dr. Digumarti Bhaskara Rao

M.Sc., M.A., M.A., M.Ed., Ph.D.
Secretary
Academy of Communication Culture
Education Science and Service
Srinivasa Nagar Colony
Guntur–522 006
Andhra Pradesh
India

DISCOVERY PUBLISHING HOUSE
NEW DELHI-110002

First Published-2004
Reprint: 2011
ISBN 81-7141-887-2

Published by

DISCOVERY PUBLISHING HOUSE
4831/24, Ansari Road, Prahlad Street,
Darya Ganj, New Delhi-110002 (India)
Phone: 23279245 • Fax: 91-11-23253475
E-mail:dphtemp@indiatimes.com

Printed at:
Dynamic Printers, Delhi

Dedicated
To
Mr. Ch. V.K. Narasimha Rao, B.E.
Mr. Ch. Vasu Prakash, M.B.A.
Mr. Ch. Ajay Prakash, M.S. (USA)
Mr. Ch. Vijay Prakash, M.Sc.
The Founders of
Sri Prakash Vidya Niketan
S.V. College of Education
Sri Prakash Junior College
SPACES Degree College
SPACES Institute for PG Studies
Sri Prakash Residential Model High School
Sri Prakash Vidya Niketan
Sri Prakash Engineering College
Tuni–Payakaraopeta–Visakhapatnam
Andhra Pradesh
India

Foreword

The Universal Declaration of Human Rights calls upon every individual and every institution of society to promote respect for human rights and to strive for their universal and effective recognition. This call was reiterated during the World Conference on Human Rights in 1993 and given an institutional framework with the proclamation of the United Nations Decade for Human Rights Education (1995-2004).

During the Decade, Governments, international organisation, national institutions, non-governmental organisations, professional associations, all sectors of civil society and individuals are asked to establish partnerships and to concentrate their efforts on promoting a universal culture of human rights through human rights education, training and public information. The "International Plan of Action for the Decade" sets out detailed objectives for the international community: the assessment of needs and formulation of effective strategies; the building and strengthening of programmes and capacities for human rights education at the international, regional, national and local levels; the coordinated development of effective materials; the strengthening of the role and capacity of the mass media; and the global dissemination of the Universal Declaration of Human Rights.

I have made human Rights education one of my highest priorities, not only in the context of fulfilling my mandate to coordinate the implementation of the Plan of Action, but also because I firmly believe in the fundamental role of human rights education in empowering individuals to defend their rights and those of others. This empowerment can also make a critical contribution to the prevention of human rights violations.

The Decade for Human Right Education provides us with an important common framework. It focuses on the development and strengthening of comprehensive, effective and sustainable educational programmes at the local, national, regional and implementation levels. National and local initiatives should be supported and encouraged by the international community.

The proclamation of the Decade reaffirms, as already stated in several international human rights instruments, that educational in and for human rights is a right in itself, i.e., the right of all to learn about the rights and dignity of all and about means to ensure their respect. This should be our common commitment, since all organisations and individuals have a role to play in the organisation of and participation in formal and non-formal human rights education programmes, at all levels of society.

The decade, undoubtedly, constitutes a formidable challenge, I count on the support of all partners, I wish to encourage the cooperation of all institutions, organisations and individual working for the purposes and principles on which the Decade is based. The Decade for Human Rights Education is our common project, and its success is entirely dependent on the contribution of each and every one of us to this global effort.

Mary Robinson
United Nations
High Commissioner for Human Rights

Preface

The United Nations proclaimed the United Nations Decade for Human Rights Education (1995-2004) in order to realise the objectives of the Universal Declaration of Human Rights (1948) and to respect the call made during the World Conference on Human Rights (1993).

The governments, international organisations, professional associations, all sectors of civil society and individuals have been especially encouraged to establish partnerships and concentrate efforts for human rights education during the Decade through the International Plan of Action for the Decade. By following and implementing the Plan of Action, almost all the world nations put the human rights education on a right track and it is sailing smoothly.

This book on the United Nations Decade for Human Rights Education presents some of the important documents of the United Nations and the Office of the United Nations High Commissioner for Human Rights to make the readers aware of the objectives and the Plan of Action of the Decade and the initiatives taken up by the individual countries in implementing the Plan of Action. An inclusion is also made of the International Bill of Human Rights and the status of the rights mentioned in the Universal Declaration of Human Rights.

This book will be of the great use to the people and personnel involved in the promotion and popularisation of human rights and human rights education.

I am very much thankful to Ms. Mary Robinson, United Nations High Commissioner for Human Rights for her kind encouragement in every endeavour. I am also thankful to the Department of Public Information of the United Nations and office of the United Nations High Commissioner for Human Rights for the prompt responses they give to my queries. All of these made this publication possible.

Dr. Digumarti Bhaskara Rao
Research Director in Education
Nagarjuna University
br_digumarti@rediffmail.com

Sai Soudha
D-43, S.V.N. Colony
Guntur– 522 006
Andhra Pradesh (India)

Contents

1

Human Rights Education Decade: UN General Assembly Resolution

Human Rights Education Decade

General Assembly Resolution 48/127 of 20 December 1993

The General Assembly,

Guided by the fundamental and universal principles enshrined in the Charter of the United Nations and the Universal Declaration of Human Rights,

Reaffirming article 26 of the Universal Declaration of Human Rights, according to which education shall be directed to the full development of the human personality and to the strengthening of respect for human rights and fundamental freedoms,

Recalling the provisions of other international human rights instruments, such as those of article 13 of the International Covenant on Economic, Social and Cultural Rights and article 20 of the Convention on the Rights of the Child, that reflect the aims of the aforementioned article,

Convinced that human rights education is a universal priority in that it contributes to a concept of development consistent with the dignity of the human person, which must include consideration of the diversity of groups such as children, women, youths, persons with disabilities, the ageing, indigenous people, minorities and other groups,

Aware that human rights education involves more than providing information but rather is a comprehensive life-long process by which people at all levels of development and in all strata of society learn respect for the dignity of others and the means and methods of ensuring that respect within a democratic society,

Taking into account the efforts made by educators and non-governmental organisations in all parts of the world, as well as by intergovernmental organisations, including the United Nations Educational, Scientific and Cultural Organisation, the International Labour Organisation and the United Nations Children's Fund, to promote education in accordance with the aforementioned principles,

Considering the World Plan of Action on Education for Human Rights and democracy, adopted by the International Congress on Education for Human Rights and Democracy, convened by the United Nations Educational, Scientific and Cultural Organisation at Montreal from 8 to 11 March 1993, and the statement by the Congress that education for human rights and democracy, is itself a human rights, and a prerequisite for the realisation of human rights, democracy and social justice,

Aware of the experience in human rights education of United Nations peace-building operations, including the United Nations Observer Mission in El Salvador and the United Nations Transnational Authority in Cambodia.

Taking into account Commission on Human Rights resolution 1993/56 of 9 March 1993, in which the Commission recommended that knowledge of human rights, both in its theoretical dimension and in its practical application, should be established as a priority in educational policies,

Bearing in mind the Vienna Declaration and Programme of Action, adopted by the World Conference on Human Rights at Vienna on 25 June 1993, in particular section II, paragraphs 78 to 82,

1. Appeals to all Governments to step up their efforts to eradicate illiteracy and to direct education towards the full development of the human personality and to the strengthening of respect for human rights and fundamental freedoms;

2. Urges governmental and non-governmental educational agencies to intensify their efforts to establish and implement programmes of human rights education, as recommended in the Vienna Declaration and Programme of Action;

3. Takes note of the World Plan of Action on Education for Human Rights and Democracy adopted by the International Congress on Education for Human Rights and Democracy, and recommends that Governments and non-governmental organisations consider it is preparing national plans for human rights education;

4. Requests the Commission of Human Rights, in cooperation with Member States, human rights treaty-monitoring bodies, other appropriate bodies and competent non-governmental organisations, to consider proposals for a United Nations decade for human rights education, which should be incorporated by the Secretary-General into a plan of action for such a decade and submitted, through the Economic and Social Council, to the General Assembly at its forty-ninth session, with a view to the proclamation of a decade for human rights education;

5. Requests the Secretary-General to consider the establishment of a voluntary fund for human rights education, with special provision for the support of the human rights education activities of non-governmental organisations, to be administered by the Centre for Human Rights of the Secretariat;

6. Invites the specialised agencies and United Nations programmes to develop suitable activities in their respective fields of competence to further the objectives of human rights education;

7. Requests the Secretary-General to bring the present resolution to the attention of all members of the international community and to intergovernmental and non-governmental organisations concerned with human rights and education;

8. Calls upon international, regional and national non-governmental organisations, in particular those concerned with women, labour, development and the environment, as

well as all other social justice groups, human rights advocates, educators, religious organisations and the media, to increase their involvement in formal and non-formal education in human rights and to cooperate with the Centre for Human Rights in preparing for a United Nations decade for human rights education;

9. Urges the existing human rights monitoring bodies to place particular emphasis on implementation by Member States of their international obligation to promote human rights education;

10. Decides to consider this matter at its forty-ninth session under the item entitled Human rights questions.

2

United Nations Decade for Human Rights Education

Resolution Adopted by the General Assembly

[On the Report of the Third Committee (A/49/610/Add. 2)]

49/184. United Nations Decade for Human Rights Education

The General Assembly,

Guided by the fundamental and universal principles enshrined in the Charter of the United Nations and the Universal Declaration of Human Rights[1],

Reaffirming article 26 of the Universal Declaration of Human Rights, according to which "education shall be directed to the full development of the human personality and to the strengthening of respect for human rights and fundamental freedoms",

Recalling the provisions of other international human rights instruments, such as those of article 13 of the International on Economic, Social and Cultural Rights[2] and article 28 of the Convention on the Rights of the Child[3] that reflect the aims of the aforementioned article,

---

[1] Resolution 217 A (III).

[2] See resolution 2200 A (XXI), annex.

[3] Resolution 44/25, annex.

Taking into account Commission on Human Rights resolution 1993/56 of 9 March 1993[4] in which the Commission recommended that knowledge of human rights, both in its theoretical dimension and in its practical application, should be established as a priority in education policies,

Considering Commission on Human Rights resolution 1994/51 of 4 March 1994[5] in which the Commission encouraged the United Nations High Commissioner for Human Rights to include among his specific objectives a plan of action for the United Nations decade for human rights education and invited the Secretary-General to submit to the General Assembly at its forty-ninth session, through the Economic and Social Council, a plan of action for a decade for human rights education,

Convinced that human rights education should involved more than the provision of information and should constitute a comprehensive life-long process by which people at all levels in development and in all strata of society learn respect for the dignity of others and the means and methods of ensuring that respect in all societies,

Convinced also that human rights education contributes to a concept of development consistent with the dignity of women and men of all ages that takes into account the diverse segments of society such as children, indigenous peoples, minorities and disabled persons.

Taking into account the efforts to promote human rights education made by educators and non-governmental organisations in all parts of the world, as well as by intergovernmental organisations, including the United Nations Educational, Scientific and Cultural Organisations the International Labour Organisation and the United Nations Children's Fund.

Convinced that each woman, man and child, to realise, their full human potential, must be made aware of all their human rights—civil, cultural, economic, political and social.

---

[4] See *Official Records of the Economic and Social Council, 1993, Supplement No. 3* (E/1993/23), chap. II, sect. A.

[5] Ibid., *1994 Supplement No. 4* and corrigendum (E/1994/24 and Corr. 1), chap. II, sect. A.

Believing that human rights education constitutes an important vehicle for the elimination of gender-based discrimination and ensuring equal opportunities through the promotion and protection of the human rights of women,

Considering the World Plan of Action on Education for Human Rights and Democracy[6] adopted by the International Congress on Education for Human Rights and Democracy convened by the United Nations Educational, Scientific and Cultural Organisation at Montreal from 8 to 11 March 1993, according to which education for human rights and democracy is itself a human right and a prerequisite for the realisation of human rights, democracy and social justice,

Recalling that it is the responsibility of the United Nations High Commissioner for Human Rights to coordinate relevant United Nations education and public information programmes in the field of human rights[7],

Taking note of the report of the United Nations High Commissioner for Human Rights[8] in paragraph 94 of which he declared that human rights education is essential for the encouragement of harmonious inter-community relations, for natural tolerance and understanding and finally for peace,

Aware of the experience in human rights education of United Nations peace-building operations, including the United Nations Observer Mission in El Salvador and the United Nations Transitional Authority in Cambodia,

Bearing in mind the Vienna Declaration and Programme of Action, adopted by the World Conference on Human Rights on 25 June 1993[9] in particular section II, paragraphs 78 to 82 thereof.

1. Takes note with appreciation of the report of the Secretary-General[10] on human rights education, submitted in

---

[6] See A/CONF.157/PC/42/Add. 6.

[7] See resolution 48/141, para, 4 (*c*).

[8] A/49/36.

[9] A/CONF. 157/24 (Part I), chap. III.

[10] A/49/261-E/1994/110 and Add. 1.

accordance with the request contained in General Assembly resolution 48/127 of 20 December 1993;

2. Proclaims the ten-year period beginning on 1 January 1995 the United Nations Decade for Human Rights Education;

3. Welcomes the Plan of Action for the United Nations Decade for Human Rights Education. 1995-2005, as contained in the report of the Secretary-General[11] and invites Governments to submit comments, with a view to supplementing the Plan of Action;

4. Invites the Secretary-General to submit proposals, taking into account the views expressed by Governments, for the purpose indicated in paragraph 3;

5. Appeals to all Governments to contribute to the implementation of the Plan of Action and to step up their efforts to eradicate illiteracy and to direct education towards the full development of the human personality and to the strengthening of respect for human rights and fundamental freedoms;

6. Urges governmental and non-governmental educational agencies to intensity their efforts to establish and implement programmes of human rights education, as recommended in the Plan of Action, in particular by preparing and implementing national plans for human rights education;

7. Requests the United Nations High Commissioner for Human Rights to coordinate the implementation of the Plan of Action;

8. Requests the Centre for Human Rights of the Secretariat and the Commission on Human Rights, in cooperation with Member States, human rights treaty-monitoring bodies, other appropriate bodies and competent non-governmental organisations to support efforts of the United Nations High Commission for Human Rights to coordinate the Plan of Action;

9. Requests the Secretary-General to consider establishing a voluntary fund for human rights education, with special provision for the support of the human rights education

[11] A/49/261-E/1994/110/Add. 1, annex.

activities of non-governmental organisations, to be administered by the centre for human rights;

10. Invites the specialised agencies and United Nations programmes to contribute, within their respective spheres of competence, to the implementation of the Plan of Action;

11. Requests the Secretary-General to bring the present resolution to the attention of all members of the international community and to intergovernmental and non-governmental organisations concerned with human rights and education;

12. Calls upon international, regional and national non-governmental organisations, in particular those concerned with women, labour, development and the environment, as well as all other social justice groups, human rights advocates, educators, religious organisations and the media to increase their involvement in formal and non-formal education in human rights and to cooperate with the Centre for Human Rights in implementing the United Nations Decade for Human Rights Education;

13. Requests the existing human rights monitoring bodies to place emphasis on the implementation by Member States of their international obligation to promote human rights education;

14. Decides to consider this matter at its fiftieth session under the item entitled "Human rights questions".

94th plenary meeting
23 December 1994

3

United Nations Decade for Human Rights Education: Commission on Human Rights Resolution

United Nations Decade for Human Rights Education

Commission on Human Rights Resolution 1996/44

The Commission on Human Rights,

Guided by the Charter of the United Nations and the Universal Declaration of Human Rights,

Reaffirming article 26 of the Universal Declaration of Human Rights, in accordance with which education shall be directed to the full development of the human personality and to the strengthening of respect for human rights and fundamental freedoms,

Recalling the provisions of other international human rights instruments, including article 13 of the international Covenant on Economic, Social and Cultural Rights and article 28 of the Convention on the Rights of the Child, that reflect the aims of the aforementioned article,

Taking into account Commission on Human Rights resolution 1993/56 of 9 March 1993, in which the Commission recommended that knowledge of human rights, both in its theoretical dimension and its practical, should be established as a priority in education policies,

Believing that each women, man and child, to realise their full human potential, must be made aware of all their human rights, civil, cultural, economic, political and social,

Believing also that human rights education constitutes an important vehicle for the elimination of gender-based discrimination and ensuring equal opportunities through the promotion and protection of the human rights of women,

Convinced that human rights education should involve more than the provision of information and should constitute a comprehensive life-long process by which people at all levels of development and in all strata of society learn respect for the dignity of others and the means and methods of ensuring that respect in all societies,

Convinced also that human rights education contributes to a concept of development consistent with the dignity of women and men of all ages which takes into account the diversity of society including children, indigenous people, minorities and disabled persons, bearing in mind the Vienna Declaration and Programme of Action (A/CONF.157/23) adopted by the World Conference on Human Rights, in particular Part II, paragraphs 78 to 82 thereof,

Recalling the responsibility of the United Nations High Commissioner for Human Rights to coordinate relevant United Nations education and public information programmes in the field of human rights,

Recalling General Assembly resolution 49/184 of 23 December 1994 by which the Assembly proclaimed the ten-year period beginning on 1 January 1995 the United Nations Decade for Human Rights Education, welcomed the Plan of Action for the Decade, as contained in the report of the Secretary-General (A/49/261-E/1994/110/Add. 1, annex), and requested the United Nations High Commissioner for Human Rights to coordinate the implementation of the Plan of Action,

Noting General Assembly resolution 50/177 of 22 December 1995 by which the Assembly appealed to all Governments to contribute to the implementation of the Plan of Action and, in particular, in accordance with national conditions, to establish a national focal point (national committee) for human rights education and a resource and training centre for human rights education or, where such a centre already exists, to work towards its strengthening, and to develop and implement an action-oriented national plan for human rights education, as foreseen in the Plan of Action,

1. Takes note with appreciation of the report of the United Nations High Commissioner for Human Rights on the implementation of the Plan of Action for the United Nations Decade on Human Rights Education (E/CN.4/1996/51);

2. Requests the United Nations High Commissioner for Human Rights to accelerate, within existing resources, the implementation of the Plan of Action and, in particular, to encourage and facilitate the establishment of national Plans of action, focal points and centres of human rights education in Member States in accordance with national conditions;

3. Invites all Governments to consider the establishment, in accordance with national conditions, of national focal points and plans of action for the implementation of the Plan of Action of the Decade, including the building and strengthening of programmes and capacities for formal and informal human rights education and cooperation with non-governmental organisations and the private sector in pursuing the objectives of the Plan of Action;

4. Requests human rights monitoring bodies to consider adopting a general comment on human rights education, placing emphasis on the implementation by Member States of their international obligation to promote human rights education;

5. Invites all relevant specialised agencies, in particular the United Nations Educational, Scientific and Cultural Organisation and the International Labour Organisation, United Nations programmes, especially the United Nations Children's Fund, and other intergovernmental organisations to enhance their contribution, within their respective spheres of competence, to the implementation of the Plan of Action and to continue cooperating with the High Commissioner for that purpose;

6. Calls upon international, regional and national non-governmental organisations, in particular those concerned with women, children, indigenous people, minorities, labour, development and the environment, as well as other social justice groups, human rights advocates, educators, religious and community organisations and the media, to increase their involvement in formal and non-formal education in human rights and to cooperate with the High Commissioner and the Centre for Human Rights in implementing the Plan of Action;

7. Invites the United Nations High Commissioner for Human Rights to seek the views of States on ways and means to increase support to the Decade, with special emphasis on activities of non-governmental organisations in the field of human rights education, and on the advisability of establishing a voluntary fund for this purpose, and to include this information in this report to the fifty-third session of the Commission on Human Rights;

8. Decides to continue consideration of the question of human rights education at its fifty-third session under the same agenda item.

52nd meeting 19 April 1996

[Adopted without a vote]

4

International Plan of Action for the United Nations Decade for Human Rights Education 1995-2004

I. Normative Basis and Definition

1. The United Nations Decade for Human Rights Education shall be based upon the provisions of the international human rights instruments, with particular reference to those provisions addressing human rights education, including article 26 of the Universal Declaration of Human Rights, article 13 of the International covenant on Economic, Social and Cultural Rights, article 29 of the Convention on the Rights of the Child, article 10 of the Convention on the Elimination of All Forms of Discrimination against Women, article 7 of the Convention on the Elimination of All Forms of Racial Discrimination, paragraphs 33 and 34 of the Vienna Declaration and paragraphs 78 to 82 of its Programme of Action.

2. In accordance with those provisions, and for the purposes of the Decade, human rights education shall be defined as training, dissemination and information efforts aimed at the building of a universal culture of human rights through the imparting of knowledge and skills and the moulding of attitudes and directed to:

   (a) The strengthening of respect for human rights and fundamental freedoms;

(*b*) The full development of the human personality and the sense of its dignity;

(*c*) The promotion of understanding, tolerance, gender equality and friendship among all nations, indigenous peoples and racial, national, ethnic, religious and linguistic groups;

(*d*) The enabling of all persons to participate effectively in a free society;

(*e*) The furtherance of the activities of the United Nations for the maintenance of peace;

II. General Guiding Principles

3. The United Nations Decade for Human Rights Education shall be guided by the definition and normative basis set out in part I of the present Plan of Action and shall further be directed towards creating the broadest possible awareness and understanding of all of the norms, concepts and values enshrined in the Universal of Human Rights, the International Covenant on Civil and Political Rights, the International Covenant on Economic, Social and Cultural Rights and in other relevant international human rights instruments. The Decade is placed within the context of action of States and others to eradicate illiteracy and understands education to be a constant factor in the multidimensional life of individuals and of society of which human rights are an integral part.

4. A comprehensive approach to education for human rights, including, civil, cultural, economic, political and social rights and recognising the indivisibility and interdependence of all rights, as defined by the United Nations, shall be adopted for all activities under the Decade.

5. Education for the purpose of the Decade shall be conceived to include the equal participation of women and men of all age groups and all sectors of society both in formal learning through schools and vocational and professional training, as well as in non-formal learning through institutions of civil society, the family and the mass media.

6. In order to enhance their effectiveness, human rights education efforts for the Decade shall be shaped in such a way as to be relevant to the daily lives of learners, and shall seek to engage learners in a dialogue about the ways and means of transforming human rights from the expression of abstract norms to the reality of their social; economic, cultural and political conditions.

7. In recognition of the interdependence and mutually reinforcing nature of democracy, development and human rights education under the Decade shall seek to further effective democratic participation in the political, economic, social and cultural spheres, and shall be utilised as a means of promoting economic and social progress and people-centred sustainable development.

8. Human rights education under the decade shall combat and be free of gender bias, racial and other stereotypes.

9. Human rights education under the Decade shall seek both to impart skills and knowledge to learners and to affect positively their attitudes and behaviour, consistent with all other principles set forth in the present Plan of Action and in the international human rights instruments upon which it is based.

III. Objectives

10. The objectives of the decade shall include:

(a) The assessment of needs and the formulation of effective strategies for the furtherance of human rights education at all school levels, in vocational training and formal as well as non-formal learning;

(b) The building and strengthening of programmes and capacities for human rights education at the international, regional, national and local levels;

(c) The coordinated development of human rights education materials;

(d) The strengthening of the role and capacity of the mass media in the furtherance of human rights education;

(e) The global dissemination of the Universal Declaration of Human Rights in the maximum possible number of languages and in other forms appropriate for various levels of literacy and for the disabled.

IV. Principal Actors

11. Governments should play an active role in the implementation of the programme of the Decade through the development of national plans of action for human rights education, the introduction or strengthening of national human rights curricula in their formal educational systems, the conducting of national information campaigns on human rights and the opening of public access to human rights resource, information and training centres, as well as through enhanced donor support for relevant voluntary funds and international and national human rights education programmes.

12. National human rights institutions, such as human rights commissions, offices of the ombudsman and human rights research and training institutes should play a central role in the development, coordination and implementation of human rights education programmes at the national level.

13. The active engagement of national non-governmental organisations, grass-roots organisations, professional associations and interested individual, shall be encouraged to assist in the realisation of the goals of the Decade. To that end, national organisations should be given the full support of international programmes. Governments and others to assist them in their human rights educational activities, both through technical assistance and training and through financial support to aid them to strengthening their role in civil society.

14. The United Nations High Commissioner for Human Rights is the highest official of the United Nations dealing with human rights matters and is specifically responsible for coordinating relevant United Nations education and public information programmes in the field of human rights, in keeping with General Assembly resolution 48/141 of 20 December 1993.

15. The United Nations High Commissioner for Human Rights, in consultation with the United Nations Educational, Scientific and Cultural Organisation (UNESCO), shall continue to provide Governments, on request, with human rights education, training, information, fellowships and advisory services programmes. The Office of the High Commissioner for Human Rights should continue to place emphasis, in this regard, on the training of teachers, police, prison, officials, lawyers, judges, government officials, the media, the military, non-governmental organisations, electoral officials and the general public. The Office should also continue to provide human rights training to international civil servants, development officers and peacekeepers.

16. United Nations human rights treaty monitoring bodies, the Commission on Human Rights, the Sub-Commission on Prevention of Discrimination and Protection of Minorities and all other United Nations human rights bodies and programmes shall, in the course of their mandated functions during the decade, encourage the furtherance of human rights education, including through appropriate recommendations to States, to the High Commissioner for Human Rights and to others involved in human rights education.

17. UNESCO, by reason of its long experience in education educational methodology and human rights and through its network of UNESCO schools, clubs, human rights chairs and national commissions, shall play a central role in the design, implementation and evaluation of projects under the Plan of Action. Accordingly, UNESCO will be called upon to cooperate closely with the Office of the High Commissioner for Human Rights in the implementation of the Plan.

18. Similarly, other United Nations specialised agencies, units of the Secretariat and programmes involved in human rights educational activities, including the United Nations Children's Fund (UNICEF), the International Labour Organisation (ILO), the Office of the United Nations High Commissioner for Refugees (UNHCR), the United Nations Development Programme (UNDP), the United Nations

Voluntary (UNV), the United Nations Environment Programme (UNDP), the United Nations Centre for Human Settlements (Habitat), the Centre for Social Development and Humanitarian Affairs, the United Nations University (UNU) and various United Nations institutes engaged in research and training shall be encouraged to work with the High Commissioner for Human Rights in order that existing capacities for human rights education may be fully coordinated and mobilised towards the objectives of the Decade.

19. Other international organisations, including intergovernmental and non-governmental organisations active in the field of human rights shall be encouraged to continue and enhance their activities in the area of human rights education and to avail themselves of the coordination of the High Commissioner for Human Rights for the purposes of the Decade.

V. Target Groups

20. Activities carried out under the Decade shall be designed to bring the objectives of the Decade to as wide an audience as possible, through both formal and non-formal education and, to this end, should encourage an approach that is designed to build permanent capacity, including through the training of trainers.

21. The general public shall be the subject of far-reaching human rights information efforts to inform them of their rights and responsibilities under the international human rights instruments.

22. Human rights education initiatives taken under the Decade shall include the use of audiovisual and multimedia materials, with a view to the effective delivery of human rights education to people at all levels of literacy and education and to persons with disabilities.

23. Special emphasis shall be given in human rights education activities under the Decade to the human rights of women, children, the aged, minorities, refugees, indigenous peoples, persons in extreme poverty, persons with HIV infection of AIDS and other vulnerable groups.

24. Special attention shall be given to the training of the police, prison officials, lawyers, judges, teachers and curriculum developers, the armed forces, international civil servants, development officers and peacekeepers, non-governmental organisations, the media, government officials, parliamentarians and other groups that are in a particular position to effect the realisation of human rights.

25. Schools, universities, professional and vocational training programmes and institutions should be encouraged and assisted in developing human rights curricula and corresponding teaching and resource materials, with the help of Governments and international donors and programmes, for incorporation into formal education at the early childhood, primary, secondary, post-secondary and adult education levels.

26. Appropriate institutions of civil society, including non-governmental organisations, workers' and employers' organisations, labour unions, the mass media, religious organisations, community organisations, the family, independent information, resource and training centres and others, for the purpose of incorporating human rights education into non-formal programmes, should be encouraged and assisted in developing and delivering such non-formal programmes, with the help of Governments and international donors and programmes.

VI. Structure for Coordination and Implementation

27. The United Nations High Commissioner for Human Rights will promote and coordinate the implementation of the present Plan of Action. The High Commissioner shall consult with the United Nations human rights treaty-monitoring and Charter-based human rights bodies regarding the Plan of Action and consider ways of supporting any recommendations made by those bodies in the area of human rights education. The High Commissioner will also consult closely with Governments, regional organisations, national institutions, specialised agencies, non-governmental organisations grass-roots and professional associations, and will prepare an annual report on the progress made at all levels based on information supplied by those sources.

28. In recognition of the fact that action at the national and local levels is crucial to the effective promotion of human rights education, as is an effective international coordination structure, the Plan of Action envisages that:

(a) National focal points for human rights education should be designated in each State, according to national conditions. Such focal points may consist of specially constituted committees including representatives or relevant government agencies, non-governmental organisations, the private sector and educators; or alternatively, existing appropriate structures or organisations, such as ombudsman offices, national human rights commissions or national human rights training and research institutes may be designated to perform this function;

(b) Each national focal point should be charged with identifying national human rights education needs, developing a national plan of action, raising funds, coordinating with regional and international bodies involved in implementing the objectives of the Decade and reporting to the High Commissioner for Human Rights on needs, proposals and progress made towards the realisation of the goals of the Decade;

(c) Each national focal point shall also serve as a conduit for the channelling of international and regional input, information and support to the local and grass-roots levels in their respective countries;

(d) Each State shall be encouraged to establish a national human rights resource and training centre of engaging in research, training of trainers, preparation, collection, translation, and dissemination of human rights materials, and organisations of conferences, workshops and courses or, where such centres already exist, to work towards their strengthening.

(e) International programmes and activities, including those of the United Nations and other international agencies, donor Governments and intergovernmental and non-

governmental organisations should provide stimulus and support to national and local efforts in advancing the objectives of the Decade.

VII. Programme of Implementation

29. The particular objectives of the Decade, the programme of implementation for the realisation of those objectives and the means for follow-up and assessment of each programme element shall be as described below.

A. COMPONENT ONE: ASSESSING NEEDS AND FORMULATING STRATEGIES

Objectives

30. The objective of component one is to assess needs and to formulate effective strategies for the furtherance of human rights education at the international, regional, national and local levels.

Programme Elements

31. The Office of the High Commissioner for Human Right, in co-operation with UNESCO, shall conduct, in 1995, a preliminary survey and evaluation of existing human rights education programmes and initiatives at the international, regional and national levels, and shall issue a report of the results of that survey and evaluation.

32. The preliminary report shall take into account all available information on existing programmes and initiatives, shall identify shortcomings and needs for the realisation of the goals of the Decade and shall make recommendations for action to address those needs effectively during the Decade.

33. For the purposes of the High Commissioner's preliminary report, all participating national focal points, international and regional organisations, non-governmental organisations, specialised agencies and programmes, and other interested partners, shall be requested to provide relevant information to the High Commissioner, based upon their own independent assessments and activities. National focal points, in particular, shall be requested to conduct detailed assessments in their own countries and to report thereon to the High Commissioner.

34. The survey and evaluation and the resulting, preliminary report shall seek to identify with particular, at the international, regional and national levels, *inter alia,* the number and types of human rights educational materials available, existing human rights educational institutes, centres and permanent focal points, national percentages of teachers trained in human rights education, the percentage of schools having adopted human rights curricula at the primary, secondary and post-secondary levels, and number and types of human rights education components in professional training and non-formal education programmes.

35. The preliminary report shall identify, as well, the needs and requirements of Members States, non-governmental organisations and other implementing partners for the enhancement of existing human rights education programmes and for the creation of new programmes in order to contribute to the objectives of the Decade and shall make recommendations to those ends.

36. The report should also explore other aspects of the socialisation process, outside of traditional education, with a view to expanding human rights education in new directions so that human rights values may become more effectively integrated throughout society.

37. Annexed to the report should be a roster of national focal points, international and regional organisation cooperating in the Decade, existing human rights research and training institutes and centres, and other Decade partners. Information should also be provided on agencies, organisations, foundations and institutions providing financial and technical assistance to national governmental and non-governmental educational institutions and organisations engaged in human rights education.

Assessment and Follow-up

38. Following the publication of the preliminary report of the High Commissioner, the Office of the High Commissioner for Human Rights shall convene an international planning conference on the Decade, with the participation of UNESCO,

other United Nations agencies and human rights bodies participating in the Decade, representatives of regional and international organisations, non-governmental organisations, donor Governments, educators and other experts from all parts of the world.

39. The conference will review the preliminary report of the High Commissioner and develop detailed plans for the implementation of its recommendations and for the allocation of responsibilities to that end. Such plans will include timetables, designation of local, national, regional and international implementing agencies, budgets and implementation and funding strategies.

40. The High Commissioner will use the meeting as an opportunity to appeal to donors to support the funding of the various programmes resulting from the preliminary report and the conference.

41. The conclusions of the meeting will be contained in a report, which will be complementary to the preliminary report of the High Commissioner and which will be made available together with the preliminary report to all organisations, Governments and national focal points participating in the Decades.

42. Upon receipt of the complementary reports, all national focal points will be requested to develop a five-year detailed national implementation plan for human rights education including target groups, methodologies, timetables, budgets and funding strategies, covering efforts to meet the objectives of the Decade up to the mid-term evaluation period in the year 2000.

B. COMPONENT TWO: STRENGTHENING INTERNATIONAL PROGRAMMES AND CAPACITIES

Objectives

43. The objective of component two is to build and strengthen programmes and capacities for human rights education at the international level.

Programme Elements

44. The Office of the High Commissioner for Human Rights will continue and enhance its activities relating to programme development in the field of targeted human rights education, including the production of handbooks and training manuals on human rights for selected audience. The Office will ensure the broad distribution of its manuals and handbooks on human rights and social work, human rights and elections, human rights and pre-trial detention, and human rights reporting, and will produce further manuals and handbooks on human rights and national institutions, human rights and the police, human rights and prisons, human rights and the administration of justice, human rights and the armed forces, human rights and constitutions, human rights and conflict resolution, human rights and teachers, human rights and the media, and human rights and parliament. In these materials, the universality, indivisibility and interdependence of all rights should be reflected, and they should specifically address economic, social and cultural rights.

45. The Office of the High Commissioner for Human Rights will continue and enhance its technical cooperation activities relating to human rights education, both for the general public and for specialised audiences, under the programme of advisory services and technical assistance in the field of human rights.

46. The Office of the High Commissioner for Human Rights, in co-operation with UNESCO, will develop model human rights curricula, pedagogical techniques and teaching materials for primary and secondary schools. The Office, under its programme of advisory services and technical assistance in the field of human rights, will utilise these materials in its provision of technical assistance to requesting States.

47. Each specialised agency will be requested to enhance its efforts in the area of human rights education and to appoint a human rights education liaison officer to work with the Office of the High Commissioner for Human Rights in the Development of joint educational activities relating to human

rights in the areas of competence of each agency. Each agency will provide information to the High Commissioner on programmes undertaken and materials produced in the field of human rights education for the High Commissioner's preliminary, mid-term and final reports.

48. The Office of the High Commissioner for Human Rights will promote the organisation of international workshops to identify concepts, materials and methods for human rights education on priority human rights themes.

49. Consistent with the directions of the World Conference on Human Rights in its Vienna Declaration and Programme of Action the Office of the High Commissioner for Human Rights will continue and enhance its activities aimed at assisting peacekeepers, international civil servants and development officers in integrating human rights standards, concepts and methods into the planning and implementation of their work. To that end, the Office should develop specific training programmes for each of these groups, and should cooperate with the relevant agencies and departments of the United Nations in incorporating such programmes into their activities.

50. The Office of the High Commissioner for Human Rights, as well as relevant sepcialised agencies and international programmes, will explore possibilities for the development and use of advanced technologies, including telecommunications networks, electronic mail databases and data exchange to facilitate networking among international programmes, national focal points, educators and resource and training centres involved in the Decade.

51. The Secretary-General shall be requested to establish a United Nations voluntary fund for human rights education, to be administered by the Office of the High Commissioner for Human Rights through the programme of advisory services and technical assistance. The fund shall be used to support activities under the Decade, including support for building human rights education organisation capacities in governmental institutions and non-governmetal organisations at the national level.

Assessment and follow-up

52. The High Commissioner will report on progress and developments in all of these programmes elements in preliminary, mid-term and final reports and will also make recommendations for advancing the objectives of these elements in each such report. Each international actor associated with these programme elements will accordingly be called upon to provide updated and detailed information to the High Commissioner.

C. COMPONENT THREE: STRENGEHENING REGIONAL PROGRAMMES AND CAPACITIES

Objectives

53. The objective of component three is to build and strengthen programmes and capacities for human rights education at the regional level.

Programme Elements

54. All regional and subregional human rights organisations will be requested to enhance their efforts in the area of human rights education and will also be requested to appoint a human rights education liaison officer to work with the Office of the High Commissioner for Human Rights in the development of joint educational activities relating to human rights in the respective regions of each organisation. Liaison officers will, as well, be requested to report to the High Commissioner, on behalf of each organisation, on programmes undertaken and materials produced in the field of human rights education, for purposes of the High Commissioner's preliminary, mid-term and final reports.

55. In regions or subregions where such organisations do not yet exist, the Office of the High Commissioner will encourage their establishment through the convening of workshops and through the provision of technical assistance, where appropriate.

Assessment and Follow-up

56. The High Commissioner will report on progress and developments in all of these programmes elements in

preliminary, mid-term and final reports and will also make recommendations for advancing the objectives of these elements in each such report. Each regional organisation participating in these elements will accordingly be called upon to provide up-dated and detailed information to the High Commissioner.

D. COMPONENT FOUR: STRENGTHENING NATIONAL PROGRAMMES AND CAPACITIES

Objectives

57. The objectives of component four is to build and strengthen programmes and capacities for human rights education at the national level.

Programme Elements

58. Every State will be requested to draw up a national plan of action for human rights education, reflecting the principles and objectives of this international plan and forming an integral part of a comprehensive national plan of action for human rights. Such national plan of action for human rights education, should be completed during 1995, in consultation with all relevant national and local actors and groups, and should be transmitted to the High Commissioner for Human Rights for purposes of effective coordination and cooperation in their implementation. Each national plan should contain specific objectives, strategies and programmes for the enhancement of human rights education in pre-schools, primary and secondary schools, higher education, professional schools, the training of public officials and in non-formal learning, including general public information. National focal points should periodically review the implementation of the frameworks and revise them as necessary.

59. As described in paragraph 28 above, every State will be requested to designate a national focal point for human rights education, which shall assist in the identification of needs, the development of a national plan of action, fund-raising and international and local liaison and coordination with the High Commissioner for Human Rights.

60. Every State will be encouraged to establish a national public access human rights resource and training centre or, where such centres already exist, to take concrete steps to strengthen their capacity to support human rights education at the national and local levels. International and regional programmes and organisations should assist in the establishment and strengthening of such centres, including through the provision of financial and technical assistance. States should provide the High Commissioner, for purposes of preliminary, mid-term and final reports, with all available information on the existence, operation, functions and resources of such centres.

61. National human rights resource and training centres, in cooperation with national focal points, should engage, *inter alia*, in the following tasks:

(a) Research on human rights and human rights education;

(b) Translation and culturally appropriate adaptation of training materials;

(c) Outreach towards professional groups and community workers;

(d) Gender-sensitive training of trainers;

(e) Organisation of internship programmes for students and teachers interested in developing projects in human rights education;

(f) Organisation of special cultural events for art, music and theatre performances, and the production of journals, popular books and audiovisual materials on human rights;

(g) Maintenance of a roster of national experts and institutions in human rights education;

(h) Assistance in the implementation of internationally sponsored technical cooperation projects for human rights education;

(i) Establishment of a human rights extension services for making consultations, publications and teaching materials available to individuals and groups requesting

assistance in matters relating to human rights education. Assistance in the development of guidelines and materials for these extension services should be provided for national resource and training centres by competent international programmes and organisations on request.

Assessment and Follow-up

62. The High Commissioner will report on progress and developments in all of these programme elements in preliminary, mid-term and final reports and will also make recommendations for advancing the objectives of these elements in each such report. Each national focal point participating in these programme elements will, accordingly, be called upon to provide updated and detailed information to the High Commissioner.

63. The reports of the High Commissioner will be made available to all national focal points in order that they may take into account the recommendations contained therein and make use of other information contained in those reports, for purposes of programme development, identification of sources of funding and technical assistance, and liaison with other actors in the Decade.

E. COMPONENT FIVE: STRENGTHENING LOCAL PROGRAMMES AND CAPACITIES

Objectives

64. The objective of component five is to build and strengthen programmes and capacities for human rights education at the local level.

Programme Elements

65. National focal points will be encouraged, in the interest of building local and community-based capacities for human rights education, to include all local and community-based organisations in the national roster described in component four above, and to direct their efforts and resources, including support received from international sources, to enabling such

local and community-based organisations to deliver effective human rights education to their constituencies.

66. With the support of national focal points and national resource and training centres, local and community-based organisations should be prepared to deliver popular human rights education, through vocational and adult education, literacy training, local non-governmental organisations, family outreach and religious education.

67. In the context of the foregoing, national focal points should be charged with organising regular consultations and annual meetings with local groups and representatives, and with soliciting their active input for purposes of national evaluations, plans of action, projects and reports to the High Commissioner.

68. Local and community-based groups should also be fully involved in the implementation of national projects for human rights education, with a view to delivering the benefits of the Decade to all levels and sectors of society.

Assessment and Follow-up

69. The High Commissioner will report on challenges, progress and developments in the delivery of human rights education to the local level in preliminary, mid-term and final reports and will also make recommendations for advancing these efforts in each such report. Each national focal point participating in these programme elements will accordingly be called upon to provide updated and detailed information to the High Commissioner on the number and types of local and community-based groups cooperating with each national focal point and the kind of support delivered to the local level, as well as challenges and difficulties encountered.

F. COMPONENT SIX: COORDINATED DEVELOPMENT OF MATERIALS FOR HUMAN RIGHTS EDUCATION

Objective

70. The objective of component six is to ensure the coordinated development of effective human rights education materials.

Programme Elements

71. The Office of the High Commissioner for Human Rights shall develop and publish, in cooperation with UNESCO and all other actors in the Decade, a current and periodically updated listing of available human rights educational materials, including manuals, handbooks, curricula, audiovisual tools and other such materials, concurrent with preliminary, mid-term and final reports. The listing shall also contain information on how such materials may be obtained by interested organisations and individuals. The listing should be made available on an electronic database as soon as possible. The educational material collected in connection with the listing should be maintained at the Office of the High Commissioner for Human Rights and made available upon request to interested parties.

72. UNESCO and other international and regional organisations and agencies will be requested to enhance their activities directed towards the development of such materials, with priority attention to be directed to any lacunae revealed in the compilation of the High Commissioner's listing and to the strengthening of existing materials where necessary.

73. Educational materials developed at the international and regional levels should benefit from the review and input of national focal points and national resource and training centres and should be made available to national and local programmes for translation, cultural adaptation, testing and revision, with the financial and technical assistance of international and regional programmes.

74. Every national resource and training centre should be provided with a full set of such materials for use in the development of national and local programmes; and national focal points, in their reports to the High Commissioner, should identify national needs in this regard. National focal points will, in turn, be responsible for making such materials available to local and community-based groups, national professional training programmes, national non-governmental organisations and other national actors in the Decade.

75. In the development of new materials for specialised audience, the following considerations should be taken into account, in addition to the normative basis, definition, guiding principles, objectives and target groups described in parts I and V of the present Plan of Action:

(a) *Collegial Presentations*. Where possible, effective training efforts should draw from a list of experts which is practical in orientation. As an alternative to panels composed entirely of professors and theorists, consideration should be given to preparing practitioners in the relevant field to deliver human rights education, by they lawyers, judges or police officers. Much more can be accomplished through the collegial approach of, for example, police discussing with police, than could be gained by a professor-student model of training;

(b) *Training the Trainers and Capacity-building*. Participants in targeted human rights courses should be selected with the understanding that their responsibilities will continue after completion of the training exercises. They should be charged with conducting their own training or dissemination efforts after returning to their normal duty station. In this way, the impact of such courses is multiplied several fold, as the information imparted is disseminated throughout the institutions concerned;

(c) *Pedagogical Techniques*. Courses developed under the Decade, in each case, should include a section designed to introduce a variety of effective techniques for the training of specific audiences. Suggestions should be made, in particular, for the use of creative, interactive teaching methods, which offer the best means of securing the active, committed involvement of programme participants Such techniques may include the use of working groups, lecture-discussions, case studies, panel discussions, round-table discussions, brainstorming sessions, simulation and role-playing, field trips, practice and the use of audio and visual aids, as culturally appropriate to the specific audience;

(d) *Audience Specificity*. The mere recitation of vague principles of general applicability offers little hope of affecting the actual behaviour of a given audience. To be effective, indeed, at all worthwhile, training and education efforts must be directly targeted at and appropriately addressed to a particular audience, be they the police, health-care workers, lawyers, students or others. Accordingly, the content of the Decade's teaching activities should focus more on the standards directly relevant to the daily work or role in the community of the audience and less on distant theoretical notions;

(e) *Practical Approach*. According to the report of a recent parliamentary commission investigating violations at one country's police stations when confronted with evidence of abuses the police said that they lacked understanding of interrogation methods and techniques, that they carried out interrogations by outdated methods and that they did not know how interrogations were carried out in other countries. In order to compare their methods and improvement them, they wanted the opportunity for research and observation of interrogation methods in other countries. Such accounts reveal two important areas of focus, extendable by analogy to audiences other than police trainees. Firstly, offering justifications of any kind for serious violations such as torture demonstrates a lack of familiarity with the most fundamental of standards for human rights. There are no legitimate justifications for such activities. Secondly, the police (and other groups) in the real world want to know not merely what the rules are, but also how to function effectively within the confines of those rules. Training efforts that ignore either of these areas will often be neither credible nor effective. Accordingly, educational efforts under the Decade should include practical information on proven techniques for the performance of the target audience's duties, as derived from the recommendations of experts and literature on current best practices for the profession in question;

(f) *Comprehensive Presentation of Standards.* Courses and materials developed under the Decade should be thorough in their presentation of the relevant international standards. To that end, relevant instruments and simplified learning tools should be translated for the benefit of trainees;

(g) *Teaching to Sensitise.* The goals of materials and courses developed under the Decade should not be limited to the imparting of standards and practical skills, but should also include exercises designed to sensitise trainees to their own potential for violence-prone behaviour, however unintentional. For example, well-developed exercises that can have the effect of making trainees aware of gender or racial bias in their own attitudes or behaviour can be quite valuable. Similarly, the special import of particular standards as they apply to women (for example) is not always readily obvious. Trainees should be made to understand, for example, that the term "degrading treatment", as found in the various international instruments, may have different practical implications when applied to women as compared to men, or when applied to one cultural group vis-à-vis another;

(h) *Flexibility of Design and Application.* To be universally, useful, training courses and materials must be designed to facilitate their flexible use, without imposing a single rigid focus or approach on the trainers. Such courses must be adaptable to the particular cultural, educational, regional and experimental needs and realities of a diverse range of potential audiences within the target group;

(i) *Evaluation Tools.* Training materials and courses should include pre-and post-training evaluation exercises, such as testing questionnaires, which severe three crucial purposes. Pre-course questionnaires, when properly utilised, allow a trainer to tailor his or her course to the particular educational needs of the audience. Post-course questionnaires and evaluation sessions with both

allow trainees to gauge what they have learned and assist in the continuous (crucial) modification and improvement of courses offered under the Decade.

Assessment and Follow-up

76. The High Commissioner, concurrently, with preliminary, mid-term and final reports, will make available for distribution to all international organisations, regional, organisations and national focal points the current listings of available materials described in this component.

77. The High Commissioner, based upon information to be provided in reports by national focal points and other partners in the Decade, will encourage the development and distribution of new materials, as indicated by evolving needs.

G. COMPONENT SEVEN: STRENGTHENING THE ROLE OF THE MASS MEDIA

Objective

78. The objective of component seven is to strengthen the role and capacity of the mass media in the furtherance of human rights education.

Programme Elements

79 In recognition of the important role of the mass media in bringing human rights education to all sectors of society, including to persons at all levels of literacy and those living or working in remote areas, journalists, broadcasters and other media professionals should, during the course of the Decade, benefit from increased training and assistance in incorporating human rights information and public education into their work. All programmes and organisations engaged in the provision of training and technical cooperation under the Decade should consider contributing to these efforts. The Office of the High Commissioner for Human Rights, in particular produce a manual on human rights for the media and increase its media training activities.

80. All sectors in the Decade shall encourage, in their contacts with the media, enhanced public coverage of human rights issues and the development of programmes that provide

information and ideas on human rights and contribute to a public dialogue on human rights, in full respect for the independence of the media and the freedoms of information and expression.

81. It consultation with the Office of the High Commissioner for Human Rights, the Department of Public Information of the United Nations will increase significantly the production of United Nations television and radio educational programmes on human rights. The Department will be requested to produce videos, films and programmes for radio broadcasting on human rights themes.

82. The Office of the High Commissioner of Human Rights, with the cooperation of the Department of Public Information, will establish a media advisory board for public information and education on human rights and will develop a mass media campaign to publicise human rights standards and mechanisms.

83. In the context of the World Public Information Campaign for Human Rights, and in cooperation with relevant non-governmental organisations and agencies, the Office of the High Commissioner for Human Rights will intensify the publication of fact sheets, studies and other public information human rights materials. It will also organise or participate in public human rights events such as the fiftieth anniversary of the United Nations, in 1995, and the fiftieth anniversary of the Universal Declaration of Human Rights, in 1998. The High Commissioner will encourage global media coverage of these events.

Assessment and Follow-up

84. The High Commissioner, in preliminary, mid-term and final reports will provide information on measures undertaken to increase media attention to human rights issues at the international, regional and national levels. All national focal points will be requested to maintain a review of national press coverage of human rights issues and to report to the High Commissioner on such coverage. A similar press review, at the international level, will be maintained by the Office of

the High Commissioner for Human Rights and the Department of Public Information.

H. COMPONENT EIGHT: GLOBAL DISSEMINATION OF THE UNIVERSAL DECLARATION OF HUMAN RIGHTS

Objectives

85. The objective of component eight is to achieve the global dissemination of the Universal Declaration of Human Rights in the maximum number of languages possible and in other forms appropriate for various levels of literacy and for the disabled.

Programmes Elements

86. The Office of the High Commissioner for Human Rights in co-operation with UNESCO, the Department of Public Information and its United Nations information centres, will conduct a global survey of existing printed language versions of the Universal Declaration of Human Rights, as well as of existing versions in pictorial, audiovisual or other formats, and will ascertain the availability of the various versions for distribution in each Member State, commencing in 1995.

87. Based upon the results of the survey, a plan, will be developed by the High Commissioner for the production of further language versions of the Universal Declaration, with priority attention to be given to ensuring the existence of at least one printed format version for the main language of each Member State, and at least one audio or other appropriate version for persons of various levels of literacy and for the disabled in each Member State. Additional versions, in minority and other national languages, and in other formats for persons of other levels of literacy and for the disabled, should immediately follow the production of these versions.

88. Under the coordination of the High Commissioner and the respective national focal points for human rights education, and according to the plan development following the survey. Governments and national non-governmental organisations, universities and institutions, will be called upon to carry out translation, publication and distribution of appropriate

versions of the Universal Declaration of Human Rights with technical and financial assistance from international organisations and programmes, where necessary. Such international organisations and programmes, including the advisory services and technical assistance programme of the Office of the High Commissioner for Human Rights, UNESCO, other United Nations agencies and international non-governmental organisations, will be encouraged by the High Commissioner for Human Rights to make available assistance of the type identified and the international donor community will be called upon to support these efforts.

89. On the occasion of the fiftieth anniversary of the Universal Declaration of Human Rights, in 1998, major celebratory events will be organised at the international, regional and national levels, emphasising the importance of universal knowledge and understanding of the provisions of the Universal Declaration. At the international level, the High Commissioner for Human Rights will convene an international conference on dissemination of the Universal Declaration, for the purpose of devising strategies for ensuring that the Declaration is globally available and effectively incorporated into human rights education at all levels and in all Member States Regional organisations and national focal points will be called upon to hold corresponding events and to contribute to and implement the recommendations of the international conference.

Assessment and Follow-up

90. The results of the survey conducted by the High Commissioner and report of the international conference to be held in 1998 will be distributed to all regional organisations, national focal points and other interested parents in the Decade on their completion.

91. All regional organisations, national focal points and other interested parents in the Decade, will be requested to report to the High Commissioner for purposes of the mid-term evaluation in the year 2000, and again for the final report in 2004, on progress made since the completion of the survey,

including celebratory events held and versions of the Universal Declaration available, and on continuing needs and challenges in the achievement of the objectives of these programme elements.

92. The High Commissioner will incorporate all such information into the mid-term and final reports, and all programme partners will be called upon to redirect their efforts according to the information and recommendations set out in those reports.

VIII. Mid-term Global Evaluation

93. During the year 2000, a mid-term global evaluation of progress made towards the achievement of the objectives of the Decade shall be undertaken by the Office of the High Commissioner for Human Rights, in cooperation with all other principal actors in the Decade. The High Commissioner shall report to the General Assembly on the results of that evaluation.

94. The evaluation report shall take into account all available information on what has been accomplished at the international, regional, national and local levels, identify remaining shortcomings and needs, and make recommendations for action during the five remaining years of the Decade.

95. For purpose of the High Commissioner's report, all participating national focal points, international and regional organisations, non-governmental organisations, specialised agencies and programmes, and other interested partners, shall be requested to provide relevant information to the High Commissioner, based upon their own independent assessments and activities. National focal points, in particular, shall be requested to conduct detailed assessments in their own countries, and to report thereon to the High Commissioner.

IX. Conclusion of the Decade

96. The year 2004 shall mark the final year of the United Nations Decade for Human Rights Education. That year shall, accordingly, be set as the target date for achievement of

generalised human rights education programmes through the implementation of State action plans. It shall also be the target date for the completion of a comprehensive collection of human rights education materials and their broad distribution throughout all Member States. By the conclusion of the Decade, effective national capacities for the delivery of the human rights education should be secured worldwide.

X. Follow-up to the Decade

97. At the conclusion of the Decade, the Office of the High Commissioner for Human Rights, in cooperation with UNESCO, should issue a final report on the state of human rights education at the local, national, regional and international levels. The High Commissioner, in the final report, should seek to identify, as precisely as possible, progress in the various areas, including in which languages the Universal Declaration of Human Rights is available, the number and types of human rights educational manuals, handbooks and teaching materials developed by international and regional organisations and programmes, the number of human rights educational institutes, centres or permanent focal points established at the national level, the national percentages of teachers trained in human rights, the number of schools having adopted human rights education curricula and the number and kinds of education in the professional fields and in informal and non-formal education. The report should also provide precise information on how various language versions of the Universal Declaration of Human Rights and human rights teaching materials may be obtained by interested groups and individuals.

98. The national, regional and international structures and network established under the Decade should continue to serve as permanent focal and contact points for international cooperation in the field of human rights education, and the Office of the High Commissioner for Human Rights, in co-operation with UNESCO, should maintain, and make available on request, a current roster of such organisations and focal points.

99. Human rights educational materials developed under the Decade should be subject to periodic review, supplementation and revision to take into account changing needs and realities, and should continue to be made available on the widest possible basis.

5

Guidelines for National Plans of Action for Human Rights Education

Preface

1. The present "Guidelines for National Plans of Action for Human Rights Education" have been developed by the Office of the High Commissioner for Human Rights (OHCHR) in the framework of the United Nations Decade for Human Rights Education (1995-2004). The Guidelines are intended to assist States in responding to several resolutions of both the General Assembly and the Commission on Human Rights, in which States were called upon to develop national plans of action for human rights education[1].

2. In its resolution 49/184 proclaiming the Decade for Human Rights Education, the General Assembly welcomed a related Plan of Action submitted to the Assembly by the Secretary-General, and requested the United Nations High Commissioner for Human Rights to coordinate its implementation. The final version of the Plan of Action (see A/51/506/Add.1, appendix) seeks to stimulate and support national and local activities and initiatives. It is the realisation of the idea to promote a partnership between Governments,

---

[1] See General Assembly resolutions 49/184, 50/177 and 51/104; and Commission on Human Rights resolutions 1995/47 and 1996/44 and decision 1997/111.

intergovernmental organisations, non-governmental organisations (NGOs), professional associations, individuals and large segments of civil society.

3. The Plan of Action has five objectives:

   (a) The assessment of needs and formulation of strategies;

   (b) Building and strengthening human rights education programmes at the international, regional, national and local levels;

   (c) Developing educational materials;

   (d) Strengthening the role of the mass media;

   (e) Global dissemination of the Universal Declaration of Human Rights.

4. With regard to the building and strengthening of human rights education programme at the national and local levels, Members States are urged to establish a national committee for human rights education and to draw up a national plan of action.

5. Since governmental and non-governmental organisations and individuals have important roles to play in ensuring that human rights are respected, national human rights education strategies and plans of action should be developed and implemented by a creative mixture of all of such entities. These Guidelines are not intended as a blueprint for a nationally coordinated effort in human rights education. Rather, they aim at providing concrete suggestions for developing and implementing, a comprehensive (in terms of out-reach), effective (in terms or educational strategies) and sustainable in the long term national plan of action.

6. In those countries with a federal system, plans of action, may be developed at both the federal and state/provincial levels. Therefore, "national plan", as used in this document, may refer to state/provincial plans as well.

7. The Guidelines are defined in the following sections:

   (a) Introduction;

   (b) Principles governing a national plan of action for human rights education;

(c) Step towards a national plan of action for human rights education.

8. The preparation of the Guidelines has benefited from the valuable input of several experts and practitioners in the area of human rights education, including Mr. Carlos Basombrio, Mr. Clarence J. Dias, Mr. Frej Fenniche, Ms Nancy Flowers, Mr. Chris Madiba, Mr. Abraham Magendzo, Mr. Vitit Muntarbhorn, Mr. Marek Nowicki, Mr. Ralph Pettman, Ms. Magda Seydegardt, Ms. Cristina Sganga, Ms. Felisa Tibbitts, Mr. David Weissbrodt and Ms. Louisa Zondo. The United Nations Educational, Scientific and Cultural Organisation (UNESCO) and the Council of Europe also participated in the process of discussing and drafting the Guidelines.

9. Three complementary documents to these Guidelines have also been prepared and will made available by OHCHR:

(a) *Human Rights Education Programming,* a paper which includes ideas and suggestions for the implementation of targeted human rights education programmes regarding (i) public awareness; (ii) the schooling sector; (iii) other priority groups, and a resource guide to assist in programme implementation;

(b) *The Rights to Human Rights Education,* a compilation of the full text of excerpts from international instruments pertaining to human rights education;

(c) *Human Rights Trainers Guide,* a methodological approach to the human rights training of professional groups.

I. Introduction

A. DEFINITION OF HUMAN RIGHTS EDUCATION

10. References to the concept of education in and for human rights appear in a number of international human rights instruments, including the Universal Declaration of Human Rights (art. 26), the International Covenant on Economic, Social and Cultural Rights (art. 13), the Convention of the Rights of the Child (art. 29) and, most recently, the Vienna Declaration and Programme of Action (sect. D, paras 78-82). Taken together, the instruments provide a clear definition of

the concept of human rights education as agreed by the international community.

11. In accordance with those provisions, and for the purposes of the Decade, human rights education may be defined as training, dissemination and information efforts aimed at the building of a universal culture of human rights through the imparting of knowledge and skills and the moulding of attitudes, which are directed towards:

(a) The strengthening of respect for human rights and fundamental freedoms;

(b) The full development of the human personality and its inherent dignity;

(c) The promotion of understanding, tolerance, gender, equality and friendship among all nations, indigenous peoples and racial, national, ethnic, religious and linguistic groups;

(d) The enabling of all persons to participate effectively in a free society;

(e) The furtherance of the activities of the United Nations for the maintenance of peace (see A/51/506/Add.1, appendix, para 2).

B. WHY HUMAN RIGHTS EDUCATION?

12. There is growing consensus that education in and for human rights is essential and can contribute to both the reduction of human rights violations and the building of free, just and peaceful societies. Human rights education is also increasingly recognised as an effective strategy to prevent human rights abuses.

13. Human rights are promoted through three dimensions of education campaigns:

(a) Knowledge: provision of information about human rights and mechanisms for their protection;

(b) Values, beliefs and attitudes: promotion of a human rights culture through the development of values, beliefs and attitudes which uphold human rights;

(c) Action: encouragement to take action to defend human rights and prevent human rights abuses.

C. WHY NATIONAL PLANS OF ACTION FOR HUMAN RIGHTS EDUCATION?

14. National plans serve to:

(a) Establish or strengthen national and local human rights institutions and organisations;

(b) Initiate steps towards national programmes for the promotion and protection of human rights, as recommended by the World Conference on Human Rights;

(c) Prevent human rights violations that result in ruinous human, social, cultural, environmental and economic costs;

(d) Identify those persons in society who are presently deprived of their full human rights and ensure that effective steps are taken to redress their situation;

(e) Enable a comprehensive response to rapid social and economic changes that might otherwise result in chaos and dislocation;

(f) Promote diversity of sources, approaches, methodologies and institutions in the field of human rights education;

(g) Enhance opportunities for cooperation in human rights education activities among government agencies, non-governmental organisations, professional groups and other institutions of civil society;

(h) Emphasise the role of the human rights in national development;

(i) Help Governments meet their prior commitments to human rights education under international instruments and programmes, including the Vienna Declaration and Programme of Action (1993) and the United Nations Decade for Human Rights Education (1995-2004).

D. WHY GUIDELINES FOR NATIONAL PLANS OF ACTION?

15. The Guidelines are intended to:

    (a) Promote a common understanding of the purpose and content of human rights education and the Decade;

    (b) Highlight minimum standards for human rights education;

    (c) Identify processes/steps needed to design, implement, evaluate and redesign a national plan for human rights education;

    (d) Draw attention to the human, financial and technical resources needed to adopt a national approach to human rights education;

    (e) Encourage effective interaction between national and international human rights institutions and organisations and promote the implementation of international human rights standards at the national level;

    (f) Provide mechanisms for setting reasonable human rights education goals and measuring their achievement.

II. Principles Governing A National Plan of Action for Human Rights Education

A. GENERAL PRINCIPLES

16. Education in and for human rights is a fundamental human right. Governments should develop national plans that:

    (a) Promote respect for and protection of all human rights through educational activities for all members of society;

    (b) Promote the independence, indivisibility and universality of human rights, including civil, cultural, economic, political and social rights and the rights to development;

    (c) Integrate women's rights as human rights into all aspects of the national plan;

(*d*) Recognise the importance of human rights education for democracy, sustainable development, the rule of law, the environment and peace;

(*e*) Recognise the role of human rights education as a strategy for the prevention of human rights violations;

(*f*) Encourage analysis of chronic and emerging human rights problems, which lead to solutions consistent with human rights standards;

(*g*) Foster knowledge of and skills for using global, regional, national and local human rights instruments and mechanisms for the promotion of human rights;

(*h*) Empower communities and individuals to identify their human rights needs and to ensure that they are met:

(*i*) Develop pedagogies that include knowledge, critical analysis and skills for action furthering human rights;

(*j*) Promote research and the development of educational materials to sustain these general principles;

(*k*) Foster learning environments free from want and fear that encourage participation, enjoyment of human rights and the full development of the human personality.

B. ORGANISATIONAL AND OPERATIONAL PRINCIPLES

17. All procedures and practices for the elaboration, implementation and evaluation of the national plan should guarantee (*a*) the pluralistic representation of society (including NGOs); (*b*) transparency of operation; (*c*) public accountability; and (*d*) democratic participation.

18. All government authorities should respect the independence and autonomy of the various organisations in the implementation of the national plan.

C. PRINCIPLES FOR EDUCATIONAL ACTIVITIES

19. All educational activities conducted under the national plan must foster:

(*a*) Respect for and appreciation of differences and opposition to discrimination on the basis of race, national or ethnic origin, gender, region, age, social, physical or mental condition, language, sexual orientation, etc.:

(*b*) Non-discriminatory language and conduct;

(*c*) Respect for and appreciation of diversity of opinion;

(*d*) Participatory teaching and learning;

(*e*) "Translation" of human rights norms into the conduct of daily life;

(*f*) Professional training of trainers;

(*g*) Development and strengthening of national capacities and expertise for the effective implementation of the plan.

III. Steps Towards A National Plan of Action for Human Rights Education

A. STEP I: ESTABLISHING A NATIONAL COMMITTEE FOR HUMAN RIGHTS EDUCATION

Establishment

20. A national committee should be established in each country, according to national conditions and should include representatives of appropriate government agencies and non-governmental organisations with experience in human rights and human rights education or with the potential to develop such programmes.

POTENTIAL MEMBERSHIP

The members of the national committee should include institutions, organisations and individuals that intend to work in accordance with the purposes and principles of the United Nations, including the principles on which the Decade is based. A sample list might include, *inter alia:*

Representatives of nations/local bodies, such as:

- government representatives (which would then liaise with relevant ministries);

- the national commission for UNESCO and other similar national agencies (in Europe, for instance, the information and Documentation Centres on the Council of Europe);
- independent human rights national institutions (human rights commissions and/or ombudsmen);
- national human rights resource and training centres;
- national/local human rights groups/organisations, including, for example, national committees for UNICEF, and other community-based organisations, including women's and social justice groups;
- national chapters of international human rights non-governmental organisations, including, for example, national United Nations associations;
- parliamentary representatives (primarily from the education, human rights and development committees);
- key representatives of civil society, including trade and professional unions;
- representatives of the judiciary;
- the business community;
- teachers' associations/unions;
- cultural/social and community leaders;
- youth organisations;
- minority groups;
- educators and university scholars;
- media representatives.

Observers may, as appropriate, be invited, such as national representatives/offices of international agencies present in the country, including, *inter alia*:

- the United Nations resident coordinator (who often is the United Nations Development Programme resident representative);
- the United Nations information centre or service;

- the United Nations High Commissioner for Refugees (UNHCR) national delegation;
- the OHCHR field presence;
- the office of regional intergovernmental organisations (Organisation of African Unity, Organisation of American States, Council of Europe, the Commonwealth, the Agency for the French-speaking community: ACCT etc.)

21. The initiative for forming the national committee should be taken by the appropriate branch or agency of the Government. In this respect, the Government should respond the relevant initiatives from a national human rights commission, a similar national institution or non-governmental organisation.

22. The selection of a temporary liaison officer or convener could be the first step in establishing a national committee. At this stage, it is important that efforts be made to ensure that the committee comprise at least all institutions and organisations already significantly active in the area of human rights education. The Government should notify OHCHR when the national committee is convened.

Functions

23. The committee should be directly responsible for the development of the national plan, including the *(a)* commissioning/conduct of the baseline study (step 2); *(b)* formulation of a comprehensive national plan of action, including identifying objectives, strategies, programmes and financing (steps 3 and 4); *(c)* facilitation of the implementation of the national plan (step 5)' and *(d)* the periodic evaluation, review and follow-up of programmes and the achievement of national goals (step 6).

24. With regard to the international level, the committee should remain in contact with regional and international bodies involved in implementing the objectives of the Decade and channel international and regional inputs, information and support to the local and grass-roots levels. The committee should also report periodically to OHCHR on needs,

proposals and progress made towards the realisation of the goals of the Decade, so that this information can be included in the High Commissioner's reports on the implementation of the United Nations Plan of Action for the Decade and can constitute a basis for further action.

Methods of Work

25. The committee should elect a coordinator, why may be guided by a small representative advisory board. A secretariat could be established, eventually within one of the member organisations of the committee.

26. The committee should operate on the basis of a free exchange of views and information, in atmosphere of trust and collaborative interest in seeing that a comprehensive, international and multidisciplinary strategy for human rights education can be put in place in the particular country.

27. Procedures for decision-making, as well as for requesting, receiving, reviewing and discussing the contributions of concerned individuals, groups and organisations should be developed at an early stage.

Time-frame

28. A national committee should, whenever called for, be established, preferably at the beginning of 1998, the year of the fiftieth anniversary of the Universal Declaration of Human Rights. It should function at least for the period of the Decade (1995-2004).

B. STEP 2: CONDUCTING A BASELINE STUDY

Purpose

29. If is has not already been undertaken, a baseline study or needs assessment will be a critical aid in determining the most pressing local and national needs.

30. Accordingly, once the committee is constituted, one of its early activities should be to conduct or commission a systematic study on the state of human rights education in the country, including the areas where human rights challenges are most daunting, the available level of support

and the extent to which the basis elements of a national strategy are already in place. This inquiry and any subsequent activities will require that the committee have a clear understanding of what constitutes human rights education.

Content

31. The study might deal with present activities, needs and human and institutional resources for human rights education, including such basic issues as:

(a) Existing programmes for human rights education (for the general public, formal schooling sectors and specific groups);

(b) Existing curricula for human rights and democracy issues at all levels of education;

(c) Current activities of governmental and non-governmental agencies active in human rights education;

(d) Existence of legal norms concerning the promotion of human rights and their implementation;

(e) Availability of key human rights documents in national and local languages as well as in simplified form;

(f) Availability of other materials, both textual and other, for use in human rights education and their accessibility;

(g) Overall level of organisational and financial support for human rights education, including institutions and individuals most likely to assist in this area;

(h) Existence of national development plans and other relevant national plans of actin already defined (general human rights plans of action or those for women, children, minorities or indigenous peoples);

(i) Obstacles to human rights education that should be overcome;

(j) An overall needs assessment for human rights education, including identification of human rights problems in the country and consequently emerging priority groups in need for human rights education.

32. The study might also include *(a)* knowledge of human rights among the general population, as well as potential target groups; *(b)* social, political and economic conditions relevant to human rights education; *(c)* human rights educational access for marginalised groups; and *(d)* treatment of human rights issues by the mass media (including television, radio, newspapers and popular magazines).

Methods

33. As the basis for the development of the national plan of action, the baseline study must be seen as legitimate, credible and objective. This question of legitimacy extends to the organisation(s) commissioned to conduct the study, as well as to the data collection methods themselves.

34. The study can be undertaken through the distribution of questionaires,[2] interviews and the collection/review of materials. Information can also be obtained through the canvassing of existing groups, many of whom may already be on the national committee. A bottom-up approach for the assessment of needs should be encouraged, i.e. a participatory approach at the grassroots level. Local seminars and workshops among basis educators in the rural areas, for example, or the participation of representatives of NGOs working in those areas could be a means of assessing needs as widely as possible.

35. Also, the study should review State reports to the United Nations treaty bodies on the implementation of human rights education provisions of international instruments[3] as well as the observations and recommendations made by those bodies in this regard. National reports elaborated in

---

[2] A questionnaire developed by OHCHR to conduct a survey of human rights programmes, materials and organisations at the national level is available and may be requested from OHCHR.

[3] Relevant United Nations treaty bodies include the Committee on Economic, Social and Cultural Rights, the Human Rights Committee, the Committee on the Rights of the Child, the Committee on the Elimination of Racial Discrimination, the Committee on the Elimination of Discrimination against Women and the Committee against Torture.

accordance with other international or regional monitoring procedures should also be reviewed.

36. The study should make recommendations on high-priority groups in need of human rights education, purpose programmes areas to address gaps in programme coverage and put forward suggestions for improving the human rights education activities of existing groups.

37. The study must be made public and be widely disseminated and could include a useful annex of addresses of all national and local institutes and governmental and non-governmental agencies dealing with human rights education that may be contacted and may provide materials for further development of programmes[4].

C. STEP 3: SETTING PRIORITIES AND IDENTIFYING GROUPS IN NEED

38. Priorities in human rights education will need to be established for the short, medium, and long term on the basis of the findings of the baseline study. These priorities might be set on the basis of the most pressing needs (for example, among groups that are clearly in need for human rights education) and on the basis of opportunity (for example, if certain groups or institutions have requested assistance in setting up human rights education programmes).

39. Groups in need of human rights education may include:

(a) Administration of justice officials: (i) law enforcement personnel, including police; (ii) prison officials; and (iii) judges and prosecutors;

(b) Other government and legislative officials: (i) members of the legislature; (ii) public officials involved in drafting legislation; developing and implementing policy; (iii) the military and other security forces; and (iv) immigration and border officials;

(c) Key professional groups: (i) teachers and curriculum developers; (ii) social workers; (iii) the medical

---

[4] Inspiration for the content and methods of the baseline study was taken from the Italian example, as reported in A/51/506, para 44 *(e)* and the Tunisian example, as reported in E/CN.4/1997/46, para 23 *(g)*.

profession; (iv) the media and journalists; and (v) the legal profession;

(d) Organisations and groups: (i) women's organisations; (ii) indigenous peoples; (iii) minority groups; (iv) trade unions; (v) development agencies; (vi) the business community; (vii) workers' and employers' organisations; (viii) community lenders; (ix) groups with a special interest in social justice issues; and (x) religious leaders;

(e) Schooling sectors: (i) children; (ii) youth; and (iii) professional trainees;

(f) Others: (i) refugees and displaced persons; (ii) the rural and urban poor, especially women; (iii) migrant workers; (iv) other vulnerable groups; such as people with HIV/ AIDS infection, disabled persons, persons living in extreme poverty, the aged; (v) prisoners and others in detention; and (vi) the general public.

D. STEP 4: DEVELOPING THE NATIONAL PLAN

Components

40. In response to the needs identified in the baseline study and to the national context, a national plan of action should include a comprehensive set of objectives, strategies and programmes for human rights education and evaluation mechanisms.

41. Accordingly, the plan of action should include the following components:

(a) An affirmation of the overall goals or objectives for human rights education in the country (on the basis of a clear definition of human rights education, as set out in international instruments);

(b) Strategies for reaching the general public, formal schooling sectors and special target groups;

(c) Programmes for the realisation of these strategies, comprising specific activities;

(d) Short-medium-and long-term steps for carrying out the Plan;

(e) Realistic identified results to be achieved and criteria for monitoring/evaluating;

(f) Special opportunities for human rights education;

(g) The role of the National Committee in the implementation of the Plan;

(h) Mechanism for individuals and groups to contact the Committee and become part of the national human rights education effort;

(i) Contact information for key local human rights education organisations[5].

Objectives

42. The objectives of the national plan should be consistent with the principles outlined in section II above.

Strategies

43. A comprehensive national strategy for human rights education should include *(a)* a general public awareness campaign; *(b)* the infusion of human rights themes into all levels of formal schooling; and *(c)* an educational effort adapted to specific groups in need of human rights education.

---

[5] An example of a comprehensive Plan of Action for Human Rights Education which has already been developed is the Philippine case, as reported in E/CN.4/1997/46. The Philippine Plan of Action, forwarded to OHCHR by the Philippine Commission on Human Rights, includes clear objectives, target audience (organised and unorganised elements of society), strategies (trainers' training organisation of networks, integration of human rights in all educational curricula, utilisation of village-level officials to reach out to the community level, promotional campaigns including artistic and cultural activities, development of monitoring and evaluation systems etc.) and programmes, including the creation of a human rights training, documentation and research centre (the Human Rights Academy). In the elaboration of the Plan, and in view of its implementation, the Commission has entered into a number of formal agreements with other national partners for human rights education, to define in detail specific areas of responsibility. These partners include: the Department of Interior and Local Government, the Liga NG MGA Barangay (an organisation of barangay captains or village chiefs), the Department of Justice, the Department of National Defense, the Department of Education, Culture and Sports, the Commission on Higher Education and Amnesty International/Philippine Section (E/CN.4/1997/46, para 23 *(f)*).

44. The national plan of action should constitute an integral part of the national development plan and complement other relevant national plans of action already defined (general human rights plans of action or those relating to women, children, minorities, indigenous peoples, etc.)

Programmes

45. The national plan of action should include a national-specific framework for implementing and monitoring human rights education programmes. With regard to existing programmes for human rights education, the plan could indicate how those programmes should be strengthened or reformulated. Also, the plan should aim at strengthening local programmes and capacities.

46. The following types of activities and approaches could constitute courses of action in support of the attainment of national strategies goals:

(a) *Networking Support:* building practical relationships/ networks among individuals, groups and institutions; promotion of meetings and collaboration; and identification and sharing of useful resources and experiences among those conducting human rights education. A general principle for the involvement of organisations is that their complementarity should be promoted;

(b) *Institutional/organisational support:* identification, support and, if necessary, establishment of individual institutions or agencies, as well as coalitions of such organisations, to promote and coordinate human rights education training, materials' development and other means of education. This course of action should include the establishment (or strengthening) of a publicly accessible national human rights resource and training centre to support the world of the national committee (see A/ 51/506/Add. 1, appendix, para 61). The centre should be able to offer technical assistance (for example, in the form of publications, training materials and a roster of national trainers, experts and institutions) to those interested in implementing human rights education programmes. Where such a centre already exists, its work should be evaluated. In the absence of an established centre or where an existing centre is not effective for the purposes of the Decade, one could be set up, on the basis of national requirements, for instance within the framework of a university or a national institution (such as a human rights commission or an ombudsman's office). A new organisation might also be established by the committee in cases where there is no obvious vehicle for the delivery of human rights education programming:

(c) *Integration of Human Rights Education into All Levels of Formal Education:* after a thorough revision of existing programmes and curricula, key human rights themes and topics should be included in professional and technical training programmes and in professional codes of conduct or operating procedures, as well as at the pre-school and primary, secondary, university and other institutions of high learning levels of education.

(d) *Education of Groups in Need:* development and maintenance of comprehensive training programmes for the various groups in need of human rights education, including vulnerable groups, groups which are more likely to affect human rights advocacy, and influential persons/groups in the society in order to promote awareness of sectorally-based human rights challenges and actions to enhance human rights practices;

(e) *Public Awareness Campaign:* the undertaking of activities to increase public and professional access to and awareness of international human rights standards, of local, national and international mechanisms of protection and of human rights conditions locally, nationally and internationally, through the mass media, informal education techniques and existing agencies and non-governmental networks;

(f) *Production and Revision of Materials:* development of national language/simplified versions of key international human rights documents and human rights training materials, for all levels of literacy and for persons with disabilities, and revision of educational materials to bring their content in line with international human rights standards;

(g) *Research and Evaluation:* facilitation of research into and evaluation of human rights education programming in order to further its improvement and share experiences of best practices;

(h) *Legislative Reform:* promoting reform in relevant public policy sectors, including review of existing and proposed legislation and elaborating new legislation (for instance, the incorporation of human rights in the educational curricula at all levels of the formal educational system could probably entail legislative or policy action, such as changes in licensing requirements for teachers).

Resources

47. A financial strategy, for the national plan should be developed. Funding could be raised at the local, regional, national and international levels. Consideration could be given to the establishment of a national fund.

48. The development of a national plan of action should be linked to a corresponding policy declaration and the freeing up of resources to help realise programme goals. In this regard, the committee should make as much use as possible of institutional, human and financial resources already available, according to national conditions, by reorienting available resources for national programmes. Additional resources could be sought from the private sector and donor agencies.

49. Once the plan has been elaborated through a process of broad consultation an immediate task of the committee should be to identify organisations and approaches likely to promote its realisation. Partnerships with and between human rights groups and university faculties, trades unions, government agencies and other non-governmental organisations should be established.

E. STEP 5: IMPLEMENTING THE NATIONAL PLAN

50. Effective implementation is essential for the credibility of the national plan. The plan should bear in mind the possibility of a variety of inputs into federal systems of government and the relevance of the regional and local levels.

51. Implementation is linked to a number of measures including responsive policies, law, mechanisms and resources (human, financial, information and technological), and may vary from country to country. However, in each country implementation should be based on the principles covered in section II above.

F. STEP 6: REVIEWING AND REVISING THE NATIONAL PLAN

52. The plan should be reviewed periodically and revised as necessary to ensure effective responses to the needs identified by the baseline study. It is recommended that periodic reviews, through the participation of independent evaluators, be organised by the committee, the first to take place one year after the initiation of the plan of action, and thereafter at intervals. These reviews would ideally involve self-evaluation and independent evaluations. They would be a learning tool for understanding the strength and weaknesses in the design and implementation of existing programming, and for making revisions as necessary with effective follow-up.

53. Conditions vary greatly within countries regarding data, as well as the human and financial resources available for evaluation. Moreover, the methods chosen must be appropriate to local cultures. But it is always possible to build an evaluation component into educational activities, especially at the time they are taking place. Evaluating comprehension can be vary different from evaluating attitudinal change or skills development. The more participatory the methodology used for human rights education, the more effective is likely to be the evaluation.

54. Clearly, each national programme will need to devise its own plans for evaluation. What follows is intended to be purely suggestive of some of the issues and questions involved.

55. National evaluations should examine at least three areas: *(a)* the national plan of action; *(b)* programme implementation; and *(c)* the functioning of the national committee.

National Plan of Action

56. Are the objectives contained in the national plan of action being met:

    (a) In terms of programme coverage? *Data source:* contact objectives in the National Plan with current human rights education programming;

    (b) In terms of programme effectiveness (within the sectors of public awareness; education at the primary, secondary, university and professional/technical educational levels; education of groups in need)? *Possible indicators:* see "Programme implementation" below.

57. Have there been any developments in the human rights or human rights education fields, either locally, nationally or internationally, that would affect elements of the national plan of action, including the need to focus more or less on certain groups, or new opportunities for human rights education programming? *Data sources:* recent human rights reports, new national legislation or court decisions, new relationships with potential human rights education deliverers or collaborators, new communication technologies, local/national/regional international events that highlighted the need for human rights education.

Programme Implementation

58. For the various programming sectors (*e.g.* public awareness campaigns etc.), how are the programmes meeting the criteria of comprehensiveness (including non-discriminatory and affirmative action measures)? Are the programmes having maximum outreach towards target audiences and/or a core group, which in turn, has leadership, visibility and motivation to influence others in their respective sectors?

    (a) *First set of indicators:* outreach mechanisms and numbers reached:

(i) *Public Outreach:* print readership, television viewers, radio listeners (including articles, programming and advertising campaigns), use of visuals such as posters and artistic programmes;

(ii) Outreach to Key leadership in relation to the national plan of action, including possibility the media, educational authorities, governmental officials, social justice groups, trainers and others;

(iii) *Sector-specific Outreach:* (1) written: readership of professional newspapers and magazines, dissemination of special information brochures, educational materials used in awareness and training; (2) oral: participants in awareness and educational/training activities; and (3) other: dissemination of visual materials such as posters, videos;

(b) *Second Set of Indicators:* contrast numbers reached with total numbers desired;

(c) *Third Set of Indicators:* projection of further outreach based on future programming, relationship with key agencies.

59. For the various sectors of programming, are the programmes effective for educating learners in the knowledge/ understanding, attitudes/values and skills/behaviour necessary to support national respect for and protection of human rights? *Possible data sources: (a)* pre- and post-surveys of programme participants on their knowledge of and attitudes towards human rights and related issues, including relevance to everyday life (if it is not feasible to survey all participants, a random sampling of those with exposure to human rights education, including use of control groups, could be done); *(b)* individual and focus group interviews with participants concerning their knowledge of and attitudes towards human rights, evaluation of the rights education programming in which they participated and any plans for application of human rights principles; and *(c)* longitudinal data collection on impact including follow-up surveys and interviews on above topics.

60. For the various programming sectors, are the programmes sustainable?

(a) Can the human rights education programme strategies be sustained either through the direct continuation of programming and/or through the expertise catalysed by the original programme? (An example of the first are training activities conducted directly by staff; an example of the second would be training activities conducted by those originally trained by staff);

(b) Has human rights education expertise been expanded? *Possible indicators:* future programme plans (including outreach numbers and techniques, funding sources), cadre of human rights education specialists that can be drawn upon for future programming, local spin-off programming, networking and coalitions with other groups;

(c) Have the programmes been institutionalised? *Possible indicators:* insertion of human rights in all teaching institutions' curricula and the establishment and functioning of a national human rights resource and training centre.

National Committee

61. How timely and effective has the national committee been in developing the national plan of action (including commissioning the baseline study and formulating national objectives, strategies and programme priorities)? *Data source:* interviews with key members of the committee. Comparison between time-frame set (if available) and time-frame met.

62. How successful has the committee been in facilitating cooperative behaviour between government agencies, intergovernmental organisations, non-governmental organisations, professional associations, individuals and other civil society groups? *Data sources:* interviews with members of the national committee leadership of cooperating agencies and leadership of non-cooperating agencies.

63. How successful has the committee been in generating political and financial support for carrying out the national plan of action? *Indicators:* organisational representation from governmental and non-governmental organisations on the national committee itself; support and endorsement by key agencies for implementation of human rights education programming; funds or support in kind contributed from government sources, donor agencies and cooperating intergovernmental agencies and NGOs.

6

Human Rights Questions: Report of the High Commissioner for Human Rights

Fifty-first Session

Agenda Item 110 (b)

HUMAN RIGHTS QUESTIONS: HUMAN RIGHTS QUESTIONS, INCLUDING ALTERNATIVE APPROACHES FOR IMPROVING THE EFFECTIVE ENJOYMENT OF HUMAN RIGHTS AND FUNDAMENTAL FREEDOMS

Note by the Secretary-General

Addendum

The Secretary-General has the honour to transmit to the General Assembly the addendum to the report of the United Nations High Commissioner for Human Rights on the implementation of the Plan of Action for the United Nations Decade for Human Rights Education (1995-2004), issued pursuant to General Assembly resolution 50/177 of 22 December 1995 (A/51/506).

ANNEX

Report of the United Nations High Commissioner for Human Rights on the Implementation of the Plan of Action for the United Nations Decade for Human Rights Education

Introduction

1. The World Conference on Human Rights (Vienna, June 1993) in the Vienna Declaration and Programme of Action stated that human rights education, training and public information were essential for the promotion and achievement of stable and harmonious relations among communities and for fostering mutual understanding, tolerance and peace. The Conference recommended that States strive to eradicate illiteracy and direct education towards the full development of the human personality and the strengthening of respect for human rights and fundamental freedoms. It called on all States and institutions to include human rights, humanitarian law, democracy and the rule of law as subjects in the curricula of all learning institutions in formal and non-formal settings.

2. Pursuant to a suggestion of the World Conference, the General Assembly, in its resolution 49/184 of 23 December 1994, proclaimed the 10-year period beginning on 1 January 1995 the United Nations Decade for Human Rights Education, and welcomed the draft Plan of Action for the Decade contained in the report of the Secretary-General (A/49/261-E/1994/110/Add,1, annex).

3. The General Assembly appealed to all Governments to contribute to the implementation of the Plan of Action and to step up their efforts to eradicate illiteracy and to direct education towards the full development of the human personality and to the strengthening of respect for human rights and fundamental freedoms; urged governmental and non-governmental educational agencies to intensify their efforts to establish and implement programmes of human rights education, as recommended in the Plan of Action, in particular by preparing and implementing national plans for human rights education; and requested the United Nations High Commissioner for Human Rights to coordinate the implementation of the Plan of Action.

4. In the same resolution the General Assembly invited the specialised agencies and United Nations programmes to contribute, within their respective spheres of competence, to the implementation of the Plan of Action; called upon a wide

range of non-governmental organisations and others to increase their involvement in formal and non-formal education in human rights; and requested the existing human rights monitoring bodies to place emphasis on the implementation by Member States of their international obligation to promote human rights education.

5. The Plan of Action has five objectives; the assessment of needs and formulation of strategies; building and strengthening human rights education programmes; developing educational material; strengthening the mass media; and the global dissemination of the Universal Declaration of Human Rights. The Plan of Focuses on stimulating and supporting national and local activities and initiatives and is built upon the idea of a partnership between Governments, international organisations, non-governmental organisations, professional associations, individual and large segments of civil society.

6. The active engagement of non-government organisations, grass-roots organisations and professional associations in the various activities of the Plan of Action is seen as a crucial element for success. The General Assembly and the Commission on Human Rights both called upon international, regional and national non-governmental organisations, in particular those concerned with women, labour, development and the environment, as well as all other social justice groups, human rights advocates, educators, religious organisations and the media, to increase their involvement in formal and non-formal education in human rights and to cooperate with the Centre for Human Rights in carrying out the activities of the United Nations Decade for Human Rights Education.

7. The Plan of Action is set out in the appendix to the present document. It reflects comments made by Governments as requested by the General Assembly and the Commission on Human Rights.

APPENDIX

Plan of Action for the United Nations Decade for Human Rights Education, 1995-2004: Human Rights Education—Lessons for Life

Contents

Paragraph

I. Normative Basis and Definition

1. The United Nations Decade for Human Rights Education shall be based upon the provisions of the international human rights instruments, with particular reference to those provisions addressing human rights education, including article 26 of the Universal of Human Rights, article 13 of the International Covenant on Economic, Social and Cultural Rights, article 29 of the Convention on the Rights of the Child, article 10 of the Convention on the Elimination of All Forms of Discrimination against Women, article 7 of the Convention on the Elimination of all Forms of Racial Discrimination, paragraphs 33 and 34 of the Vienna Declaration and paragraphs 78 to 82 of its Programme of Action.

2. In accordance with those provisions, and for the purposes of the Decade, human rights education shall be defined as training, dissemination and information efforts aimed at the building of a universal culture of human rights through the imparting of knowledge and skills and the moulding of attitudes and directed to:

(a) The strengthening of respect for human rights and fundamental freedoms;

(b) The full development of the human personality and the sense of its dignity;

(c) The promotion of understanding, tolerance, gender equality and friendship among all nations, indigenous peoples and racial, national, ethnic, religious and linguistic groups;

(d) The enabling of all persons to participate effectively in a free society;

(e) The furtherance of the activities of the United Nations for the maintenance of peace.

II. General Guidelines Principles

3. The United Nations Decade for Human Rights Education shall be guided by the definition and normative basis set out in part I of the present Plan of Action and shall further be directed to creating the broadest possible awareness and

understanding of all of the norms, concepts and values enshrined in the Universal Declaration of Human Rights, the International Covenant on Civil and Political Rights, the International Covenant on Economic, Social and Cultural Rights and in other relevant international human rights instruments. The Decade is placed within the context of action of States and others to eradicate illiteracy and understands education to be a constant factor in the multidimensional life of individuals and of society of which human rights are an integral part.

4. A comprehensive approach to education for human rights, including civil, cultural, economic, political and social rights and recognising the indivisibility and interdependence of all rights, as defined by the United Nations, shall be adopted for all activities under the Decade.

5. Education for the purpose of the Decade shall be conceived to include the equal participation of women and men of all age groups and all sectors of society both in formal learning through schools and vocational and professional training, as well as in non-formal learning through institutions of civil society, the family and the mass media.

6. In order to enhance their effectiveness, human rights education efforts for the Decade shall be shaped in such a way as to be relevant to the daily lives of learners, and shall seek to engage learners in a dialogue about the ways and means of transforming human rights from the expression of abstract norms to the reality of their social, economic, cultural and political conditions.

7. In recognition of the interdependence and mutually reinforcing nature of democracy, development and human rights, human rights education under the Decade shall seek to further effective democratic participation in the political, economic, social and cultural spheres, and shall be utilised as a means of promoting economic and social progress and people-centred sustainable development.

8. Human rights education under the Decade shall combat and be free of gender bias, racial and other stereotypes.

9. Human rights education under the Decade shall seek both to impart skills and knowledge to learners and to affect positively their attitudes and behaviour, consistent with all other principles set forth in the present Plan of Action and in the international human rights instruments upon which it is based.

III. Objectives

10. The objectives of the Decade shall include:

(a) The assessment of needs and the formulation of effective strategies for the furtherance of human rights education at all school levels, in vocational training and formal as well as non-formal learning;

(b) The building and strengthening of programmes and capacities for human rights education at the international, regional, national and local levels;

(c) The coordinated development of human rights education materials;

(d) The strengthening of the role and capacity of the mass media in the furtherance of human rights education;

(e) The global dissemination of the Universal Declaration of Human Rights in the maximum possible number of languages and in other forms appropriate for various levels of literacy and for the disabled.

IV. Principal Actors

11. Governments should play an active role in the implementation of the programme of the Decade through the development of national plans of action for human rights education, the introduction, or strengthening of national human rights curricula in their formal educational system, the conducting of national information campaigns on human rights and the opening of public access to human rights resource, information and training centres, as well as through enhanced donor support for relevant voluntary funds and international and national human rights education programmes.

12. National human rights institutions, such as human rights commissions, offices of the ombudsman and human rights research and training institutes should play a central role in the development, coordination and implementation of human rights education programmes at the national level.

13. The active engagement of national non-governmental organisations, grass-roots organisations, professional associations and interested individuals shall be encouraged to assist in the realisation of the goals of the Decade. To that end, national organisations should be given to full support of international programmes, Governments and other to assist them in their human rights educational activities, both through technical assistance and training and through financial support to aid them in strengthening their role in civil society.

14. The United Nations High Commissioner for Human Rights is the highest official of the United Nations dealing with human rights matters. He is specifically responsible for coordinating relevant United Nations education and public information programmes in the field of human rights, in keeping with General Assembly resolution 48/141 of 20 December 1993.

15. The United Nations High Commissioner for Human Rights and the Centre for Human Rights are a unity whereby the High Commissioner sets the policy direction and the priority of action and the Centre implements those policies. In this connection, the Centre for Human Rights, in consultation with the United Nations Educational, Scientific and Cultural Organisation (UNESCO), shall continue to provide to Governments, on request, human rights education, training, information, fellowships and advisory services programmes. The Centre should continue its emphasis, in this regard, on the training of teachers, police, prison officials lawyers, judges, government officials, the media, the military, non-governmental organisations electoral officials and the general public. The Centre should also continue to provide human rights training to international civil servants, development officers and peacekeepers.

16. United Nation human rights treaty monitoring bodies, the Commission on Human Rights, the Subcommission on Prevention of Discrimination and Protection of Minorities and all other United Nations human rights bodies and programmes shall, in the course of their mandated functions during the Decade, encourage the furtherance of human rights education, including through appropriate recommendations to States, to the High Commissioner for Human Rights and to other involved in human rights education.

17. UNESCO, by reason of its long experience in education, educational methodology and human rights and through its network of UNESCO schools, clubs, human rights chairs and national commissions, shall play a central role in the design, implementation and evaluation of projects under the Plan of Action. Accordingly, UNESCO will be called upon to cooperate closely with the High Commissioner and the Centre for Human Rights in the implementation of the Plan.

18. Similarly, other United Nations specialised agencies, units of the Secretariat and programmes involved in human rights educational activities, including the United Nations Children's Fund (UNICEF), the International Labour Organisation (ILO), the Office of the United Nations High Commissioner for Refugee (UNHCR), the United Nations Development Programme (UNDP), the United Nations Volunteers (UNV), the United Nations Environment Programme (UNDP), the United Nations Centre for Human Settlements (Habitat), the Centre for Social Development and Humanitarian Affairs, the United Nations University (UNU) and various United Nations institutes engaged in research and training shall be encouraged to work with the High Commissioner for Human Rights in order that existing capacities for human rights education may be fully coordinated and mobilised towards the objectives of the Decade.

19. Other international organisations, including intergovernmental and non-governmental organisations active in the field of human rights, shall be encouraged to

continue and enhance their activities in the area of human rights education and to avail themselves of the coordination of the High Commissioner for Human Rights for the purposes of the Decade.

V. Target Groups

20. Activities carried out under the Decade shall be designed to bring the objectives of the Decade to as wide an audience as possible, through both formal and non-formal education and, to this end, should encouraged an approach that is designed to build permanent capacity, including through the training of trainers.

21. The general public shall be the subject of far-reaching human rights information efforts designed to inform them of their rights and responsibilities under the international human rights instruments.

22. Human rights education initiatives taken under the Decade shall include the use of audiovisual and multimedia materials, with a view to the effective delivery of human rights education to people at all levels of literacy and education and to persons with disabilities.

23. Special emphasis shall be given in human rights education activities under the Decade to the human rights of women, children, the aged, minorities, refugees, indigenous peoples, persons in extreme poverty, persons with HIV infection or AIDS and other vulnerable groups.

24. Special attention shall be given to the training of police, prison officials, lawyers, judges, teachers and curriculum developers, the armed forces, international civil servants, development officers and peacekeepers, non-governmental organisations, the media, governmental officials, parliamentarians and other groups that are in a particular position to effect the realisation of human rights.

25. Schools, universities, professional and vocational training programmes and institutions should be encouraged and assisted in developing human rights curricula and corresponding teaching and resource materials, with the help

of Governments and international donors and programmes, for incorporation into formal education at the early childhood primary, secondary, post-secondary and adult education levels.

26. Appropriate institutions of civil society, including non-governmental organisations workers' and employers' organisations, labour unions the mass media, religious organisations, community organisations, the family, independent information, resource and training centres and others, for the purpose of incorporating human rights education into non-formal programmes, should be encouraged and assisted in developing and delivering such non-formal programmes, with the help of Governments and international donors and programmes.

VI. Structure for Coordination and Implication

27. The United Nations High Commissioner for Human Rights, with the assistance of the Centre for Human Rights, will promote and coordinate the implementation of the present Plan of Action. He shall consult with the United Nations human rights treaty-monitoring and Charter-based human rights bodies regarding the Plan of Action and consider ways of supporting any recommendations made by those bodies in the area of human rights education. He will also consult closely with Governments, regional organisations, national institutions, specialised agencies, non-governmental organisations and grass-roots and professional associations, and will prepare an annual report on the progress made at all levels based on information supplied by those sources.

28. In recognition of the fact that action at the national and local levels is crucial to the effective promotion of human rights education, as is an effective international coordination structure, the Plan of Action envisages that:

   (a) National focal points for human rights education should be designated in each State, according to national conditions. Such focal points may consist of specially constituted committee including representatives of relevant government agencies, non-governmental

organisations, the private sector and educators; or, alternatively, existing appropriate structures or organisations, such as ombudsman offices, national human rights commissions or national human rights training and research institutes may be designed to perform this function;

(b) Each national focal point should be charged with identifying national human rights education needs, developing a national plan of action, raising funds, coordinating with regional and international bodies involved in implementing the objectives of the Decade and reporting to the High Commissioner for Human Rights on needs, proposals and proposals and progress made towards the realisation of the goals of the Decade;

(c) Each national focal point shall also serve as a conduit for the channeling of international and regional input, information and support to the local and grass-roots levels in their respective countries;

(d) Each State shall be encouraged to established a national human rights resources and training centre capable of engaging in research, training of trainers, preparation, collection, translation and dissemination of human rights materials, and organisation of conferences, workshops and courses or, where such centres already exist, to work towards their strengthening;

(e) International programmes and activities, including those of the United Nations and other international agencies, donor Governments and intergovernmental and non-governmental organisations should provide stimulus and support to national and local efforts in advancing the objectives of the Decade.

VII. Programme of Implementation

29. The particular objectives of the Decade, the programme of implementation for the realisation of those objectives and the means for follow-up and assessment of each programme element shall be as described below:

A. COMPONENT ONE: ASSESSING NEEDS AND FORMULATING STRATEGIES

Objectives

30. The objective of component one is to assess needs and to formulate effective strategies for the furtherance of human rights education at the international, regional, national and local levels.

Programme Elements

31. The High Commissioner for Human Rights, with the assistance of the Centre for Human Rights and in cooperation with UNESCO, shall conduct, in 1995, a preliminary survey and evaluation of existing human rights education programmes and initiatives at the international, regional and national levels, and shall issue a report of the results of that survey and evaluation.

32. The preliminary report shall take into account all available information on existing programmes and initiatives, shall identify shortcoming and needs for the realisation of the globals of the Decade and shall make recommendations for action to address those needs effectively during the Decade.

33. For the purposes of the High Commissioner's preliminary report, all participating national focal points, international and regional organisations, non-governmental organisations, specialised agencies and programmes, and interested others, shall be requested to provide relevant information to the High Commissioner, based upon their own independent assessments and activities. National focal points, in particular, shall be requested to conduct detailed assessments in their own countries and to report thereon to the High Commissioner.

34. The survey and evaluation and the resulting preliminary report shall seek to identify with particularly, at the international, regional and national levels, *inter alia*, the number and types of human right educational materials available, existing human rights educational institutes, centres and permanent focal points, national percentages of

teachers trained in human rights education, the percentage of schools having adopted human rights curricula at the primary, secondary and post-secondary levels, and number and types of human rights education components in professional training and non-formal education programmes.

35. The preliminary report shall identify, as well, the needs and requirements of Member States, non-governmental organisations and other implementing partners for the enhancement of existing human rights education programmes and for the creation of new programmes in order to contribute to the objectives of the Decade and shall make recommendations to those ends.

36. The report should also explore other aspects of the socialisation process, outside of traditional education, with a view to expanding human rights education in new directions so that human rights values may become more effectively integrated throughout society.

37. Annexed to the report should be a roster of national focal points, international and regional organisations cooperating in the Decade, existing human rights research and training institutes and centres, and other Decade partners. Information should also be provided on agencies, organisations, foundations and institutions providing financial and technical assistance to national governmental and non-governmental educational institutions and organisations engaged in human rights education.

Assessment and Follow-up

38. Following the publication of the preliminary report of the High Commissioner, the High Commissioner and the Centre for Human Rights shall convene an international planning conference on the Decade, with the participation of UNESCO, other United Nations agencies and human rights bodies participating in the Decade, representatives of involved regional and international organisations, non-governmental organisations, donor Governments, educators and other experts from all parts of the world.

39. The conference will review the preliminary report of the High Commissioner and develop detailed plans for the implementation of its recommendations and for the allocation of responsibilities to that end. Such plans will include timetables, designation of local, national, regional and international implementing agencies, budgets and implementation and funding strategies.

40. The High Commissioner will use the meeting as an opportunity to appeal to donors to support the funding of the various programmes resulting from the preliminary report and the conference.

41. The conclusions of the meeting will be contained in a report, which will be complementary to the preliminary report of the High Commissioner and which will be made available together with the preliminary report to all organisations, Governments and national focal points participating in the Decade.

42. Union receipt of the complementary reports, all national focal points will be requested to develop a five-year detailed national implementation plan for human rights education including target groups, methodologies, timetables, budgets and funding strategies, covering efforts to meet the objectives of the Decade up to the mid-term evaluation period in the year 2000.

B. COMPONENT TWO: STRENGTHENING INTERNATIONAL PROGRAMMES AND CAPACITIES

Objective

43. The objective of component two is to build and strengthen programmes and capacities for human rights education at the international level.

Programme Elements

44. Under the overall policy guidance of the High Commissioner for Human Rights, the Centre for Human Rights will continue and enhance its activities relating to programme development in the field of targeted human rights education, including the production of handbooks and training manuals on human

rights for selected audiences. The Centre will ensure the broad distribution of its manuals and handbooks on human rights and social work, human rights and elections, human rights and pre-trial detention, and human rights reporting, and will produce further manuals and handbooks on human rights and national institutions, human rights and police, human rights and prisons, human rights and the administration of justice, human rights and the armed forces, human rights and constitutions, human rights and conflict resolution, human rights and teachers, human rights and the media, and human rights and parliament. In these materials, the universality, indivisibility and interdependence of all rights should be reflected, and they should specifically address economic, social and cultural rights.

45. The Centre for Human Rights will continue and enhance its technical cooperation activities relating to human rights education, both for the general public and for specialised audiences, under the programme of advisory services and technical assistance in the field of human rights.

46. The Centre for Human Rights, in cooperation with UNESCO, will develop model human rights curricula, pedagogical techniques and teaching materials for primary and secondary schools. The Centre for Human Rights, under its programme of advisory services and technical assistance in the field of human rights, will utilise these materials in its provision of technical assistance to requesting States.

47. Each specialised agency will be requested to enhance its efforts in the area of human rights education and to appoint a human rights education liaison officer to work with the High Commissioner and the Centre for Human Rights in the development of joint educational activities relating to human rights in the areas of competence of each agency. Each agency will provide information to the High Commissioner on programmes undertaken and materials produced in the field of human rights education for the High Commissioner's preliminary, mid-term and final reports.

48. The Centre for Human Rights will promote the organisation of international workshops to identify concepts, materials

and methods for human rights education on priority human rights themes.

49. Consistent with the directives of the World Conference on Human Rights in its Vienna Declaration and Programme of Action, the Centre for Human Rights will continue and enhance its activities aimed at assisting peacekeepers, international civil servants and development officers in integrating human rights standards, concepts and methods into the planning and implementation of their work. To that end, the Centre should develop specific training programmes for each of these groups, and should cooperate with the relevant agencies and departments of the United Nations in incorporating such programmes into their activities.

50. The Centre for Human Rights, as well as relevant specialised agencies and international programmes, will explore possibilities for the development and use of advanced technologies, including telecommunications, networks, electronic mail databases and data exchange to facilitate networking among international programmes, national focal points, educators and resource and training centres involved in the Decade.

51. The Secretary-General shall be requested to establish a United Nations voluntary fund for human rights education, to be administered by the Centre for Human Rights through the programme of advisory services and technical assistance. The fund shall be used to support activities under the Decade, including support for building human rights education capacities in governmental institutions and non-governmental organisations at the national level.

Assessment and Follow-up

52. The High Commissioner will report on progress and developments in all of these programmes elements in his preliminary, mid-term and final reports. He will also make recommendations for advancing the objectives of these elements in each such report. Each international actor implicated in these programme elements will accordingly be called upon to provide updated and detailed information to the High Commissioner.

C. COMPONENT THREE: STRENGTHENING REGIONAL PROGRAMMES AND CAPACITIES

Objectives

53. The objective of component three is to build and strengthen programmes and capacities for human rights education at the regional level.

Programmes Elements

54. All regional and subregional human rights organisations will be requested to enhance their efforts in the area of human rights education and will also be requested to appoint a human rights education liaison officer to work with the High Commissioner and the Centre for Human Rights in the development of joint educational activities relating to human rights in the respective regions of each organisation. Liaison officers will, as well as, be requested to report to the High Commissioner, on behalf of each organisation, on programmes undertaken and materials produced in the field of human rights education, for purposes of the High Commissioner's preliminary, mid-term and final reports.

55. In religions or subregions where such organisations do not yet exist, the High Commissioner, with the assistance of the Centre for Human Rights, will encourage their establishment through the convening of workshops and through the provision of technical assistance, where appropriate.

Assessment and Follow-up

56. The High Commissioner will report on progress and developments in all of these programme elements in his preliminary, mid-term and final reports. He will also make recommendations for advancing the objectives of these elements in each such report. Each regional organisation participating in these programme elements will accordingly be called upon to provide updated and detailed information to the High Commissioner.

D. COMPONENT FOUR: STRENGTHENING NATIONAL PROGRAMMES AND CAPACITIES

Objectives

57. The objective of component four is to build and strengthen programmes and capacities for human rights education at the national level.

Programme Elements

58. Every State will be requested to draw up a national plan of action for human rights education, reflecting the principles and objectives of this international plan and forming an integral part of a comprehensive national plan of action for human rights. Such national plans of action for human rights education should be completed during 1995, in consultation will all relevant national and local actors and groups, and should be transmitted to the High Commissioner for Human Rights for purposes of effective coordination and cooperation in their implementation. Each national plan should contain specific objectives, strategies and programmes for the enhancement of human rights education in pre-schools, primary and secondary schools, higher education, professional schools, the training of public officials and in non-formal learning, including general public information. National focal points should periodically review the implementation of the framework and revise them as necessary.

59. As described in paragraph 28 above, every State will be requested to designate a national focal point for human rights education, which shall assist in the identification of needs, the development of a national plan of action, fund-raising and international and local liaison and coordination with the High Commissioner for Human Rights.

60. Every State will be encouraged to establish a national public access human rights resource and training centre or, where such centres already exist, to take concrete steps to strengthen their capacity to support human rights education at the national and local levels. International and regional programmes and organisations should assist in the

establishment and strengthening of such centres, including through the provision of financial and technical assistance. States should provide to the High Commissioner, for purposes of his preliminary, mid-term and final reports, all available information on the existence, operation, functions and resources of such centres.

61. National human rights resource and training centres, in cooperation with national focal points, should engage, *inter alia*, in the following tasks:

(*a*) Research on human rights and human rights education;

(*b*) Translation and culturally appropriate adaptation of training materials;

(*c*) Outreach to professional groups and community workers;

(*d*) Gender-sensitive training of trainers;

(*e*) Organisation of internship programmes for students and teachers interested in developing projects in human rights education;

(*f*) Organisation of special cultural events for art, music and theatre performances, and the production of journals, popular books and audiovisual materials on human rights;

(*g*) Maintenance of a roster of national experts and institutions in human rights education;

(*h*) Assistance in the implementation of internationally sponsored technical cooperation projects for human rights education;

(*i*) Establishment of a human rights extension service for making consultations, publications and teaching materials available to individuals and groups requesting assistance in matters relating to human rights education. Assistance in the development of guidelines and materials for these extension services should be provided to the national resource and training centres by competent international programmes and organisations on request.

Assessment and Follow-up

62. The High Commissioner will report on progress and developments in all of these programmes elements in his preliminary, mid-term and final reports. He will also make recommendations for advancing the objectives of these elements in each such report. Each national focal point participating in these programme elements will accordingly be called upon to provide updated and detailed information to the High Commissioner.

63. The reports of the High Commissioner will be made available to all national focal points in order that they may take into account his recommendations, and so that they may make use of other information contained in those reports, for purposes of programme development, identification of sources of funding and technical assistance, and liaison with other actors in the Decade.

E. COMPONENT FIVE: STRENGTHENING LOCAL PROGRAMMES AND CAPACITIES

Objective

64. The objective of component five is to build and strengthen programmes and capacities for human rights education at the local level.

Programme Elements

65. National focal points will be encouraged, in the interest of building local and community-based capacities for human rights education, to include all local and community-based organisations in the national roster described in component four above, and to direct their efforts and resources, including support received from international sources, to enabling such local and community-based organisations to deliver effective human rights education to their constituencies.

66. With the support of national focal points and national resource and training centres, local and community-based organisations should be prepared to deliver popular human rights education, through vocational and adult education, literacy, training, local non-governmental organisations, family outreach and religious education.

67. To these ends, national focal points should be charged with organising regard consultations and annual meetings with local groups and representatives, and with soliciting their active input for purposes of national evaluations, plans of action, projects and reports to the High Commissioner.

68. Local and community-based groups should also be fully involved in the implementation of national projects for human rights education, with a view to delivering the benefits of the Decade to all levels and sectors of society.

Assessment and Follow-up

69. The High Commissioner will report on challenges, progress and developments in the delivery of human rights education to the local level in his preliminary, mid-term and final reports. He will also make recommendations for advancing these efforts in each such report. Each national focal point participating in these programme elements will accordingly be called upon to provide updated and detailed information to the High Commissioner on the number and types of local and community-based groups cooperating with each national focal point and the kind of support delivered to the local level, as well as challenges and difficulties encountered.

F. COMPONENT SIX: COORDINATED DEVELOPMENT OF MATERIALS FOR HUMAN RIGHTS EDUCATION

Objective

70. The objective of component six is to ensure the coordinated development of effective human rights education materials.

Programme Elements

71. The High Commissioner for Human Rights and the Centre for Human Rights shall develop and publish, in cooperation with UNESCO and all other actors in the Decade, a current and periodically updated listing of available human rights educational materials, including manuals, handbooks, curricula, audiovisual tools and other such materials, concurrent with his preliminary, mid-term and final reports. The listing shall also contain information on how such materials may be obtained by interested organisations and

individuals. The listing should be made available on an electronic database as soon as possible. The educational material collected in connection with the listing should be maintained at the Centre for Human Rights and made available upon request to interested parties.

72. UNESCO and other international and regional organisations and agencies will be requested to enhance their activities directed at the development of such materials, with priority attention to be directed to any lacunae revealed in the compilation of the High Commissioner's listing and to the strengthening of existing materials where necessary.

73. Educational materials developed at the national and regional levels should benefit from the review and input of national level points and national resource and training centres and should be made available to national and local programmes for translation, cultural adaptation, testing and revision, with the financial and technical assistance of international and regional programmes.

74. Every national resource and training centre should be provided with a full set of such materials for use in the development of national and local programmes, and national focal points, in their reports to the High Commissioner, should identify national needs in this regard. National focal points will, in turn, be responsible for making such materials available to local and community-based groups, national professional training programmes, national non-governmental organisations and other national actors in the Decade.

75. In the development of new materials for specialised audiences, the following considerations should be taken into account, in addition to the normative basis, definition, guiding principles, objectives and target groups described in parts I to V of the present Plan of Action.

   (a) *Collegial Presentations*. Where possible, effective training efforts should draw from a list of experts which is practical in orientation. Rather than assembling panels composed entirely of professors and theorists, consideration should be given to preparing practitioners in the relevant field to deliver human rights education, be they lawyers, judges or police officers. Much more can be accomplished through the collegial approach of, for example, police discussing with police, than could be gained by a professor-student model of training;

(b) *Training the Trainers and Capacity-building*. Participants in targeted human rights courses should be selected with the understanding that their responsibilities will continue after completion of the training exercises. They should be charged with conducting their own training or dissemination efforts after returning to their normal duty station. In this way, the impact of such courses is multiplied several fold, as the information imparted is disseminated throughout the institutions concerned;

(c) *Pedagogical Techniques*. Courses developed under the Decade, in each case, should include a section designed to introduce a variety of effective techniques for the training of specific audiences. In particular, suggestions should be made for the use of creative, interactive teaching methods, which offer the best hope for securing the active, engaged participation of the programme participants. Such techniques may include the use of working groups, lecture-discussions, case-studies, panel discussions, round-table discussions, brainstorming sessions, simulation and role playing, field trips, practice and the use of audio and visual aids, as actually appropriate to the specific audience;

(d) *Audience Specifically*. The mere recitation of vague principles of general applicability offers little hope of affecting the actual behaviour of a given audience. To be effective, indeed, at all worthwhile, training and education efforts must be directly targeted and appropriately addresses to a particular audience, be they police, health care workers, lawyers, students or others. Accordingly, the content of the Decade's teaching activities should focus more on the standards directly relevant to the daily work of or role in the community of the audience and less on distant theoretical notions;

(e) *Practical Approach.* According to the report of a recent parliamentary commission investigating violations at one country's police stations, when confronted with evidence of abuses the police said that they lacked understanding about interrogation methods and techniques, that they carried out interrogations by outdated methods and that they did not know how interrogations were carried out in other countries. In order to compare their methods and improve them, they wanted to have the chance to do research and observe interrogation methods in other countries. Such accounts reveal two important areas of focus, extendable by analogy to audiences other than police trainees. Firstly, offering justifications of any kind for serious violations such as torture demonstrates a lack of familiarity with the most fundamental of standards for human rights. There are no legitimate justifications for such activities. Secondly, police (and other groups) in the real world want to know not just what the rules are, but also how to do their job effectively within the confines of those rules. Training efforts that ignore either of these areas will likely be neither credible nor effective. Accordingly, educational efforts, under the Decade should include practical information on proven techniques for the performance of the target audience's duties, as derived from the recommendations of experts and literature on the current best practice for the profession in question;

(f) *Comprehensive Presentation of Standards.* Courses and materials developed under the Decade should be thorough in their presentation of the relevant international standards. To that end, relevant instruments and simplified learning tools should be translated and provided to trainees;

(g) *Teaching to Sensitise.* The goals of materials and courses developed under the Decade should not be limited to the imparting of standards and practical skills, but should also include exercises designed to sensitise trainees to their own potential for violative behaviour, however unwitting. For example, well-developed exercises that can have the effect of making trainees aware of notions of gender or racial bias in their own attitudes or behaviour can be quite valuable. Similarly, the special import of particular standards as they apply to women (for example) are not always readily obvious. Trainees should be made to understand, for example, that the term "degrading treatment", as found in the various international instruments, may have different practical implications when applied to women as compared to men, or when applied to one cultural groups vis-à-vis another;

(h) *Flexibility of Design and Application*. To be universally, useful, training courses and materials must be designed in such a way as to facilitate their flexible use, without imposing a single rigid focus or approach on the trainers. Such courses must be adaptable to the particular, cultural, educational, regional and experimental needs and realities of a diverse range of potential audiences within the target group;

(i) *Evaluation Tools*. Training materials and courses should include pre- and post-training evaluative exercises, such as testing questionnaires, which serve three crucial purposes. Pre-courses questionnaires, when properly utilised, allow a trainer to tailor his or her course to the particular educational needs of the audience. Post-course questionnaires and evaluation sessions will both allow trainees to gauge what they have learned and assist in the continuous (crucial) modification and improvement of courses offered under the Decade.

Assessment and Follow-up

76. The High Commissioner, concurrently with his preliminary, mid-term and final reports, will make available for distribution to all international organisations, regional organisations and national focal points the current listings of available training materials described in this component.

77. The High Commissioner, based upon information to be provided in reports by national focal points and from other partners in the Decade, will encourage the development and distribution of new materials, as indicated by evolving needs.

G. COMPONENT SEVEN: STRENGTHENING THE ROLE OF THE MASS MEDIA

78. The objective of component seven is to strengthen the role and capacity of the mass media in the furtherance of human rights education.

Programme Elements

79. In recognition of the important role of the mass media in bringing human rights education to all sectors of society, including to persons at all levels of literacy and those living or working in remote areas, journalists, broadcasters and other media professionals should, during the course of the Decade, be subject to increased training and assistance in incorporating human rights information and public education into their work. All programmes and organisations engaged in the provision of training and technical cooperation under the Decade should consider contributing to these efforts. The Centre for Human Rights, in particular, should produce a manual on human rights for the media and increase its media training activities.

80. All actors in the Decade shall encourage, in their contacts with the media, enhanced public coverage of human rights issues and the development of programmes that provide information and ideas about human rights and contribute to a public dialogue about human rights, in full respect for the independence of the media and the freedoms of information and expression.

81. In consultation with the High Commissioner for Human Rights and the Centre for Human Rights, the Department of Public Information of the United Nations will increase significantly the production of United Nations, television and radio educational programmes on human rights. The Department will be requested to produce videos, films and programmes for radio broadcasting on human rights themes.

82. The High Commissioner and the Centre for Human Rights, with the cooperation of the Department of Public Information, will establish a media advisory board for public information and education on human rights and will develop a mass media campaign to publicise human rights standards and mechanisms.

83. In the context of the World Public Information Campaign for Human Rights, and in cooperation with relevant non-governmental organisations and agencies, the Centre for Human Rights will intensify the publication of facts sheets, studies and other public information human rights materials. It will also organise or participate in public human rights events such as the fiftieth anniversary of the United Nations, in 1995, and the fiftieth anniversary of the Universal Declaration of Human Rights, in 1998. The High Commissioner will encourage global media coverage of these events.

Assessment and Follow-up

84. The High Commissioner, in his preliminary, mid-term and final reports will provide information on measures undertaken to increase media attention to human rights issues at the international and national levels. All national focal points will be requested to maintain a review of national press coverage of human rights issues and to report of the High Commissioner on such coverage. A similar press review, at the international level, will be maintained by the Centre for Human Rights and the Department of Public Information.

H. COMPONENT EIGHT: GLOBAL DISSEMINATION OF THE UNIVERSAL DECLARATION OF HUMAN RIGHTS

Objective

85. The objective of component eight is to achieve the global dissemination of the Universal Declaration of Human Rights in the maximum number of possible languages, and in other forms appropriate for various levels of literacy and for the disabled.

Programme Elements

86. The High Commissioner for Human Rights and the Centre for Human Rights, in cooperation with UNESCO, the Department of Public Information and its United Nations information centres, will conduct a global survey of existing printed language versions of the Universal Declaration of Human Rights, as well as of existing versions in pictorial, audiovisual or other formats, and will ascertain the availability of the various versions for distribution in each Member State, commencing in 1995.

87. Based upon the results of the survey, a plan will be developed by the High Commissioner for the production of further language versions of the Universal Declaration, with priority attention to be given to ensuring the existence of at least one printed format version for the main language of each Member State, and at least one audio or other appropriate version for persons of various levels of literacy and for the disabled in each Member State. Additional versions, in minority and other national languages, and in other formats for persons of other levels of literacy and for the disabled, should immediately follow the production of these versions.

88. Under the coordination of the High Commissioner and the respective national focal points for human rights education, and according to the plan developed following the survey, Governments and national non-governmental organisations, universities and institutes, will be called upon to carry out translation, publication and distribution of appropriate versions of the Universal Declaration of Human Rights, with technical and financial assistance from international organisations and programmes, where necessary. Such international organisations and programmes, including the advisory services and technical assistance programme of the Centre for Human Rights, UNESCO, other United Nations agencies and international non-governmental organisations, will be encouraged by the High Commissioner for Human Rights to make available such assistance, and the international donor community will be called upon to support these efforts.

89. On the occasion of the fiftieth anniversary of the Universal Declaration of Human Rights, in 1998, major celebratory events will be recognised at the international, religion and national levels, during which the importance of universal knowledge of understanding of the provisions of the Universal Declaration will be emphasised. At the international level, the High Commissioner for Human Rights will convene an international conference on dissemination of the Universal Declaration, for the purpose of devising strategies for ensuring that the Declaration is globally available and effectively incorporated into human rights education at all levels and in all Member States. Regional organisations and national focal points will be called upon to hold corresponding events and to contribute to and implement the recommendations of the international conference.

Assessment and Follow-up

90. The results of the survey conducted by the High Commissioner and the report of the international conference to be held in 1998 will be distributed to all regional organisations, national focal points and other interested partners in the Decade upon their completion.

91. All regional organisations, national focal points and other interested partners in the Decade will be requested to report to the High Commissioner for purposes, of his mid-term evaluation in the year 2000, and again for his final report in 2004, on progress made since the completion of the survey, including celebratory events held and versions of the Universal Declaration available, and on continuing needs and challenges in the achievement of the objectives of these programmes elements.

92. The High Commissioner will incorporate all such information into his mid-term and final report, and all programme partners will be called upon to redirect their efforts according to the information and recommendations contained in those reports.

VIII. Mid-term Global Evaluation

93. During the year 2000, a mid-term global evaluation of progress made towards the achievement of the objectives of the Decade shall be undertaken by the High Commissioner for Human Rights and the Centre for Human Rights, in cooperation with all other principal actors in the Decade. The High Commissioner shall report to the General Assembly on the results of that evaluation.

94. The evaluation report shall take into account all available information on what has been accomplished at the international, regional, national and local levels, shall identify remaining shortcomings and needs, and shall make recommendations for action during the five remaining years of the Decade.

95. For purposes of the High Commissioner's report, all participating national focal points, international and regional organisations, non-governmental organisations, specialised agencies and programmes, and interested others, shall be requested to provide relevant information to the High Commissioner, based upon their own independent assessments and activities. National focal points, in particular, shall be requested to conduct detailed assessments in their own countries, and to report thereon to the High Commissioner.

IX. Conclusion of the Decade

96. The year 2004 shall be the final year of the United Nations Decade for Human Rights Education. That year shall, accordingly, be set as the target date for achievement of generalised human rights education programmes through the implementation of State action plans. It shall also be target date for the completion of a comprehensive collection of human rights education materials and their broad distribution throughout all Member States. By the conclusion of the Decade, effective national capacities for the delivery of human rights education should be secured worldwide.

X. Follow-up to the Decade

97. After conclusion of the Decade, the High Commissioner, with the assistance of the Culture for Human Rights and in cooperation with UNESCO, should issue a final report on the state of human rights education at the local, national, regional and international levels. The High Commissioner, in the final report, should seek to identify, as precisely as possible, progress in the various areas, including in which languages the Universal Declaration of Human Rights is available, the number and types of human rights education manuals, handbooks and teaching materials developed by international and regional organisations and programmes, the number of human rights educational institutes, centres or permanent focal points established at the national level, the national percentages of teachers trained in human rights, the number of schools having adopted human rights education, curricula and the number and kinds of education in the professional fields and in informal and non-formal education. The report should also provide precise information on how various language versions of the Universal Declaration on Human Rights and human rights teaching materials may be obtained by interested groups and individuals.

98. The national, regional and international structures and networks established under the Decade should continue to serve as permanent focal and contact points for international cooperation in the field of human rights education, and the High Commissioner, and the Centre for Human Rights, in cooperation with UNESCO should maintain, and make available upon request, a current roster of such organisations and focal points.

99. Human rights educational materials developed under the Decade should be subject to periodic review, supplementation and revision to take into account changing needs and realities, and should continue to be made available on the widest possible basis.

7

Summary of National Initiatives Undertaken within the Decade for Human Rights Education (1995-2004)

This is a summary of information received by the Office of the UN High Commissioner for Human Rights (OHCHR) from Governments, concerning their activities in the framework of the Decade for Human Rights Education (1995-2004). The information is updated as of October 2003, and is included in related reports submitted by OHCHR to the United Nations General Assembly and Commission on Human Rights, National initiatives are presented by country, under five regions (*Africa; Arab countries; Asia/Pacific; Europe and North America; Latin America and the Caribbean*).

At the national level, the Decade's Plan of Action provides for the establishment, upon the initiatives of Governments or other relevant institutions, of a national committee for human rights education. This committee should consist of a broad coalition of governmental and non-governmental actors and should be responsible for developing and implementing a comprehensive (in terms of outreach), effective (in terms of educational strategies) and sustainable (over the long term) national plan of action for human rights education, in consultation with regional and international organisations. Such a plan should constitute an integral part of the overall national plan of action for human rights, when applicable, or should be complementary to it. The call for the establishment of such plans has been reiterated both by the General Assembly and the Commission on Human Rights.

For more information and committee, place contact us at: *hredatabase@ohchr.org*

ARFICA

Burundi

Although a national committee for human rights education has not been established, since the beginning of the Decade the Ministry of Human Rights has increasingly worked on the sensitisation of human rights issues in all socio-professional sectors. The Ministry has developed a plan of action, which forms part of an overall national plan. At the time of completion of the questionnaire, it was expected that the plan would be concluded during the summer of 2000.

Last information received on: 28 June 2000

Contact: Centre de Promotion des Droits de la Personne Humaine et de Prévention du Génocide (C.P.D.H.P.G.)

Cameroon

All overall national plan for human rights is currently being developed with the assistance of OHCHR. The Government is favourable for the integration of a national plan for human rights education and information into the overall national action plan for human rights.

Last information received on: 19 May 1999

Contact: Office of the Prime Minister

Cape Verde

The Government requested technical assistance from OHCHR for the development of an overall national plan for human rights, which would include a national plan for human rights education and information.

Last information received on: 2 February 1999

Contact: Ministry of Justice and Administration

Central African Republic

The Ministry of Justice, in close cooperation with MINURCA, organised a national seminar on "The impact of human rights in the national reconstruction process" in May/June 1999. This project was elaborated with the view to adopt a national plan of action for human rights education and promotion. The seminar gathered more than 200 participants, who included Government Officials, and members of political parties, religious communities, NGOs and the civil society.

There is no national plan of action in operation, however OHCHR and the Human Rights Department of the Bureau des Nations Unies en Centrafrique (BONUCA) are working together on plan which is expected to be completed in Jan/Feb 2001. The introduction of human rights education in schools coupled with the adoption of a national plan are the goals envisaged for the next five years of the Decade at the national level.

Since its creation in November 1999, the Human Rights Commission has disseminated information and organised seminars directed at all classes of society.

A national committee has not been established, however there are plans to do so at the beginning of the academic year 2000/01.

Last information received on: 5 July 2000.

Contact: Haut Commissariat à la Primature chargé des Droits de l'Homme

Chad

A national committee for human rights education was established on 8 May 1998, in accordance with decision number 002/PM/98. The Prime Minister acted on a proposal from the National Human Rights Committee (CNDH). The aforementioned decision did not determine the mandate of the committee, however it is anticipated that the following functions will be included:

the development of education in the human rights domain;

the adoption of an educational system which embraces peace and democracy;

to ensure that human rights concerns are promoted increasingly at all levels of society;

the strengthening of cooperation between OHCHR, African Commission on Human Rights and Populations, the Human Rights Centre, as well as all institutions and intergovernmental organisations in the area of human rights.

The committee is comprised of eleven members in total, with six representatives from the following human rights associations:

Ligue Tchadienne des droits de l'homme (LTDH)

The Chad Section of the International Observatory

Tchad non Violence

L'association jeunesse anti-clivage

The Chad Fundamental Rights Association

The Association for Defense and Promotion of Human Rights and five representatives from the following ministerial departments:

Justice

Family and Social Affairs

National Defense

Pubic Affairs

Higher Education

A plan of action, which is expected to be completed in May 2001, is underway. The principal actors include the following institutions:

National Human Rights Committee

National Education Committee

Human Rights NGOs

Government

The Plan of Action will aim to sensitize the population to human rights. It will also establish human rights education programmes in schools and promote democracy. Training for teachers and the increased use of didactical materials will be focus areas in the plan. The human rights education plan will be a component of a global action plan for Chad, which is not limited solely to human rights issues.

Technical assistance is being provided by OHCHR, UNESCO and the PUND.

Last information received on: 7 July 2000

Contact: Cabinet du Premier Ministre

Comoros

Although there is no national committee in existence, decree No. 99-001/PM calls for the establishment of a human rights declaration. Neither a national plan of action nor a human rights committee for human rights education have been established. Comoros is not in receipt of technical assistance.

Last information received on: 21 June 2000

Contact: Secretary General of Comoros Government

Ethiopia

The Government of Ethiopia reported on-going activities undertaken by different ministries. The Ministry of Justice, through its Legal Education and Training Department and Women's Affairs Department, promotes legal education, which includes a human rights component. This is accomplished through the use of the media (newspapers, radio and television), and the organisation of training programmes for judges, public prosecutors and women's groups. The Ministry of Education undertook a revision of school curricula in order that principles of human rights are included.

The Government of Ethiopia also noted the complementary role played by civil society in raising human rights awareness.

The Government of Ethiopia underlined the need for United Nations technical assistance to better integrate human rights education in its programmes and activities.

Last information received on: July 2001

Contact: Permanent Mission of the Federal Democratic Republic of Ethiopia, Geneva

Ghana

The Commission on Human Rights and Administrative Justice advised as to some of the existing activities in the area of human rights education, such as seminars and workshops for professional groups and a mass education campaign to reach out to communities. In addition, the faculty of Law at the University of Ghana has offered a course in international human rights law since 1994.

The Commissioner acknowledge the need for technical assistance in carrying out broad human rights education programmes, including the creation of a national committee for human rights education, and the establishment of a human rights resource and training centre. He expressed interest in facilitating the creation of a national committee for human rights education, and the establishment of a human rights resource and training centre. Specific proposals were made in that regard.

Last information received on: 5 September 1997

Contact: Commission on Human Rights and Administrative Justice

Lesotho

There is no national committee in existence and no plans have been made to establish such a committee.

The Human Rights Unit of the Ministry of Justice has been the key actor in human rights education at the national level. Since the beginning of the Decade, the Human Rights Unit has worked increasingly in this area, and launched a Human Rights and Democracy Programme with the Danish Centre for Human Rights (1995-1997).

Lesotho is not in receipt of technical assistance, however assistance is requested in the form of documentation regarding the development of a plan. Furthermore, it is proposed that a workshop be organised, at which an expert would assist in the construction of the plan.

Last information received on: 10 July 2000

Contact: Human Rights Unit/Ministry of Justice, Human Rights and Rehabilitation

Mauritius

The Ministry of Education has set up a curriculum panel team to revise materials, on human values education, for use in schools.

This involves working in close cooperation with a national non-governmental organisation dealing with teacher training.

Last information received on: 11 August 1998

Contact: Ministry of Education and Scientific Research

Mozambique

UNESCO provides technical assistance in the production of teaching and learning materials, and teacher training. Moreover, human rights education is integrated into the school curricula.

The creation of a national committee and a national plan are objectives for the next five years of the Decade.

Last information received on: 11 October 2000

No contact details provided.

Namibia

The Inter-Ministerial Technical Committee for Human Rights (IMTCHR), established in 1995 within the Ministry of Justice and composed by representatives of different ministries, has been developing number of human rights training programmes for police, prison and military officials since 1997. In 1998, a series of human rights training workshops for key sectors (the private sector, parliamentarians, women's organisations, regional Governors and NGOs) were also organised. Furthermore, the Committee has been active in curriculum development within the school system; a regional project involving Zimbabwe and Mozambique.

These projects were organised with the support of International Organisations, in particular OHCHR, UNESCO, the Red Cross and the Commonwealth, and through bilateral cooperation. In addition, a Human Rights Documentation Centre (HRDC) was established at the Faculty of Law of the University of Namibia, on the initiative of the Ministry of Justice. The HRDC is mandated to disseminate human rights information materials.

Two others bodies contribute to human rights education: in the first place, the Justice Training Centre (JTC), which is responsible for human rights training for magistrates, prosecutors, judges and related personnel; in the second, the Law Reform and Development Commission (LRDC), which is active in legal research and ensures that national law conforms to international human rights standards.

They reported on the establishment of a series of institutions charged with the promotion of human rights, including the Inter-Ministerial Technical Committee on Human Rights serviced by the Ministry of Justice, which comprises representatives of different ministries and which has organised training session for professional groups such as police, immigration officers, community leaders, judges and lawyers. The Human Rights Documentation Centre, located at the University of Namibia, disseminates human rights information materials; the Justice Training Centre is responsible for human rights training for magistrates, prosecutors, judges and related personnel; the Law Reform and Development Commission is active in legal research and ensures that national law conforms with international human rights standards.

Last information received on: 18 July 2002

Contact: Ministry of Foreign Affairs, Information and Broadcasting

Nigeria

The Government reported on the existence of a National Human Rights Commission, which is mandated to promote human rights education.

Last information received on: 10 September 1998

Contact: National Human Rights Commission

South Africa

The South African Human Rights Commission is promoting human rights education and is working on Decade-related issues with the Ministry of Education.

Last information received on: 4 May 1996

Contact: Human Rights Commission

Sudan

A national focal point has been established. National committee for human rights education at the state level are to be established in 1996.

Last information received on: 4 May 1996

Contact: Consultative Council for Human Rights/Ministry of Justice

Syria

The Ministry of Education reported on work undertaken towards the interrogation of international humanitarian law into academic curricula as well as the future integration in school curricula, in cooperation with the International Committee of the Red Cross, Educational activities were also undertaken to foster religious tolerance in the formal education system.

Last information received on: 8 January 2003

Tanzania

There is no national committee in existence, however there are plans to establish one during the year 2000/01.

A number of human rights agencies and the Permanent Commission of Enquiry have held responsibility at the national level for human rights education. Since the beginning of the Decade, the Tanzania Ombudsman Office has dealt to a greater degree with human rights issues. The Tanzania Ombudsman Office was established in 1996 by the government. It conducts enquiries into abuse of authority of office by public officials and submits recommendations to the present following assessment. It comprises of five members, a chairperson and four commissioners, who are appointed by the president. It has no NGO representatives.

The development of a human rights education plan before the end of the Decade is proposed.

Last information received on: 14 November 2000

Contact: Prime Minister Office

Zimbabwe

The Human Rights National Committee was set up by the Government in 1993, to serve as an advisor on human rights issues and to attend to Zimbabwe's obligations regarding international instruments to which the country is a party. The committee is composed of twenty members in total who represent various government ministries, departments and the Presidents office. The committee is chaired by the Ministry of Justice, Legal and Parliamentary Affairs. There are no NGO representatives on the committee, through NGOs often play a key role during workshops. The Inter-Ministerial committee is currently developing a national Plan of Action and it is envisaged that it will be completed by August 2002.

UNESCO is assisting the Ministry of Education, Sport and Culture with the development of curriculum materials and the integration of human rights and democracy in education.

Last information received on: 24 August 2000

Contact: Inter-Ministerial Committee on Human Rights and Humanitarian Law/Ministry of Justice, Legal and Parliamentary Affairs

ARAB COUNTRIES

Algeria

The Government has nominated the National Observatory for Human Rights as the focal point for the Decade and has translated the Universal Declaration of Human Rights into local languages.

Last information received on: 22 September 1997

Contact: National Observatory of Human Rights

Egypt

Following a National Conference on the Development of Primary-level Curricula in 1993 and of Preparatory-level Curricula in 1994, the Centre for the Development of Curricula and Teaching Materials began incorporating human rights, and in particular human rights and the prevention of discrimination, the rights of the child, in these two levels of formal education. The approach chosen was the infusion of these issues in all school subjects and textbooks rather than the creation of separate classes. As a result of meetings organised with human rights specialists, the infusion is taking place through varying courses of action: the incorporation of human rights in all schoolbooks, and the development of accompanying fascicles for students, containing practical activities, and teaching manuals for teachers. In addition, training courses for teachers, relating, to appropriate teaching strategies, have been organised. The Ministry of Education is currently planning to hold a conference on the development of Secondary-level Curricula, and preparatory studies are being conducted.

Last information received on: 1 July 2003

Contact: Permanent Mission of the Arab Republic of Egypt, Geneva

Jordan

The Ministry of Education informed that a series of laws have been passed over the period 1990-2001, focusing on the importance of creating a democratic and human rights climate in schools. Information on international and national human rights law has been incorporated into schools curricula and textbooks; teaching materials, also addressing the issue of teaching methodologies, have been developed. Human rights awareness-raising programmes have been designed to promote the role of women leaders, the rights of the child and conflict resolution methodologies, in cooperation with the Royal Human Rights Committee, the Ministry has contributed to the training of administration of justice officials. In cooperation with the Mizan Institute, human rights and children's rights clubs have been set up in a number of Jordanian schools. Jordan is further planning to develop human rights training for educational managers, in cooperation with UNESCO, and to establish a human rights education and training centre.

Last information received on: 20 March 2003

Contact: Ministry of Education

Lebanon

The 1997 Decree concerning pre-university educational curricula made provisions for the special national education and civics curricula within the school system. This provides for human rights and human-extensive coverage of the rights of the child, women rights in general. The National Centre for Educational Research and Development has been publishing related textbooks since the 1998/1999 academic year.

Last information received on: 27 September 1999

Contact: National Centre for Educational Research and Development

Morocco

The Government initiated in 1994 a partnership between the Ministry for Human Rights and the Ministry of Education with the aim to elaborate a National Programme for Human Rights Education. In this context, the following activities have been undertaken: revision of school textbooks to ensure accordance with human rights standards; training seminars for teachers and their supervisors; pilot-testing of the National Programme in both urban and rural areas of the country. Morocco further reported on the initiative to hold the first Arabic gathering on human rights education within the Decade, in cooperation with UNDP and UNESCO, which led to the adoption of the Rabat Declaration on the elaboration of a regional strategy for human rights education. In partnership with OHCHR, Morocco has also established a Human Rights Training, Information and Documentation Centre, which develops related materials and organises training sessions for prison officials, judges, NGO leaders, etc. Close working relationships have been developed with international and national NGOs as well as similar centres abroad.

The programme is at its dissemination and final phase, which aims at institutionalising programmes and materials previously tested. In 2003 the Ministry of Human Rights has also been focussing on human rights education in prisons and for police officials (in cooperation with Amnesty International/Morocco) and on non-formal awareness programmes for NGOs and political parties.

Last information received on: 19 May 2003

Contact: Permanent Mission of The Kingdom of Morocco, Geneva

Palestinian National Authority

In October 1997 Amnesty International in Gaza organised a workshop, which recommended the development of a national plan of action and the establishment of a national committee for Human Rights Education. A committee consisting of representatives of the Authority and NGOs has subsequently been launched.

Last information received on: 1997

Contact: Observer Mission of the Palestinian National Authority, Geneva

Tunisia

A National Commission for human rights education has been established. It is chaired by the Minister of Education and composed of representatives from the Higher Committee for Human Rights and Fundamental Freedoms, relevant non governmental organisations and associations, and the Ministry of Education, the Ministry of Higher Education and Scientific Research, the Ministry of Youth and Childhood, the Ministry of Women and Family, the Ministry of Culture, the Ministry of Information, the Ministry of Health, the Ministry of Justice, the Ministry of the Interior and the Ministry of Foreign Affairs.

The National Commission has prepared a preliminary report, outlining the status of human rights education in primary schools, secondary schools and higher education, and providing information on existing programmes of human rights training for professional groups (such as law enforcement agents, magistrates and lawyers). Further information has been provided in relation to programmes addressed to vulnerable groups (children, including juvenile offenders, women, people with disabilities, detainees) at professional training centres, including the creation of "human rights clubs" and "ecological clubs". Existing information relating to human rights amongst the general public, with an emphasis on the role of the media was also included.

A Human Rights Documentation, Publication, Research and Study Centre linked to the Higher Committee for Human Rights and Fundamental Freedoms has also been established.

In relation to formal education, the Government reports that human rights education takes place through the integration of human rights concepts in related programmes and materials, the organisation of specific events, and the revision and elimination, in textbooks, of stereotypes contrary to tolerance. Tunisia has also been promoting the re-valorisation of the teaching profession as part of the 1989 education reform: human rights modules have been included in pre-service training for future teachers in all subjects, while in-service human rights training sessions are also organised.

Furthermore, the Government stressed the important role of the Arab Institute for Human Rights, based in Tunis, in the dissemination of a culture of human rights. This is accomplished through the organisation of several national and regional seminars.

In conclusion, the Government illustrated its envisaged national strategy for human rights education, which includes close co-operation with United Nations agencies.

Last information received on: July 2002

Contact: Permanent Mission of Tunisia to the International Organisations

ASIA/PACIFIC

Australia

In December 1998, the Attorney General announced the establishment of a National Committee for Human Rights Education, which brings together the expertise of business, community organisations and the Government in an endeavour to enhance human rights education in Australia.

The Government provided seed funding for the Committee, whose work-plan includes: conducting a comprehensive adult of human rights education needs of the Australian Community; identifying and assessing current initiatives in human rights education; developing a national action plan for human rights education in Australia, focussing on priority needs; providing assistance in the development of comprehensive and effective human rights education programmes in priority areas, in consultation with education delivery agencies; developing effective communication strategies for human rights education; communicating with international agencies and counterparts in other countries to make available best techniques and resources; supporting human rights education initiatives addressing Asia-Pacific needs; developing effective partnerships between Government, business and community sectors; reviewing implementation and reporting progress. No national Plan of Action has been developed as of yet.

The National Committee on Human Rights Education, a cooperative venture among relevant governmental and non governmental agencies as well as the business and community sectors, is the focal point for the Decade and is financially supported by the Government. In addition to the National Committee, State Committees on human rights education have been established in most Australian States and Territories. In August 2002, the National Committee organised a National Strategic Conference on Human Rights Education, which involved many sectors and produced recommendations for a coordinated national strategy. The Committee also designed the "Citizenship of Humanity" Project, which aims at sensitising primary school students to the rights and values contained in the Universal Declaration of Human Rights.

Human right education is also a main focus of the work of the Human Rights and Equal Opportunity Commission, the Australian's national human rights institution, which in 2001-2002 developed a human rights education programme for teachers of upper primary and secondary schools. The programme is composed of a series of cross-curricular (history, legal studies, religious studies, etc.) modules and other teaching materials (videos, worksheets, etc.). In addition, the Commission developed a specific portal on its website to help teachers and other partners in their related efforts. For this programme, the Commission received the 2002 "Aware for Excellence in Educational Publishing" by "The Australian" newspaper. The Commission also runs, since 1999, a programme which brings together thousands of secondary school students and their teachers during a one-day workshop on human rights and responsibilities, in order to prevent discriminative behaviours; supporting materials are distributed during the seminars. Finally, the Commission has developed awareness raising activities in private companies to counteract sex- and race-related harassment. NGOs are involved or consulted in most of the above activities.

The Federal Government has also supported a series of educational programmes on democracy, multiculturalism, and prevention of racism targeting schools, higher education and adult community education. It has promoted human rights education in Asia by supporting training of administration of justice personnel, strengthening of legal institutions and treaty reporting training in China, Vietnam and Indonesia, as well as by providing funding to the Asia-Pacific Forum of National Human Rights Institutions.

Last information received on: 17 July 2003

Contact: Human Rights Branch/Commonwealth Attorney-General's Department

China

The Government informed that human rights education is provided through legal education programmes for all citizens, focusing on the study the law on how to apply it; in this regard, three 5-year plans have already been designed and implemented, reaching so far about 640 million people. As a result of these programmes, citizens are more familiar with the law and are increasingly using it for suing public officials, while the latter are more careful to act in accordance with the law.

In the formal education system, both moral and legal education are provided. Moral education focuses on issues such as love for the country and for life, respect for the elders and for the family, concern for the environment and for society, awareness of the moral standards of the society and willingness to abide by them, and a sense of discipline. Legal education focuses on fostering respect for the authority of constitutional law, development of awareness of democracy and the legal system, the lawful enjoyment of civil rights and the performance of civil obligations as set forth in the Constitution. Specifically trained teachers deliver such course, using specific textbooks and various methodologies; also; legal education is a compulsory subject in teacher training courses. Within universities, the subject of international law, as taught in law schools, includes human rights law; other university and college students undergo legal education programmes, also through out-of-school and community activities. Research on human rights and on human rights education is carried out in various universities.

Last information received: 8 July 2002

Contact: Permanent Mission of the People's Republic of China, Geneva

Fiji

The Government reported that the new Constitution (July 1998) provides for the establishment of a human rights commission, who tasks include the promotion of human rights education.

Last information received on: 15 October 1998

Contact: Fiji National Human Rights Commission

India

The Government of India has constituted a Coordination Committee, under the chairmanship of the Home Secretary, comprising of secretaries of other ministries and departments. The Committee requested the National Human Rights Commission to draft a national plan of action for human rights education. This task was accomplished in 2001, when the National Action Plan for Human Rights Education was finalised. The plan focuses on strategies for human rights awareness-raising and for sensitising specific target groups (students, officers in the administration of justice, etc.). Civil society is involved in the implementation of human rights education programmes, as well as the National Human Rights Commission. The Government also reported on specific activities undertaken in the secondary and higher education sector, including the establishment of a curriculum revision committee to revise textbooks; the development of a number of training modules for teachers in English, Hindi and local languages by the National Council of Teacher Education; the provision of financial assistance, by the University Grants Commission, to universities and colleges for the development of specific courses in human rights. India further reported on a project to establish a national resource centre at the Indira Gandhi Open University, which would include human rights materials, with a focus on educational tools

Last information received on: 23 May 2002

Contact: Permanent Mission of India to the United Nations Offices

Islamic Republic of Iran

In collaboration with UNDP and OHCHR, the Faculty of Law and Political Science of the University of Tehran is implementing a project for strengthening national capacities for human rights research and training, which will bring together faculty members, students and university graduates. It is expected that as a result of the project, a volume of literature on different crucial human rights subjects will be published.

In addition, the Government highlighted educational programmes carried out by NGOs (in particular, the Network of Women NGOs), the judiciary branch (which organised courses for lawyers and judges) and the Islamic Human Rights Commission (which organised courses for various groups involved in law enforcement).

Last information received on: 25 August 1999

Contact: Mission of the Islamic Republic of Iran to the United Nations, Geneva

Japan

The Headquarters for the Promotion of Human Rights Education was established in December 1995. In July 1997, a broad national plan of action for human rights education was released, which included the promotion of human rights education and training at all levels (schools, general public, corporations and civil society movements, professionals), specific programmes for special groups (women, children, the aged, people with disabilities, people with HIV infection), and the promotion of international cooperation and other public information activities, such as symposia and conferences.

The Headquarters, which is Japan's national committee, is composed of a chairperson (the Prime Minister), a vice-chairperson (the Chief Cabinet Secretary), the Minister of Justice, the Minister for Foreign Affairs, the Minister of Education, Science, Sports and Culture, the Director General of the Management and Coordination Agency Members, the Deputy Chief Cabinet Secretary, and administrative vice-ministers of all the ministries and agencies. The total number of members is 28. There are no NGO representatives on the committee as the objectives of establishing committees under the Cabinet, is to encourage each of the administrative agencies to exercise their administrative functions and to promote certain measures in a coordinated manner.

Several non-governmental organisations, such as the International Movement Against All Forms of Discrimination and Racism/Japan Committee, the Buraku Libration, the National Dowa Educators Associations, the Japan Teachers Union and the International Human Rights NGO Network, have been actively involved in these initiatives. This includes the elaboration of the Plan, the organisation of training programmes and symposia, and the production of publications.

The Ministerial Liaison Council for Training related to Human Rights Education was established in July 1998, to promote the exchange of information on training programmes and materials in related ministries and agencies.

In addition, major efforts are being undertaken at the prefectural level; 35 prefectures have established local task forces to pursue the Decade's objectives, and 26 have developed a local plan for human rights education. Municipal governments are also taking similar action.

In 2001, the National Plan was updated and evaluated by the Government. The Headquarters have promoted human rights education through different means and to different target groups. The latter include primary, junior high and high school students, as well as adults, companies and other societies and people engaged in specific occupations (such as lawyers, social workers and immigration officers). The means to carry out this plan include, apart of formal education materials and other awareness-raising activities.

Last information received on: 6 March 2001

Contact: Permanent Mission of Japan to the International Organisations, Geneva

New Zealand

Since 1993, the New Zealand Human Rights Commission, as mandated in its statute, has been developing human rights education and awareness-raising programmes. Among its activities, the following have been reported:

- preparation of education materials for parliamentarians and distribution to each member of the Parliament (1996).
- development, in consultation with the Ministry and with Teachers' Associations, of training resource materials for schools on the prevention of sexual harassment, and related training (1996-1997).

- publication of training resource materials for people with disabilities, in cooperation with the disability sector, and related training (1997-1998)

Development, in cooperation with the Ministry of Education and UNICEF, of a human rights module for primary, intermediate and secondary schools (1998-1999)

In 1999, an agreement was signed with the New Zealand Association of Citizen's Advice Bureau, who maintains more than 90 offices on the national territory, providing each office with a human rights education presence.

In addition to the Commission, the Human Rights Unit of the Ministry of Foreign Affairs and Trade has been engaged in raising awareness of human rights issues in the country.

Last information received on: 6 September 1999

Contact: New Zealand Permanent Mission to the United Nations, Geneva

Pakistan

Although a national committee has not been set up, plans are underway to do so.

The Human Rights wing of the Ministry of Law, Justice and Human Rights has been entrusted with the responsibility of Human Rights Education at the national level. The Human Rights wing has only recently been assigned this task, but has launched a human rights awareness campaign and held a Human Rights Convention in April, 2000.

The Human Rights wing is currently preparing the national plan for human rights education and it will be finalised in a few months, upon the establishment of the national committee. The national plan of Action will introduce the subject of human rights through curriculum development at school, college and university levels, and through extra curricular activities such as debates, essays, paintings, puppet shows, songs plays, community service and linkages with under privileged school children.

In relation to technical assistance, UNESCO is providing material to approximately 300 schools involved in the project on human rights education.

Last information received on: 21 June 2000

Contact: Ministry of Law, Justice and Human Rights/Human Rights Wing

Philippines

A National Plan of Action for human rights education was prepared by the Philippine Commission on Human Rights. The Plan includes clear objectives, target audiences (organised and unorganised elements of society), strategies (trainers' training, organisation of networks, integration of human rights in all education curricula, utilisation of village-level officials to reach out to the community level, promotional campaigns including artistic and cultural activities, development of monitoring and evaluation systems) and programmes, including the creation of a human rights training, documentation and research centre (the Human Rights Academy).

In the implementation of the Plan, the Commission has entered into a number of formal agreements with other national partners for human rights education, to define specific areas of responsibility. They include Amnesty International/Philippine Section, the Department of Interior and Local Government, the Liga NG MGA Barangay (an organisation of barangay captains or village chiefs), the Department of Justice, the Department of National Defence, the Department of Education, Culture and Sports, and the Commission on Higher Education.

This coalition has conducted consultative workshops to elaborate human rights education plans at the national and regional levels, since November 1996. A national gathering of all regional delegates, human rights practitioners and advocates from both the private, non-governmental and government sectors was hosted by Amnesty International/Phillippine Section in February 1997, in order to produce a long-term national plan inclusive of a national vision, mission and objectives for human rights education in the Philippines. Among the recommendations of the consultation were: the passing of an executive order creating a national inter agency committee to implement the national plan; the establishment of an ad hoc inter agency task force for each region; the development of a memorandum of agreement with all concerned agencies; the creation of the National Association of Human Rights Educators, formed by all participants to the consultation and endowed with specific responsibilities in the implementation of the Plan.

Finally, the years 1998-2007 have been proclaimed the Decade for HRE in the Philippines.

Last information received on: 18 January 1998

Contact: Philippines Commission on Human Rights

Republic of Korea

A variety of measures have been undertaken to promote human rights awareness, including the dissemination of human rights treaties publication and translation into Korean, the intensified provision of human rights education to public officials, the organisation of a national programme of public lectures and symposia on human rights, and the provision of legal aid services, through which fundamental human rights are publicised and small-sized cities coupled with farming and fishing communities.

In addition, South Korea hosted a sub-regional Training Workshop on Human Rights Education in Northeast Asia (Seoul, Republic of Korea), from 1 to 4 December 1999. The Workshop, organised by OHCHR in cooperation with the Government, aimed at providing a forum within which selected participants from Northeast Asia occupying a position of influence in their respective educational systems could explore and discuss strategies and components for the development of human rights education in schools. It was organised both as a follow-up to the Asia-Pacific Framework for Regional Technical Cooperation agreed upon in Teheran in 1998 and as a contribution to the Decade.

No national committee for human rights education has been established, however a bill has been passed in the National Assembly providing that a national commission for human rights shall be established to promote human rights education. There is no other institution which holds responsibility at the national level for this area. No national Plan of Action has been developed as attention has been directed at the passing of a national human rights law in the National Assembly. With the passage of the law, the Republic of Korea will take a series of measures to promote human rights education over the next five years of the Decade. A national committee will be set up to strengthen human rights programmes both in formal education settings and in non-formal education. This committee will also take the responsibility for elaborating a national human rights education plan which is to be implemented by relevant government authorities.

Last information received on: 24 July 2000

Contact: Permanent Mission of the Republic of Korea, Geneva

Ministry of Foreign Affairs/Human Rights Division

Ministry of Education

Sri Lanka

A management committee responsible for the formulation of a national plan of action for human rights education has been established. The committee is composed of ten members, five representing the governmental sector, and five the non-governmental and civil society sector. The committee was established with the technical assistance of OHCHR and UNDP.

Last information received on: May 2001

Contact: Ministry of Constitutional Affairs and Industrial Development

Thailand

A sub-committee on the Rights of the Child was established following Thailand's ratification of the Convention on the Rights of the Child. It promotes child rights education and other issues.

The office of the National Commission on Women's Affairs (ONCWA), as the secretariat body of the national machinery for the advancement of women, has implemented legal literacy programs for local women and published materials on the topic of Women and the Law.

In 1998, a National Committee was set up to draft the National Policy and Plan of Action on Human Rights, which was completed and approved by the Parliament in October 2000. One of the 11 sections of the document concerns human rights education. The National Policy and Plan of Action on Human Rights is implemented through inter-ministry coordination, and the Ministry of Education is the focal point for the specific section on human rights education.

The Government has also advised of educational activities undertaken by the Office of the Attorney-General (focusing on public information activities for vulnerable groups and training of legal professionals), the Ministry of Education (focusing on children's rights, including the development of school curricula, materials and training for teachers, and the elaboration of related legislation) and the Ministry of Interior (focusing on the empowerment of community organisations).

Last information received on: August 2001

Contact: Permanent Mission of Thailand to the United Nations Office and other International Organisations in Geneva

EUROPE AND NORTH AMERICA

Austria

In 1997, the Federal Ministry for Foreign Affairs, the Federal Ministry for Education, Science and Culture and the Ludwig Boltzmann, Institute for Human Rights jointly established the Service Centre for Human Rights Education, Austria's leading institution for the development of human rights education in schools and for advice and assistance to teachers. It has focused on the introduction of human rights education in Austrian schools, a programme supported by the Department of Civic Education. Among the various activities undertaken, workshops and training of teachers are organised, and appropriate material, such as the UNESCO publication Human Rights Questions and Answers, are disseminated. The Service Centre has also developed networking and information tools such as a website and an electronic newsletter, as well as educational and training programmes (teacher training, peer training) and materials.

Human rights education is incorporated into national legislation concerning the formal education system; in primary and secondary schools, human rights are included in subjects such as civic education, legal education, history and philosophy, and specific anti-discrimination and anti-racism educational programmes are carried out. The Ministry for Education, Science and Culture regularly encourages provincial educational authorities and teachers to develop human rights education programmes and celebrate specific occasions, such as the

Anniversary of the adoption of the Convention on the Rights on the Child and Human Rights Day.

At the local level, in February 2001 the Municipal Council of Graz has proclaimed the city of Graz a human rights city, with the aim of mainstreaming human rights into all activities and decision-making processes of the City's administration. This includes the organisation of human rights training for local government officials. In addition, the Graz's European Research and Training Centre for Human Rights and Democracy develops and implements human rights training worldwide.

At the national level, the Service Centre for human Rights Education continues to provide systematic assistance and advice to school teachers on human rights issues, including the development of special projects and a newsletter. Anti-racism educational efforts are also reported. The Government reported on the creation of a network of human rights coordinators (one in each Federal Ministry) responsible, *inter alia*, for questions related to human rights education; they attend periodic seminars organised by the Federal Academy of Public Administration, whose objective is to increase network efficiency as well as human rights education efforts in the public administration.

Human rights education is incorporated into national legislation concerning the formal education system; in primary and secondary schools, human rights are included in subjects such as civic education, legal education, history and philosophy, and specific anti-discrimination and anti-racism educational programmes are carried out. The Ministry of Education, Science and Culture regularly encourages provincial educational authorities and teachers to develop human rights education programmes and celebrate specific occasions, such as the anniversary of the adoption of the Convention on the Rights of the Child and Human Rights Day.

A major contribution to the Decade is the human rights program offered by the Federal Academy of Public Administration since 1999. The program is open to civil servants and employees from all branches of government including teachers, the police, the army, immigration, prison staff, social workers, judges and prosecutors, and foreign service officials.

The Austrian Government is working together with a wide range of actors in the field of human rights education. The aforementioned Service Centre for Human Rights Education co-operates with the Ministry of Education, Science and Culture, the Ministry of Foreign Affairs and other relevant Ministries and government agencies, including school authorities at all levels. The Ministry of the Interior and the Ministry of Justice work with NGOs, that are active in human rights education by elaborating and implementing training courses for government officials, including police officers, judges and prosecutors. The Security-Academy of the Ministry of Interior coordinators and develops training activities for Ministry's personnel, notably police and gendarmerie.

In 1988 the Federal Government provided 5 million ATS to support human rights projects proposed by Austrian NGOs, several of which were projects in the area of human rights education.

At the international level, the Government promotes human rights education in the framework of the Stability Pact for South Eastern Europe, the Human Security Network and bilateral development cooperation projects. In 1999, the Federal Ministry for Foreign Affairs launched an international initiative aiming at strengthening human security through human rights education. The Ministry of Foreign Affairs is engaged in highlighting human rights education in United Nations fora. Also, during the Austrian Presidency of the Human Security Network, human rights education has been declared as a priority item; in this context, the manual "Understanding Human Rights" is being developed and a governmental declaration on the strengthening of human rights education will be adopted in Graz in 2003. In addition, Human rights education activities are part of various development cooperation programmes carried out with various countries.

There exists a network of human rights coordinators (one in each Federal ministry) responsible, *inter alia*, for questions related to human rights education; they attend periodic seminars organised by the Federal Academy of Public Administration, whose objective is to increase network efficiency as well as human rights education efforts in the public administration.

The Ministry of Foreign Affairs is engaged in highlighting human rights education in United Nations forums. Also, during the Austrian presidency of Human Security Network, human rights education has been declared as a priority item; in this context, the manual *Understanding Human Rights* is being developed, and a governmental declaration on the strengthening of human rights education will be adopted in Graz in 2003. Human rights education activities are also part of various development cooperation programmes carried out with several countries.

Finally, the Security Academy of the Ministry of the Interior coordinates and develops training activities for the Ministry's personnel, notably police and gendarmerie.

Last information received on: 13 July 2002

Contacts: Service Centre for Human Rights Education/ Ludwig Boltzmann Institute of Human Rights

Permanent Mission of Austria to the United Nations, Geneva

Azerbaijan

In June 1998, State Programme for Human Rights Protection, which at the President approved the provides for the Government to take specific measures in the following areas:

- development of specialised training in human rights, in particular through international exchanges
- infusion of human rights in the school curricula, and publication of related materials
- organisation of various events with a human rights theme, such as school competitions and art exhibitions
- publication in the national language of international human rights instruments
- production of specific material (newspapers, magazines, posters) to increase human rights awareness

In July 1998, the Government signed a technical co-operation project with OHCHR, which also included human rights education and training activities.

Last information received on: 28 September 1999

Contact: Permanent Mission of the Republic of Azerbaijan, Geneva

Republic of Belarus

In March 1999, the Council of Ministers approved a National Plan on the Development of Education in Human Rights, covering the period 1999-2004. The Plan focuses on the school system and has six components:

- a public information component, including the dissemination of main United Nations and UNESCO instruments, and relevant national legislation
- the inclusion of human rights in the school curricula, as part of the subjects "Man and the World", "Man, Society and the State", and "Fundamentals of the Law of the Republic of Belarus"
- the development of human rights courses at the higher education level
- the organisation of other educational activities, such as competitions, exhibitions, film festivals and tours
- the development of relevant school textbooks and teaching materials, and the carrying out of related research at the National Education Institute, the Republican Institute for Higher Schools, the Belarusian State Pedagogical University and a number of regional universities
- the training of teachers, facilitated by international symposia, and national seminars, training courses and conferences

Cooperation with other countries and international organisations such as the ICRC and UNICEF

The Ministry of Education, together with other institutions, has commenced work on the development of textbooks for schoolchildren, the organisation of seminars for teachers from various educational establishments, and a National Conference on Human Rights in the Structure and Contents of Professional Education.

The Ministry of Education established The National Commission for Children's Rights on 18 March 1996, which serves as a national committee for human rights education. One of the main tasks of the Commission is to provide wide-ranging information to children, parents and the public at large regarding the Rights of the Child Act and other international and national human rights instruments, and to promote the study of these instruments in educational establishments. The Commission comprises of representatives from the Presidential Administration, the Council of Ministers, the National Assembly, the Supreme Court, the Procedures Office, ministries, other central government agencies, local authorities and administrative bodies, and voluntary associations concerned with the protection of children's rights. The total number of members of the committee is 25; there is one representatives from an NGOs.

The Belarus government is receiving technical assistance from the UN office in Belarus.

In 1995, the government established a National Plan of Action for the Protection of Children's Rights, which included the introduction of a special 10-hour course on children's rights at all school levels, as well as in teacher training institutes; in 1998, a course on human rights was included in all education establishments; in 1999, the government ratified the National Plan for the Development of Human Right Education (1999-2004), which outlines the contents of the human rights course, i.e. human rights, the rights of the child and humanitarian law; specific university courses, in particular for law and pedagogy faculties, were introduced and related materials, such as textbooks, support materials for teachers and pamphlets on the Universal Declaration of Human Rights, the Convention on the Rights of the Child and national relevant legislation, were prepared and widely disseminated. In 2000, the government also organised a competition to award the most original contribution for human rights education; it also held international conferences under the auspices of the Council of Europe.

Last information received on: 8 January 2003

Contacts: Ministry of Education

Permanent Mission of the Republic of Belarus, Geneva

Canada

Canada has prepared and is making available to the public a thematic and country by country human rights report, based on

United Nations sources, entitled for the Record (available at http://www.hri.ca).

On the occasion of the 50th Anniversary of the Universal Declaration of Human Rights, the federal Department of Canadian Heritage, in partnership with provincial ministries of education and non-governmental organisations, delivered several human rights awareness campaigns and programmes aimed at all ages. The Canadian Human Rights Commission also advised that human rights education is a regular part of its work and that it would support the establishment of a national plan, if such an initiative were undertaken in Canada.

Last information received on: 22 February 1999

Contact: Federal Department of Canadian Heritage

Croatia

The Government of the Republic of Croatia established a National Committee for Human Rights Education in 1996. This is a consultative body headed by the Minister of Education and consisting of 17 experts. The Committed has established a National Programme of Human Rights Education based on national and international human rights instruments, and focusing on integration with programmes carried out in the framework of co-operation with international organisations (UNICEF, UNESCO).

The Croatian Programme has been developed on the basis of a survey of other countries' programmes conducted by a group of pedagogical science experts from the University of Zagreb and is composed of two sections. The first section has been completed and is now being implemented in all schools: it targets pre-school education, lower and higher school classes and all types of secondary schools. A cross-curricular approach was adopted, with the integration of human rights and civil education topics in all suitable school subjects, and various extracurricular activities. Furthermore, a project with UNESCO entitled "Peace and human rights education for Croatian primary schools" has begun. Its implementation has been entrusted to the Department of Pedagogical Sciences within the Zagreb University Faculty of Arts. This project incorporates field research and the publication of textbooks.

The second section of the Programme, which deals with human rights education for adults and the media, has recently been completed; the university level is still to be approached.

The implementation of the programme is the responsibility of governmental authorities, educational establishments and NGOs. The Government of Croatia, in cooperation with OHCHR, opened a Human Rights Documentation and Education Centre in October 2000 in Zagreb, which is accessible to all interested citizens, offers a range of books and documentation and organises seminars and roundtables, as well as training for human rights educators. The Government also reported the organisation of a series of public information activities, such as dissemination of human rights documents and publications. The programme is currently being implemented in all schools. The second part of the Programme, which deals with human rights education for adults and the media, has recently been completed; the university level is still to be approached.

Last information received on: 15 July 2002

Contact: National Committee for Human Rights Education

Ministry of Foreign Affairs

Permanent Mission of the Republic of Croatia to the United Nations Office, Geneva

Cyprus

The Government has taken the initiative to set up a National Institute for Human Rights aiming at the widest possible representation. The main objectives of the institute are:

- to raise public awareness for human rights
- to further educate civil servants, teachers, lawyers on human rights
- to strengthen human rights education in Cyprus educational system at all levels
- to strengthen to capacity of the mass media for human rights education through the use of appropriate means
- to promote active engagement of national NGOs in the realisation of the goals of the Decade

- to establish a human rights library in order to enhance public awareness

Furthermore, the Ministry of Education, having reviewing the current status of human rights education in schools, is developing new curricula and new teaching methods.

Last information received on: 25 November 1998

Contacts: Ministry of Education and Culture

National Institution for the Protection of Human Rights

Czech Republic

The Government Human Rights Council was established in 1998 by the Government (resolution No. 809 of December 9, 1998), to monitor the democratic compliance with fundamental human rights standards. It is comprised of Government representatives and representatives of civil society. In 1999 it created an expert Working Group for Human Rights Education. The Working Group was tasked to act as a focal point for the purposes of the Decade and played a significant role in drafting a comprehensive report on human rights education in the Czech Republic, which was commissioned by the Government in the year 2000.

The report builds on materials submitted by the Ministries of Education, Justice, Finance, Labour and Social Affairs, Interior, Defense, Culture and Foreign Affairs. The Working Group also included information received from specialised educational establishments, institutes of higher education, professional organisations and non-governmental organisations. It focused on human rights educational efforts in schools and higher education establishments, and on the human rights training of teachers, Ministry of Finance's employees, police, Army, prison officials, legal professionals, social workers and health professionals.

The structure of the Government Human Rights Council permits and active participation of the general public in the protection of human rights: it comprises of an equal number of representatives of state administration authorities at the level of deputy ministers and of representatives of the general public. Currently, the Council has 21 members, including the chairman. Each Section that the Council administers, consists of representatives of relevant ministries, other state of academic institutions and NGOs.

The Section (Working Group) on Human Rights, which currently plays the role of the national committee for human rights education, has 17 members and the coordinator from the Office of the Government. The coordinator also heads the secretariat of the Human Rights Council. Apart from the ministerial representatives, there are 4 representatives of various civic associations, 1 representatives of UNHCR, 4 representatives of various universities and one independent expert.

A national Plan of Action is to be completed by the end of 2000, when the Human Rights Commissioner is to submit a report on activities in the Czech Republic to the Government. The Commissioner will submit a draft resolution to the Government based on the findings of the report. While the report will analyse activities already undertaken, it will also propose steps to be taken to improve efforts in this area.

Last information received on: 29 June 2000

Contact: Office of the Czech Republic Government/Human Rights Council

Denmark

As a joint project between the Ministry of Education and the Danish Centre for Human Rights, a plan of action has been established with the purpose of strengthening human rights education in Danish primary and lower secondary schools, and among the youth. The aim of the plan is to enable key personnel from training institutions and professional organisations to carry out their own training of teachers. This will be the basis for concrete training courses and the development of human rights education programmes in schools. Two courses for teachers were held in the Spring 1997 with the participation of representatives from teaching aid centres, country resource centres, teacher training colleges, the Royal Danish School of Educational Studies, the Danish Red Cross, the Danish Refugees Council, Amnesty International, DanChurchAid and a number of experts. As a resource tool for those courses, a bibliography of human rights education materials (including textbooks and magazines, audiovisual materials and databases) was compiled. Furthermore, a human rights education bibliography will be published.

Implemented activities led to a variety of projects on human rights in schools, educational resource centres and teacher training institutions. Furthermore, in December 1998, the Ministry of Education hosted an International Conference on Human Rights Education, organised in cooperation with the Danish Centre for Human Rights and the National Commission for UNESCO, which gathered teachers from all levels of education. Further initiatives to be launched during the second half of the Decade are new being considered.

Last information received on: 27 June 2000

Contacts: Danish Centre for Human Rights

Ministry of Education/Department of Adult Education

Finland

There is no national committee in existence. The National Board of Education devises the framework curricula for schools. The activities of the UNESCO Associated Schools Project are coordinated by National Board of Education.

Last information received on: 31 July 2000

Contact: Finnish National Commission for UNESCO/ Ministry of Education

France

A National Committee for Human Rights Education and Training has been established jointly by the National Commission for UNESCO and the National Consultative Commission for Human Rights. It includes representatives from 11 relevant Ministries, such as Justice, Education, Defence, Foreign Affairs, Social Affairs, Interior, Culture, Youth and Humanitarian Action. Its mandate consists of:

- conducting a survey on past/current activities in the area of human rights education
- assessing needs
- elaborating a plan of action

Four working groups have been constituted within the Committee to assess the state of human rights education in the following areas: primary and secondary schools; universities and higher education; adult education, including several professional groups (police, armed forces, judges, teachers, social workers); and activities undertaken by NGOs, associations and trade unions. The Committee presented a report on the civic and human rights education curricula at the secondary school level, which illustrates the pedagogical objectives, and the contents and reference materials for such courses. It is also organising a series of colloqula (2001/2003) for experts and educators on various human rights education issues.

In addition, a national centre for information and training on human rights, publicly accessible and provided with a broad range of human rights documentation, was inaugurated in November 1996.

Last information received on: November 2001

Contact: French Committee for Human Rights Education and Training

Germany

The Government of Germany informed the Office that its contribution to the Decade is focusing on three areas. The first area is human rights education in schools. The Basic Law, Lander Constitutions, laws, legal and administrative regulations, and several resolutions of the conference of Ministers of Education and Cultural Affairs, specify human rights education as one of the educational objectives in all federal states, even where those states have sovereignty over their school systems. Accordingly, human rights education is deeply rooted in a number of subjects in schools, of all types and at all levels.

Secondly, a public relations and information campaign, aimed at encouraging the integration of foreigners and the dismantling of mutual prejudices among citizens, has commenced. This is accomplished through an information service, editorial services for local newsletters, radio programmes for foreigners and Germans, and seminars for people working with foreigners.

Finally, some development cooperation projects aim at creating learning conditions, which will enable broad sections of the population to gain an insight into social and administrative processes, and thus to exercise their rights.

The Government of Germany stressed the importance of human rights education in combating racism and xenophobic attitudes. Among the activities undertaken at the Länder (State) level, which is primarily responsible for schools, it mentioned the inclusion of intercultural education in school curricula and the incorporation of the contents of the Convention on the Rights of the Child, in school programmes and textbooks, as well as the adoption, by the Standing Conference of Ministers of Education and Cultural Affairs of the Länder, of a revised "Recommendations for the Promotion of Human Rights Education" (2000), which made human rights education a priority in all state constitutions and laws on education. The Federal Ministry for Education and Research has launched a series of anti-discrimination and anti-violence programmes at all levels of the school system, including pilot research, evaluation projects and the development of multi-media tools. The government mentioned three specific educational programmes. The programme XENOS has been designed especially for the labour market; it targets companies, trade unions, firms and other institutions and supports projects in the areas of conflict management and intercultural training. The programme ENTIMON, which focuses on Youth, aims at combating violence and right-wing extremism and supports local activities such as conference, theatre festivals and workshops which have a great impact through media coverage. The programme CIVITAS support similar projects in the five eastern federal Länder.

Other actors involved in human rights education in Germany are the German Institute for Human Rights, founded in 2001 by a broad range of civil society actors, the German Commission for UNESCO and the UNESCO Chair of Human Rights Education, also founded in 2001 at the Magdeburg University, they undertake studies and conduct human rights awareness-raising activities.

Last information received on: 9 December 2002

Contact: Conference of Ministers of Education and Cultural Affairs

Greece

Greece reported that the Greek National Commission for Human Rights has undertaken a series of initiatives to promote human rights education at the university level, with the aim to establishing specific courses on human rights. Also, in 2001/2 the

Commission promoted a research study on national mass media and the promotion of stereotypes and discrimination attitudes, held consultations with the Ministry of Public Order and the National School of Public Administration concerning the establishment of human rights education programmes for policemen and civil servants, and undertook the translation of OHCHR's related materials.

Last information received on: 14 July 2003

Holy See

The Holy See undertook surveys on the existing human rights education programmes within the network of Catholic institutions (schools, colleges, training centres and institutes). These surveys demonstrated the special attention given to the foundations of human rights in general, the legal aspects of human rights and the promotion of economic and social rights.

Catholic educational institutions focus on specific human rights issues (such as bioethics and the right to development) or on specific groups (such as disabled persons, indigenous peoples and minorities). In order to carry out human rights education programmes, which are directed not only towards members of the clergy but also to children and students attending Catholic schools, partnerships have been established with United Nations agencies, the International Committee of the Red Cross and civil society. The Holy See stressed that in some Catholic schools children and teachers from other religions are present in large numbers, and this promotes tolerance and peaceful coexistence.

Last information received on: July 2001

Contact: Sezione per i Rapporti con gli Stati/Segreteria di Stato

Hungry

No national Committee for human rights education has been established, although plans to do so are under consideration. There is no national plan of action for human rights education.

Human rights education has been incorporated at all levels of education through the legislative process. Such education exists in the presentation and study of national Constitution and relevant international human rights treaties; however, human rights are not taught as a separate subject.

Hungry is a participant in the European Community Action Programme in the field of Education, Training and Youth, the CIVITAS Programme, and other programmes co-organised, *inter alia*, with the Soros Foundation.

Various specific programmes targeted at specific social or professional groups are also implemented.

Last information received on: August 2000

Contact: Head of Department of International Organisations/ Ministry of Foreign Affairs

Ireland

The Government provided information regarding two initiatives, developed within the Department of Foreign Affairs and in consultation with NGOs, towards the elaboration of a national plan of action.

In addition, it referred to the work of the National Committee for Development Education (NCDE), which is composed of representatives from a broad range of groups involved in development education. This includes the former education sector, women's and community groups, and NGOs. NCDE provides grant support for activities, including human rights education projects, undertaken by these groups. It is also involved in the integration of human rights in the school curricula.

Last information received on 23 October 1998

Contact: Office of the Taoiseach

Italy

A joint effort of the National Academy of Scientists and the Italian Government has produced a survey of human rights education and information in Italy. This contains information on human rights education in primary schools, secondary schools and higher education (collected through specific questionnaires), on existing programmes for human rights training for professional groups (police, prison personnel, magistrates and lawyers, teachers, health personnel), and on human rights among the public in general, emphasising the role of the media.

All the current activities of governmental and non governmental agencies active in this area are reviewed, and detailed suggestions for improvement are addressed to the Italian Government. Annexed to the survey is a list of documents relating to human rights education translated into Italian (including the Universal Declaration of Human Rights and several United Nations documents, including the Plan of Action for the Decade). A list of the addresses of all institutes and governmental and non governmental agencies dealing with human rights education, which can be contacted and can provide materials for developing further programmes, is also attached. The survey has been published and has been disseminated throughout the country, particularly in all educational establishments.

Last information received on: 1996

Contact: Presidency of the Council of Ministers

Kazakhstan

Kazakhstan has not established a national committee for human rights education, and no national plan of action for human rights education has been developed, thus far.

The Government emphasised the need for technical assistance on the part of relevant UN bodies.

Human rights have been integrated into school curricula at all levels of education; such integration involves the study and the use of relevant international human rights treaties. Moreover, three universities have developed programmes on human rights teaching and research.

Last information received on: June 2000

Contact: Department of International Law and Protocol

Latvia

Within the school system, human rights and taught in primary schools as part of the compulsory Civics subject, and in secondary schools as an optional course "Politics and Rights".

In September 1995, as a contribution to the Decade, the University of Latvia established, within its Faculty of Law, a Human Rights Institute. The purpose of which is to provide human rights education to law students and students from other faculties; carry out human rights research; publish study materials, monographs and articles on human rights; establish a human rights library; and organise conferences and seminars.

In 1995, the Centre for the Protection of the Rights of the Child was also established at the Ministry of Education and Science. It organised related seminars for school personnel and s rights-conferences on children

Furthermore, the Government highlighted the on-going human rights education activities carried out by the Latvian National Human Rights Office, such as the production of publications, a series of TV broadcasts, and the maintenance of an Information and Documentation Centre.

Last information received on: 23 November 1998

Contact: Office of the Prime Minister

Lithuania

There is no national Committee for human rights education established in the country. Human Rights education activities are predominantly under the responsibility of the Lithuanian Centre for Human Rights. Numerous activities (seminars, lectures, workshops) take place, and are conducted both by governmental entitles and civil society members, as well as UN agencies and programmes.

The Consultative Council of Children's Affairs was set up in 1996. It deals with all aspects relating to the human rights of children and has a large education and information component.

Human rights are incorporated into school curricula at all levels of the education system; laws and policies were passed to that end.

Last information received on: August 2000

Contact: International Co-operation and European Integration Department

Luxembourg

In addition to specific activities undertaken within the commemoration of the 50th Anniversary of the Universal

Declaration of Human Rights, the Ministry of National Education informed of various initiatives, such as the creation of a multi-disciplinary working group for the integration of human rights in the school curricula, the training of teachers in human rights and the support of human rights initiatives undertaken independently by various schools, in collaboration with NGOs.

Last information received on: 30 December 1998

Contact: Ministry of National Education

Malta

Malta's authorities informed of the inclusion of human rights principles in the National Minimum Curriculum; they are reflected in the syllabuses of subjects like social studies, European studies, history and Personal and Social Education. Related training sessions for teachers are organised. Activities aimed at sensitising students to human rights issues are regularly held in the classes. A particular emphasis is put on citizenship and global education, in cooperation with the Council of Europe; in this context, Maltese schools organised events in 2001 on the occasion of the Council of Europe's Global Education Week, entitled "Children and Youth Rights Now". The government of Malta underlined the cooperation developed with NGOs in the area of human rights education, as that between the Social Sciences Unit of the Department of Education of Malta and national non governmental organisations. In this case, the result of this cooperation has been a broad programme of human rights awareness in schools and the preparation of training materials on thc rights of thc child, on tolerance and on human rights in general. It has also promoted in service courses for teachers on human rights, tolerance and peace.

Last information received on: 12 July 2002

Contact: Office of the Prime Minister

Moldova

Human Rights have been incorporated into the primary and secondary school curricula. Activities are developed accordingly: seminars, workshops, and essay competitions. A specific course on human rights is also available for law students at the State University of Maldova.

The Department of National Relations and Languages of the Republic of Maldova regularly organised meetings, workshops, conferences, seminars, and art festivals on ethnic and minority rights.

Last information received on: August 2000

Contact: Department of International Relations/Ministry of Education and Science

Monaco

There is no national Committee for human rights education or a national action plan for human rights education.

Human rights education is included in curricula, particularly in history and civic education classes, at all levels of education (except at university as there is no university in Monaco), with a focus on children's rights.

Cooperation on human rights education takes place through partnerships with NGOs.

Last information received on: August 2000

Contact: Directeur de l'Éducation nationale, Monaco

The Netherlands

The Government is continuing discussions on the possible establishment of a national platform for human rights education.

However, various related activities are currently being undertaken: in relation to the school system, teaching materials are prepared mainly by NGOs on their initiatives or in cooperation with the authorities, while the level of teaching human rights in the classroom is often left to the teacher's discretion. At the university level, as a result of the collaboration of several law faculties, the School of Human Rights Research was established. Human rights training for public officials, police and the military is institutionalised, as well as for people from developing countries.

Public information campaigns are organised on relevant issues, such as refugees and immigrations.

Last information received on: 7 December 1998

Contact: Office of the President

Norway

In 1980 a Working Group on Human Rights Education was established within the Advisory Committee on Human Rights, under the direction of the Foreign Affairs. It was assigned new terms of reference in 1995, in connection with the proclamation of the Decade. The Group, which has an advisory role, considers and discusses, on its own initiative or upon request from the Ministry, issues relating to human rights education. The UN Association in Norway serves as the secretariat for the working group and is composed of representatives from relevant ministries (the Ministry of Foreign Affairs, the Ministry of Education, Research and Church Affairs), the Norwegain National Commission for UNESCO, Amnesty International, the Norwegian Red Cross, teachers' unions, the Norwegian Agency for International Development, the Norwegian Refugee Council and the Norwegian UNICEF Committee.

A national Plan of Action has been developed within the framework of a more general plan for Human Rights, which is entitled "Focus on Human Dignity". It was submitted to the Government in December 1999 as a White Paper. The Plan of Action was developed in response to a request from parliament to the Government to draw up a "general plan of action to provide information, instruction and education with a view to protecting and promoting human rights in Norway". An inter-ministerial working group, chaired by the Ministry of Education developed the Plan in conjunction with various ministries, including the Ministry of Justice, the Ministry of Social Affairs, and the Ministry of Children and Family Affairs. The Plan of Action has been summarised as follows:

"The Government will implement measures to increase the expertise of the teaching staff at the teacher training institutions and teachers in primary, lower secondary and upper secondary schools. Measures will also be carried out to enhance the knowledge of human rights to employees in the central government administration, the defence forces and the legal profession. The Government will take steps to ensure that instruction in human rights is included to a greater extent in continuing education for various professional groups, and will evaluate the instruction in human rights that is provided at certain educational institutions. Emphasis is placed on providing information on and promoting sound attitudes towards human rights, and the Government will initiate information campaigns to encourage commitment to and create awareness of human rights among the population at large. The Government places emphasis on research as an important source of knowledge and expertise, and will strengthen the Norwegian Institute for Human Rights".

Last information received: 28 June 2000

Contacts: Norwegian Ministry of Education, Research and Church Affairs UN Association of Norway

Poland

Human rights, focusing on children's rights and other rights defined to treaties to which Poland is a party, are a component of curricula at all school levels. Poland works in close partnership with UNESCO and the Associated School Project, through which particular emphasis is given to human rights education.

Two human rights chairs have been created at two universities and the Annual Students Human Rights Knowledge Contest has been launched.

Human rights training is compulsory for many professional groups such as civil servants, border guards, fire fighters, judges, prosecutors, police officers, prison officials, social workers and teachers.

The Government of Poland has enhanced cooperation with NGOs in the area of civil education.

Last information received on: August 2000

No contact details.

Portugal

The "National Commission for the Commemoration of the 50th Anniversary of the Universal Declaration of Human Rights and the United Nations Decade for Human Rights Education" was created through a resolution of the Council of Ministers in April 1998. Although functioning within the framework of the Council of Ministers, the Commission in independent from the

Government, due to its statute and the majority of its members, who are institutional representatives, of NGOs or independent individuals.

The Commission is presided over by the former President Mário soares and is composed of representatives from the Parliament, the Ombudsman office, the Ministry of Foreign Affairs, the Ministry of Internal Affairs, the Ministry of Justice, the Ministry of Education, the Office, the Secretary of State of the Council of-Deputy Prime Minister Ministers and the Secretary of State for the Media. In addition, all major national human rights non-governmental organisations (Civitas-Association for s Rights, the Forum for Justice and-the Defence and Promotion of Citizen Liberties, Amnesty International/Portuguese Section, Law and Justice-Portuguese Section of the International Commission of Jurists, and the Portuguese Association of Women Jurists) are represented in the National Commission.

The National Commission has developed a broad Plan of Action for the Decade, which covers the period 1999-2004. The Plan comprises of eight strategic areas:

- main instruments for promoting the UN decade for human rights education
- activities to be undertaken with the sovereign bodies, namely government departments
- organisation of seminars, congresses and other events for human rights dissemination
- activities to be developed with schools and learning establishments
- activities to be developed with the civil society
- activities to be developed with the municipal authorities
- activities to be developed with the media
- publications promoted by the national commission, or with its sponsorship or cooperation.

At the national level, the National Commission is planning to publish educational dossiers aimed at students (of different school levels) and teachers. During the first half of the Decade, publications were mainly intended to disseminate general human rights matters. The National Commission now intends to dedicate the second half of the Decade to publish materials targeted at specific groups.

The Commission also disseminates human rights education information, either directly or through communities present in the African Portuguese-speaking countries, as well as East Timor. Apart from information and training activities, the committee promotes seminars and conferences, and publishes materials specifically aimed at those societies and their particular concerns.

Last information received on: 19 June 2000

Contact: Gabinete de Documentação e Direito Comparado/ Procuradorie-Geral de República

Romania

Romania has informed OHCHR of the establishment of a National Committee in February 1996, whose secretariat is assured by the Romanian Institute for Human Rights, and whose members are representatives of relevant ministries and non-governmental organisations.

Human rights education has been incorporated into all levels of the school system: mostly in civic education classes, through legislative procedures. Relevant teaching materials have been produced.

There are specialised courses on human rights available at the University of Bucharest and at the National Institute for Human Rights (Bucharest).

Last information received on: September 2000

Contacts: Direction de l' intégration européenne/Ministère de l'Éducation nationale

Romanian National Committee for Human Rights Education for the UN Decade of Human Rights Education

c/o Romanian Institute for Human Rights

Republic of San Marino

The Government distributed a copy of the Universal Declaration of Human Rights to every secondary school student in the country in December 1998. In addition, it has financially contributed to project for the global dissemination of the Universal Declaration of the OHCHR Human Rights, which constitutes one of the objectives of the Decade.

There is no national Committee in existence. The Ministry of Foreign Affairs and the Ministry of Education have been jointly responsible for human rights education at the national level. These institutions have adopted initiatives and launched programmes in this area since the beginning of the Decade.

Given the limited size of the Republic of San Marino (61 sq. km, population 27,000) and in light of past experiences, the San Marino Government has considered it inappropriate to establish a national committee and ad-hoc bureaucratic structures for the Decade. They believe that the system adopted enables the government and NGOs to cooperate in a rapid and fruitful manner.

Last information received on: 30 June 2000

Contact: Department of Foreign Affairs/Directorate of Cultural Affairs and Information

Slovak Republic

The Slovak Republic presented a survey on human rights education in schools, at the university level, and for armed forces and police officials. As far as the formal education system is concerned, activities recently undertaken included the "Human Rights Olympiad for Secondary Schools", the development/ adaptation of methodological guides for teachers (such as First steps, a guide developed by Amnesty International and endorsed by the Ministry of Education), the organisation of seminars for methodologists and teachers of civic education and training courses for teachers organised by the Human Rights Department of the Comenius University of Bratislava.

There is no national committee in existence, however there are plans underway to establish such a committee as soon as the Board of Directors of Slovak National Centre on Human Rights has completed its reform process.

The Ministry of Education has worked increasingly in this area since the last parliamentary elections in autumn 1998. Previously, NGOs did the majority of the work in the human rights education domain.

No national Plan of action has been developed in the Slovak Republic. The relevant public administration body for human rights education is the Ministry of Education. The Ministry believes that human rights education is well integrated into the educational system at all levels.

Last information received on: 20 July 2000

Contact: Section on Human Rights and Minorities/ Government Office of the Slovak Republic

Sweden

In January 1998, the Ministry of Education appointed a committee to survey human rights education at the national level and to make recommendations for improvements. Meanwhile, human rights are taught in schools at all levels, and related materials (including free access to the Internet) are made available. At the university level, several law faculties have compulsory courses in human rights (at Lund University the Raoul Wallenberg Institute of Human Rights and Humanitarian Law in active).

Specific public information campaigns against racism and xenophobia and on the Holocaust have recently been launched. Various human rights publications are widely disseminate, such as a bibliography of human rights literature published in Sweden over the past 50 years, which is a joint project between the Ministry of Education and various NGOs. Furthermore, training material for teachers have been developed by a broad NGO coalition. There is no national committee for human rights education. However, the Government has initiated work towards an overall national action plan for human rights education. The consultation process involves representatives from governmental institutions as well as representatives from civil society, including NGOs, trade, unions, academics and Ombudspersons. Special attention to the Decade will be given in this context.

Last information received on: September 2000

Contact: Division for Democratic Issues/Ministry of Justice

Switzerland

The Federal Department of the Interior has appealed to the Swiss Conference of Cantonal Directors of Public Education to enhance human rights education in schools. In addition, it has advised various national agencies and non governmental organisations, such as the Federal Commission against Racism, the Swiss Foundation "Education and Development" and the Swiss League for Human Rights, who regularly organise human rights education and public information campaigns.

Switzerland has not established a national committee for human rights education. However, there are consultations within the country on the opportunity to create a specialised governmental body dealing with all issues related to human rights, including human rights education. The federal system prevailing in Switzerland does not necessarily favour such an establishment at the federal level because education issues are under the responsibility of the cantons. However, the federal authorities do play a role by encouraging the cantons to educate and inform on the treaties to which Switzerland is a party, and monitoring the content of teaching materials. Human rights education is dealt by the cantonal entities, although human rights have not been incorporated into the cantonal laws related to education. NGOs are also very active in this area and work together with the relevant public bodies.

Last information received on: September 2000

Contact: Section de la politique des droits de l'homme/ Département fédéral des Affaires étrangères

Republic of Tajikistan

A national human rights education programme is being established.

Last information received on: June 2001

Contact: Centre for Strategic Research

Turkey

In May 1998, the Human Rights Coordinating High Committee adopted the "Regulation on the establishment of the National Committee for the Decade for Human Rights Education" and established a national advisory committee for the Decade. The committee consists of representatives of the Prime Minister's Office, the Ministries of Justice, the Interior, Foreign Affairs,

National Education, Health, and Culture, four representatives of relevant voluntary institutions, and academics with experience in this field.

In July 1999, the National Committee published the Human Rights Education Programme of Turkey (1998-2007), which is composed of the following parts:

- introductory chapters
- priorities of human rights education in Turkey and main target groups
- present state of human rights education and relevant proposals of the National Committee, directed to the following sectors: primary schools, high schools and universities
- law enforcement officers attached to the Ministry of Justice
- law enforcement officers attached to the Ministry of Internal Affairs
- 'the mass media
- NGOs

Among the activities mentioned, there are:

- the training of trainers for civil society entitles and for the police
- the inclusion of human rights issues in in-service training and entrance examinations for civil service posts
- the conduct of research on human rights concepts, with the support of UNESCO
- various awareness-raising activities

The programme is now being implemented in cooperation with different partners, including intergovernmental organisations (United Nations, Council of Europe) and civil society organisations.

Following the proclamation of the Plan, a circular was issued by the Prime Minister in August 1999 to ensure implementation of the Plan by the Ministries of National Education, Interior and Justice, who will report periodically on this issue to the Human Rights Coordinating High Council.

The Government of Turkey reported on the recent activities of the National Committee on the Decade for Human Rights Education, which is composed of university professors, representatives of ministries and NGOs. From September 2001 to June 2002 the Committee organised human rights seminars for deputy governors of several provinces of the country; training sessions, in partnership with the Council of Europe, for police and gendarmerie trainers, as well as in-service training programmes for judges and public prosecutors; essays and drawing competitions for prisoners and prison officials, as well as poster and cartoon competitions for young people; and human rights training for social workers working with street children.

Last information received on: 8 July 2002

Contact: Turkish National Committee on the Decade for Human Rights Education

Ukraine

In May 1995, the Government issued a decree, regarding the programme of legal education for the population of Ukraine, which provides for a wide range of activities in the field of human rights education. In pursuance of this resolution, educational programmes in the field of human rights targeted to different age groups are being developed throughout the country. However, priority is given to children. Within this general framework, the Government has requested OHCHR to provide a number of institutions (ministries, institutions of higher education and libraries) and human rights publications, in order that governmental officials, students, researchers and readers, may have easy access to international instruments and information on human rights.

There is no national Committee in existence to serve as the focal point for the Decade, however there are plans under way to establish one.

The Ministry of Education and Science is the responsible institution at the national level for human rights education. The Ministry of Education and Science is developing a national Plan of Action as part of an overall national plan for human rights. It is expected to be completed by the beginning of 2001.

Last information received on: 1 July 2000

Contact: Ministry of Education and Science

Ministry of Justice

United Kingdom

With regards to the school sector, the July 1997 White Paper "Excellence in schools" provided for collaborative consultations in order to review the National Curriculum. Within that framework an Advisory Group on Education for Citizenship and the Teaching of Democracy in Schools, including human rights education, was set up.

The coming into force of the Human Rights Act in 2000 has been accompanied by several training programmes and materials.

They reported that the Department for Education and Skills has introduced citizenship education into the national curriculum for England; it was first introduced in primary school teaching in 2000 and became a statutory national curriculum subject in secondary schools in 2002. All schools have received guidelines on how to implement the curriculum; more information is available on-line at the address: http://www.dfes.gov.uk/citizenship.es.gov.uk/citizenship.

Last information received on: 27 November 2002

Contact: UK Mission to the UNOG

Department for Education and Employment

LATIN AMERICA AND THE CARIBBEAN

Antigua and Barbuda

A national plan for human rights education is in preparation; a national consultation is being undertaken so as to reform relevant constitutional law and to adopt a national policy. Activities such as meetings, workshops and media education addressing human rights issues are regularly organised by the Ministry of Social Improvement and the Ministry of Education, and are directed particularly towards police and prison guards, teachers, children, parents, nurses, and trainers.

The study of human rights is incorporated at all levels of education; components on human rights education as such, are also provided in sociology and social studies classes. Awareness-raising campaigns on human rights questions, specifically on the Universal Declaration of Human Rights, children's rights and prisoners' rights also take place in the country. Civil society is involved in these activities.

Since 1995, the government developed new curriculum materials for school education related to human rights, designed training workshops for specific professional groups, conducted national consultations for a national plan and a national policy and disseminated materials on human rights.

The Government highlighted the need for a broader regional cooperation and policy on human rights education, and the need for emphasised education programmes for professional groups and specific vulnerable groups (migrant workers, people living with HIV/AIDS, the disabled, the elderly).

Last information received on: November 2001

Contact: Ministry of Education

Argentina

Argentina designated the National Direction for the Promotion of Human Rights, within the Office of the Under Secretary of Social and Human Rights, of the Ministry of Interior, a focal point for human rights education. Through a project of technical cooperation established with OHCHR, it has carried out, in collaboration with non governmental organisations, a series of activities. These includes:

- training courses on human rights for teachers aimed at the establishment of a national network of teachers for human rights education
- the dissemination of human rights documents, such as the Vienna Declaration and Programme of Action, the Universal Declaration of Human Rights and the Convention on the Rights of the Child
- the establishment of a publicly accessible National Documentation Centre

- the preparation and dissemination of a bibliography on human rights education, which has been distributed to all educational establishments, governmental and non governmental agencies, libraries and international organisations
- human rights training for police officials and trainers
- workshops on human rights and the penitentiary system
- human rights training for lawyers and other members of the legal profession
- the establishment of a series of agreements with provincial and national universities in order to carry out joint projects
- the production of a publication on human rights ("Facts and rights)

Recent activities have included:

- human rights training for administration of justice officials (police, security forces, judges), teachers and governmental officials
- conclusion of cooperation agreements with private and public universities and organisation of joint initiatives
- development of education plans at the provincial level
- special events, such as school competitions, conferences and sports games
- public dissemination of the Universal Declaration, also through a television and radio campaign

Argentina has also developed a national Plan of Action. Since 1992, the program on the Rights of the Child and the Youth have developed educational strategies and disseminated information in order to sensitise teachers and give guidelines to schools on the subject of the International Convention on the Rights of the Child. A variety of manuals were produced for this program containing teaching resources, audio-visual materials and a number of different information leaflets aimed at young children. Some of these manuals also dealt with activities for long distance teaching. Furthermore, pamphlets were distributed regarding the maltreatment of children, giving examples of conceptual and methodological tools to deal with such situations.

In addition, since 1995 the Government has incorporated human rights in the school curricula, as part of the content of Ethics and Citizenship Education. Among the issues dealt with are the respect and the dignity of the person, respect of differences, dissemination as a violation of human rights, peace and international human rights documents. Democracy, rule of law and justice, as well as individual responsibility in the promotion and the protection of human rights, are also included, and analysis of concrete cases and current events in envisaged.

In 1997/98, the Federal Council of Education also included human rights as a compulsory topic in the training of all teachers.

In 2000, the Federal Council of Culture and Education decided to devote 19 April as day of conviviality and cultural diversity. In this context, numerous events were organised on 19 April 2001; a forum on the Holocaust, meetings on literature and culture diversity.

In 2001 the programme "Learning to Live Together" was initiated, which supports schools in their efforts to strengthen citizenship education. This programme is implemented together with *inter alia*, UNICEF and UNESCO. It provides schools with information and teaching materials on conflict resolution and culture of peace. Other activities undertaken within this programme are as follows: organisation of educational experiences involving children playing the role of policy makers, and regular gathering of teachers, students, partners and other actors.

The Government of Argentina is undertaking the following projects for the period 2001-2003:

- strengthening working partnerships with NGOs (through increased provision of documentation, training and workshops)
- elaborating projects focused on teenagers
- organising a network of partners to better circulate information on human rights throughout the country

The Federal Law on Education (1993) provides a legislative framework for human rights education in schools. Specific measures have been taken to combat discrimination in schools, for instance addressing access to education in rural areas and for children with special needs, as well as introducing multilingualism and the teaching of indigenous people languages and cultures to promote mutual understanding among different cultures. The Ministry of Education also promoted the training of 106 provincial trainers on "Ethical and Citizenship Education", who then trained teachers in local schools. Other initiatives in this area included: the development of classroom materials; the proclamation, within the school calendar, of 19 April as "Day of Living Together in Cultural Diversity" and the development of a number of related activities in schools, throughout the country. In addition the Ministry of Education has devoted a special attention to eradicating gender-based stereotypes and to reproductive rights and sexual health. Finally, work has been undertaken to introduce in various schools the "School System of Coexistence", *i.e.* democratic principles, norms and practices ruling the relationship among members of each educational establishment.

Last information received on: 17 July 2003

Contact: Ministry of Education

Ministry of Foreign Affairs

Chile

Chile forwarded some general information on human rights education in schools. The establishment of an interministerial committee for the Decade is under consideration. The Ministry of Education in Chile has informed the Office that some related activities have been undertaken at the school level, such as the implementation of the education and democracy and women programmes, which include the dissemination of human rights pedagogical materials in schools, the training of teachers and the organisation of school competitions.

The Educational Reform currently being undertaken in order to include, within the school system, education for democracy, peace and human rights, involves four specific areas:

- programmes for improvement and pedagogical innovation
- curricular reform
- professional development of teachers
- Full-Time School Day

In addition, relevant complementary extracurricular activities are envisaged.

The Ministry noted, however, that in order to implement Decade activities at the national level correctly, and inter ministerial task force would need to be created.

Since the 1980's many activities take place in the country. Some are organised by the Ministry of Education, others are conducted by NGOs. The following ministries also take part in such initiatives: Interior, Foreign Affairs, Justice, and Army school. The Government emphasises the role played by NGOs in the democratic reconstruction process of the country. NGOs built a network on human rights and education in 1993, with the aim of obtaining technical support on the part of the State.

Human rights are a component of curricula at all educational levels; presentations on the foundations of human rights, international human rights law and judicial procedures to have one's rights respected. At university, specific courses on human rights are offered to students in various areas. There is also an initiative, which aims at educating children from indigenous groups both in their language and in Spanish.

Specific activities were undertaken, as follows:

- national competition of students on human rights education (1992)
- international seminar on methodologies for human rights education (1993)
- specialised course on human rights education for education supervisors (1993-1994)
- national seminar on human rights education (1994-1995)
- design of methodological tools for human rights education (1993-2000)
- national essay competition 'Jorge Millas Annual Prize" for intellectuals and writers (1993-2000)

They highlighted the integration of human rights as a cross-curricular topic in the basic and middle education system, in particular in social sciences and history, as well as the pilot project "Exploring International Humanitarian Law", developed in 2002 in 32 upper secondary schools and supported by the International Committee of the Red Cross. A specific focus of other educational activities has been the promotion of a positive school climate with the development of activities aimed at the peaceful coexistence of all actors, including training of teachers on conflict resolution methodologies and the involvement of parents.

Last information received on: 14 January 2003

Contact: Ministry of Education

Colombia

The vice-president of the Human Rights Office in Colombia initiated the establishment of a national Committee for human rights education. The committee's main function is to assist in the formulation of the pedagogical strategy and human rights training. The committee is comprised of 13 members from NGOs, academic Institutions at the national level, journalists, politicians, private enterprise and universities.

Colombia has received technical assistance in the elaboration of the national Plan of Action, as well as a number of other projects.

The Government of Colombia highlighted a number of activities undertaken by the Ministry of Interior aimed at raising awareness on human rights and humanitarian law. This was accomplished through radio programmes, distribution of publications and television sports, with a focus on the protection of human rights defends and on the respect of differences. The target audiences were: the general public (both in cities and in rural areas) police forces, NGOs, indigenous communities, and other actors.

Capacity-building programmes and training sessions for civil servants working for the central and the local Government are also organised, often in partnership with UN agencies, including UNHCR and OHCHR.

The Government of Colombia further reported on the role played by the *Defensoría* del Pueblo in human rights education. This institution produces and disseminates relevant publications and audio-video materials, organises training sessions for governmental and municipal civil servants, designs and implements, awareness-raising campaigns, and undertakes other related efforts. Each programme focuses on a specific right or issue (such as reproductive health or domestic violence) or on a set of rights (economic and social rights, political rights, children's rights).

Last information received on: November 2001

Contact: Vice President of the Republic of Colombia

Costa Rica

The infusion of human rights education in the school system is a process which began in 1986 in cooperation with the Inter-American Institute for Human Rights. Then, between 1990-1994, a Curricular Reform was implemented, which included the integration of the Convention on the Rights of the Child in the judicial and educational system.

Between 1994-1998, the "Comisión Nacional para la Formación y el Fortalecimiento de los Valores", responsible for the development of values education, including human rights education, was strengthened. In 1995, a course on the promotion and defence of the human rights and responsibilities was included in the Open Education Programmes for Youth and Adults, through a self-learning modules.

Finally, in 1998 the Ministry of Education, in cooperation with other Ministries within Central America, published a series of modules for adult literacy, one of which was dedicated to the promotion of human rights.

In cooperation with IHCHR, Costa Rica organised an international Consultation on Pedagogical Foundations of Human Rights Education from 22 to 26 July 1996.

The Government of Costa Rica reported that, according to Article 63 of the 1997 Children and Youth Code, which is based on the provisions of the Convention on the Rights of the Child, teaching institutions shall promote children's rights among the students, and teaching and administrative personnel.

In addition, the National Education Plan of the Ministry of Public Education promotes human rights awareness-raising among students.

Cooperation between the Government and other bodies, such as the University for Peace, the Interamerican Institute for Human Rights and UNESCO, have resulted in joint human rights education projects. These include workshops for teachers, members of NGOs and representatives of governmental institutions and the development of educational materials.

The Government further reported the setting up of a specific room, devoted to the rights of the child, in the Costa Rica's Child Museum. Furthermore, a survey in the country and in Panama was undertaken to analyse the state of human rights education in the secondary school system, which prompted a publication and a regional meetings of educators.

A national committee for human rights education was initiated at the beginning of 2000 by the Minister of Education. NGOs are represented in the committee.

One of the main objectives of the National Education Plan in Costa Rica is that pupils know their rights; to this end, the "Values" and the "Culture of Peace" Projects are implemented. Special attention is devoted to pre-service human rights training for teachers; in this area, the Government highlighted the work of the Institute for Interdisciplinary Studies on Childhood and Adolescence (INEINA) within the National University (UNA). At a University level, human rights education programmes are carried out by, among others, the Law Faculty of the Costa Rica University, the National University and the State Distance University (UNED); the University for Peace offers a Master degree in International Law and Human Rights. Human rights training for administration of justice officials is organised by the Judicial School (whose activities are also occasionally open to the public), the National Police Academy as well as the National School of Penitentiary Police. The Government of Costa Rica also highlighted the many educational activities undertaken by the Inter-American Institute for Human Rights, which include training courses, production and distribution of materials, the development of a human rights section within the Children's Museum, etc.

The national Plan of Action was initiated by Counsellor Dr. Flor de María Pérez, of the Ministry of Education. Other third level educational institutions also participated in the development of the Plan.

The Costa Rican government has received technical assistance from the OEI and UNESCO.

The Costa Rican government reported that one of the main objectives of the national education plan is that pupils should know their rights; to this end, the "Values" and the "Culture of Peace" Projects are implemented. Special attention is devoted to pre-service human rights training for teachers; in this area, the Government highlighted the work of the Institute for Interdisciplinary Studies on Childhood and Adolescence (INEINA) within the National University (UNA).

Last information received on: 18 August 2002

Contact: Ministry of Education

Permanent Mission of Costa Rica, Geneva

Cuba

Cuba has reported some initiatives in the area of HRE, in cooperation with international organisations such as UNESCO and UNICEF. The Government has focused on the goal of making education accessible to all Cubans.

Cuba reported that the development of responsible citizens respectful of human rights, democracy and peace has been a permanent objective of Cuban educational policy, as part of the realisation of the right to education. Specific subjects in the school curricula are aimed at values education, including civic education in secondary schools. The Government of Cuba also stressed the need to educate law enforcement agencies and the judiciary in human rights, and human rights have been integrated into the pre-service training of governmental officials. Cuba further noted the active role played by civil society in human rights education. For example, the National Union of Jurists of Cuba, in cooperation with relevant ministries, regularly organises human rights workshops for legal professionals; it has also organised human rights seminars for Cuban and Latin-American legal and academic professionals. In January 2002, the Union and the Ministry of Foreign Affairs jointly issued a compilation of human rights instruments that are in force in Cuba, which was disseminated nationwide.

In Cuba, the primary school curricula include values education, aiming at promoting peace and respect for others and for nature; a civic education subject is taught in secondary schools. Specific related programmes include "Educate your Child", "For Life" and the Audiovisual Programme, which consists of television programmes on various themes to stimulate analysis and debates on human rights-related issues. A major achievement of the educational system, according to the government, has been the full eradication in the country of any race- or gender-based discrimination. The government also stressed the need to target law enforcement agencies and the judiciary; training on national and international law related to human rights is included in the general training programmes of relevant academies. Civil society's active role in human rights education is exemplified by the work of the National Union of Jurists which, in cooperation with relevant ministries, the Parliament or judicial institutions, organises regularly seminars and debates for professionals working in the administration of justice, with the participation of academicians from Latin-American countries, and has issued and disseminated, as a joint projects with the Ministry for Foreign Affairs, a compilation of human rights instruments in force in the country.

Last information received on: 6 June 2002

Contact: Ministry of Foreign Relations Permanent Mission of Cuba, Geneva

Ecuador

A national action plan for human rights education should be finalised in 2002. The National Permanent Commission on Human Rights is designing it and it comprises of both State and civil society representatives. The Ministry of Education will implement the Plan, in cooperation with other State and civil society actors. The national action plan for human rights education is part of the national plan for human rights, adopted in 1998. The national action plan for human rights education will reach all levels of the educational system, by revising curricula and education tools to eliminate intolerance stereotypes.

The following State actors work on human rights education:

- the National Council of women

- the Defensoría del Pueblo
- the Ministry of Education and Culture
- the Ministry of Police
- the Ministry of Foreign Affairs

In civil society, the following partners work on human rights education:

- ALDHU
- SERPAJ
- Defensa de Niños Internacional
- Instituto Nacional del Niño y la Familia
- Foro Nacional de la Niñez
- Centro de Investigaciones de la Mujer Ecuatoriana
- CEPAM, Tribuna del Consumidor
- Centro de Derechos Económicos
- Sociales y Culturales
- Fundación Pueblo Indio
- Centro Afroeccuatoriano
- universities
- camaras productivas

Governmental and non-governmental human rights specialists jointly undertake may activities.

Human rights education components have been included at all levels of education, and studies are conducted with specific and appropriate means and tools. Specific courses and programmes have also been designed for police and army forces, judges and lawyers, fiscal agents, teachers, and journalists. The following vulnerable groups are also targeted by specific programmes: niñez, teenagers, women, indiegnous people, refugees, migrant workers and the elderly. All these courses and programmes are designed and implemented by governmental entities in full partnerships with NGOs.

Five human rights awareness raising campaigns took place or are still taking place in the country, through schools, media, workshops, conferences.

Last information received on: November 2001

Contact: Ministry of Education

Ministry for Foreign Affairs

El Salvador

In April 1999, a National Committee for Human Rights Education was established, with the objective to formulate and implement a National Plan of Action for Human Rights Education. The Committee was also created to improve relations between the Government, inter-government organisations, NGOs, professionals, individuals and civil society in general. The following are a list of the committee's functions:

- to develop and approve a National Plan of Action having held national consultations
- to develop and approve regular action plans
- to authorise activities, including those that are not expressly included in the Plan of Action
- to conduct the activities included in the Plan of Action
- to initiate the participation of different sectors of El Salvadorian society
- to delegate activities to institutions or organisations that are active in the committee, or request the cooperation of other entities or persons
- to receive and authorise the report of activities
- to allocate resources so that activities may be conducted
- to modify the present guidelines and instructions
- to deal with anything that may be considered relevant to the area

The committee is compared of representatives from the following:

- the Ministry of Education

- the Ministry of External Affairs
- the Procuraduría para la Defensa de los Derechos Humanos
- the Executive Technical Unit of the Coordinating Commission of the Justice Sector
- the Doctorate program of Human Rights and Peace Education at the University of El Salvador
- a consortium of human rights NGOs
- the International Defence of the Child (DNI)
- the Institute of Women's Studies (CEMUJER)

The Plan of Action is being prepared at present and is expected to be completed by July 2000. The objectives of the plan are:

- to consolidate the national reconciliation
- to promote the culture of peace based on the respect of human rights and fundamental freedoms
- to prevent human rights violations, survey vulnerable sectors and to prevent potential agents from committing human rights violations
- to promote democracy, sustainable development, the importance of law and the protection of the environment and peace

The main topics:

- basic conceptual aspects of human rights
- fundamental rights
- democratic rights
- the rights of victims of crimes and abuse of power
- rights of women
- rights of children
- rights of elderly people
- right to a healthy environment
- duties of man

The targets:

- the formal education system
- staff of the department of justice
- the public administration
- civil society
- NGOs
- Labour organisations
- Community organisations

Principal Activities:

- undertake consultations regarding the human rights education plan of action
- undertake analysis of human rights education in El Salvador
- promote, stimulate and support development of education in the area of human rights
- sensitise the state departments and civil society to human rights
- organise a campaign to disseminate information regarding human rights and the culture of peace
- set up libraries and documentation centres dealing specifically with human rights
- promote a culture of peace
- aware persons and institutions for their work in the area of human rights and culture of peace

The National Committee for Human Rights organised a National Consultation, with the participation of representatives of governmental institutions and non-governmental organisations in July 1999, in order to identify the needs and priorities for human rights education in the country.

Last information received on: 3 July 2000

Contact: Ministry of Education

Guatemala

Guatemala informed the Office of a broad range of activities undertaken by various actors in the country. In particular it affirmed that the signing of the Peace Agreement in 1996 created a new impetus to human rights education. The following most recent initiatives can be highlighted: the Ministry of Education elaborated textbooks for human rights education in schools, developed related training for its staff and courses by correspondence for adults.

The Presidential Commission of Human Rights (COPREDEH) commissioned several human rights publications, organised seminars and radio programmes, and a produced a CD-ROM containing more than 400 human rights and related documents. In addition, it organised seminars for trainers of the Ministry of Education and activities involving the general public, such as seminars and conferences, which totalled 170 in 1998. In 1999, it began the development of a Documentation Centre and the implementation of a General s personnel and judges=Cooperation Agreement with OHCHR to train the Commission and lawyers.

The Procuraduría de los Derechos Humanos, together with the Ministry of Education, is developing a programme for the integration of human rights education at the primary school level. In addition, it is implementing three specific training programmes targeting community leaders, public officials and the Procuraduría's staff.

At the university level, professors training, development of postgraduate programmes, the establishment of human rights chairs and related activities have been assumed, under the coordination of the Consejo Superior Universitario Centroamericano. Most of the activities referred to were carried out with the support of various international organisations and aid agencies, such as UNESCO, OHCHR, UNDP, the European Union and DANIDA.

There is no national committee for HRE in existence, however the Ministry of Education and COPREDEH are working together and envisage the committee being established by July 2001.

Both the Ministry of Education and the Attorney's Office for Human Rights are currently responsible at the national level for Human Rights Education. COPREDEH has been increasingly active since the beginning of the Decade, principally in the dissemination of information on human rights instruments and contributes in the area of capacity building of civil servants, particularly the armed forces and police. Furthermore, they have circulated information regarding the content and obligations of the Plan of Action for the Decade, and on the declaration and program of action of the Culture of Peace of the UN.

Although no national Plan of Action has been developed, the government of Guatemala has made proposals of educational reform at the national level and have undergone a rethinking of the education system generally, placing emphasis on the teaching of human rights through both formal and informal education. Similarly, at the University level, the curricula are being re-evaluated to integrate the theme of human rights. Two UNICEF experts have been working full-time on the restructuring of the curricula, however there is a need for further technical assistance regarding the remuneration of experts working on the formulation of an education plan.

The establishment of a National Committee to serve as a mechanism of communication between institutions and other human rights organisations is seen as an important task to be met in the next five years of the Decade.

Last information received on: July 14, 2000

Contact: Presidential Commission on Human Rights

Guyana

From 1994 to 1997, the National Centre for Educational Resource and Development of the Ministry of Education, the Guyana Human Rights Association and Amnesty International/ Guyana Section developed the Programme "Human Rights Education for Citizenship", for primary and secondary schools.

It was adopted in the form of three cycles of national workshops. The aims of these workshops were the training of teachers and other school personnel, and curriculum and materials development. In addition, campaigns to sensitise parents and the general public regarding human rights education were developed.

In 1999, the Teachers' Manual for Caribbean Schools was published as a result of the project, and was launched during the

First Caribbean Human Rights Education Conference for Chief Education Officers and Curriculum Specialists (Trinidad and Tobago, April 1999).

Last information received on: September 1999

Contact: Ministry of Education

Haïti

There is no national committee for HRE in existence, however it is expected that one will be established by the incoming government.

Rather than one particular institution holding the sole responsibility for human rights education, it appears that various government departments engage themselves with the issues.

The failure to implement a national NRE Plan of Action in the framework of the Decade is attributed to the socio-political crisis that has affected the country since 1996. However, it has been noted that during this time, different national entities have nonetheless developed programmes in the area of human rights education. Most notably the following institutions: MCI, MENJS, MJSP, MCFAG and the Ministry of Social Affairs (MAS).

Last information received on: 26 June 2000

Contact: Office of the Prime Minister

Mexico

On the initiative of the National Human Rights Commission, and the cooperation with various governmental agencies, a broad series of activities were undertaken in 1997, 1998, including:

- training courses for public officials (immigration officers, police, security force, prison officials, armed forces, health personnel)
- courses on the rights of particularly vulnerable groups, in cooperation with those groups (women, indigenous peoples, children, migrants, prisoners, persons with disabilities and with HIV/AIDS)
- within the formal education system (including higher education and vocational training institutes), integration of human rights in the curricula, training of trainers, conferences and other activities

- a public information campaign (including the development of the documentation centre of the National Commission, television and radio programmes, the development of the Commission Website, national awards and various publications)

The Government of Mexico informed OHCHR that as part of the 1993 education reform, human rights principles have been infused in the primary and secondary school curricula, in different subjects such as history (political rights), geography (environment related rights, ethical diversity, biodiversity) and natural sciences (right to life, health related rights). Such integration has been in accordance with the age of the children and with an approach relevant to their daily life. Since the 1999-2000 school year, a course of civic and ethics studies, which aims at raising awareness among teenagers on risks which can affect the free exercise of their rights, has been introduced. Furthermore, the Ministry of Public Education has developed materials for students and for teachers, which address human rights issues, and has revised textbooks and teaching guides accordingly.

The Government of Mexico reported of a series of initiatives, including: the establishment in 2001 of a working group on human rights education involving governmental and non-governmental representatives, in order to strengthen human rights education nationally, as part of a broader cooperative initiative in the area of human rights; the request, in August 2002, of the Mexican President to the Secretary of Public Education to set up a national programme on human rights education; and the signature, still in 2002, of an agreement between the government and UNESCO to implement a series of human rights educational activities including surveys, research and organisation of seminars, in collaboration with the Universal Nacional Autónoma de México and the Universidad Iberoamericana.

Last information received on: December 2002

Contact: National Commission on Human Rights

Nicaragua

Nicaragua reported the inclusion of human rights, as contained in international, regional and national human rights documents, in pre-school and school curricula, as a cross-cutting issues and in specific subjects such as moral and civic education; related programmes involve also teachers and parents. In secondary schools, "student governments" have been established so as to prepare students to civic and political responsibilities. Nicaragua has also been promoting democracy education since 1990 through training sessions for teachers and social workers, both on principles as well as appropriate teaching methodologies; elaboration of teaching materials; organisation of drawing and essay competitions; strengthening of governmental bodies responsible for this area; development of extra-curricular activities; and other public awareness activities, for instance through the media. Educational programmes are also specifically elaborated on the rights of specific groups such as people living with HIV/ AIDS and the disabled.

Last information received on: 19 September 2002

Contact: Ministry of Education, Office of Human Values

Panama

Panama, in cooperation with the Inter-American Institute for Human Rights, UNESCO and DANIDA, has developed a comprehensive national plan of action for human rights education in schools. It includes:

- a survey on the state of human rights education in schools
- a revision of textbooks
- training of teachers
- workshops
- the establishment of both a network of human rights trainers and of a National Commission to Promote Human Rights Education and Learning.

An agreement between the Ministry of Education and the Inter-American Institute of Human Rights was signed, concerning technical cooperation for human rights education related activities. The Ministry of Education and the Panamanian Electoral Tribunal have concluded a civic electoral education agreement, with the aim of fostering democracy among young Panamanians through education.

A five-year community project was initiated in 1995, with the support of Tolerance and Education UNESCO and the Celestin

Freineth Institute, entitled, as part of the United for Democracy, Human Rights, Peace, and Development Nations Year of Tolerance.

Last information received on: 1995

Contact: Ministry of Education

Peru

The National Council for Human Rights reported on initiatives undertaken within:

- the school system (in particular, the scope and content of the New Curricular Proposal for secondary schools),
- the Ministry of Justice (events targeted at administration of justice officials, such as judges and lawyers, and at teachers and students; preparation of publications)
- the Ministry of Defence and the Interior (training courses for armed forces and police, and the elaboration of related materials; and the development of specific joint programmes with NGOs, UNICEF and the Ministry of Education for the training of governmental officials on the rights of the child).

In May 2002, Peru adopted Law No. 27741, which establishes a national human rights educational policy. The law provides that human rights education is compulsory at all levels of education, whether civil or military, in Spanish and also in various indigenous languages. The law also requests the executive power to develop a related national plan of action. As a follow-up, all educational establishments, including universities and police and military training institutions, will have six months to revise their curricula in order to comply with the law.

Last information received on: 24 June 2002

Contact Details: National Council on Human Rights

Trinidad and Tobago

There is no national committee for HRE in the country. However, human rights education is being developed by the following Ministries, which undertake specific activities:

- *Ministry of Education:* includes human rights education as part of its Social Studies curriculum in secondary schools; a relevant booklet has been produced in this regard;

- *Ministry of Communications and Information Technology:* disseminates information on human rights to the general public through TV and radio broadcasts, including retransmission of the UN Secretary Generals speeches on occasions commemorating human rights issues;
- *Ministry of Community Empowerment, Sport and Customer Affairs:* chairs an inter-ministerial National Plan of Action Committee, which strives for the attainment of the goals of the 1990 World Summit for Children; relevant Divisions have developed educational programmes (including workshops and lectures) on children's rights, on women's rights, gender-based violence, and the use of drugs;
- *Ministry of Health:* published a draft Patient's Charter of Rights, and also develops a National AIDS Programme, which includes public education aspects;
- *Ministry of Labour, Manpower, Development and Industrial Relations:* works *inter alia* on child labour issues, together with the ILO Office in the Country

A Human Rights Unit was established in 1998 at the Ministry of the Attorney General and Legal Affairs. The aims of the Unit are to promote the rights contained in the treaties to which the country is a party and to prepare the periodic reports that have to be submitted to the relevant UN Treaty Bodies. The Unit is composed of six persons, four professionals and two non-professionals.

The Government is planning to launch a Children's Authority, which was created by statute, and which will play the role of advocate for the rights of children in the country.

The Government works in partnerships with UNESCO towards human rights education at all levels of the educational system, through the UNESCO Associated Schools Projects. Activities consist of workshops with children and parents, and distribution of leaflets, information and documentation on children's rights, including copies of the convention on the Rights of the Child.

On 10 December 1999 (Human Rights Day), the Government held a commemoration at the closing ceremony of a one-week workshop on human rights reporting, co-organised with the ILO Training Centre of Turin.

The Government emphasises the role played by the civil society, including NGOs, in raising awareness on human rights issues; grants are regularly allocated to such entities so as to empower them in their activities (organisation of workshops, dissemination of human rights related information).

Last information received on: November 2001

No contact details.

Venezuela

Human rights education is being introduced as an integral part of the national human rights plan. It is developed as a joint effort of governmental authorities, non-governmental organisations and the National Commission of Human Rights. An inter-sectorial committee developed the plan, in conjunction with the government and civil society. Technical assistance was given to assist in the development of the plan.

Workshops and regional meetings of teachers are organised by the Ministry of Education in cooperation with various NGOs, such as Amnesty International/Venezuela, the Red de Apoyo para la Justicia y la Paz and the Programa Venezolano de Educación Acción en Derechos Humanos (PROVEA).

Relevant materials (such as the Valija Didáctica: Educando en Valores developed by Amnesty International/Venezuela) are disseminated in all schools.

An International Seminar on Human Rights, in which representatives of different sectors and NGOs involved in educational activities participated, was organised in July 1998.

The Ministry of Education informed OHCHR that various school programmes, activities and educational materials on the rights of the child have been developed in cooperation with UNICEF and the Centros Comunitarios de Aprendizaje (CECODAP).

There is no national committee for HRE, however the National Commission of Human Rights, which was set up in 1997, is working on the establishment of a national committee.

The Defensoría del Pueblo and relevant governmental entities regularly organise activities aimed at raising awareness on human rights; fora, seminars, training sessions and workshops. The target audiences of such activities are: judges and lawyers, civil servants, and police officers. Specific programmes and activities are carried out for vulnerable groups; children, women, indigenous groups, refugees and prisoners. Numerous information campaigns and workshops were held on human rights in general, and on children's and teenagers' rights.

Last information received on: November 2001

Contact: Department of Environment, Education and Community Participation/Ministry of Education.

8

The International Bill of Human Rights

Introduction

Five major United Nations legal instruments exist to define and to guarantee the protection of human rights: the Universal Declaration of Human Rights (1984), the International Covenant on Economic, Social and Cultural Rights (1966), the International Covenant on Civil and Political Rights (1966) and the two Operational Protocols to the latter Covenant. The Declaration is a manifesto with primarily moral authority. The Covenants are treaties binding on the States which ratify them. Together they constitute the document known as the International Bill of Human Rights.

Preparation of an International Bill of Rights was a fundamental preoccupation of the United Nations. The Charter of the United Nations, agreed to in San Francisco in 1945, in seven different articles declared United Nations support for human rights and set up a Human Rights Commission. In its first session in January 1946, the General Assembly called for the Commission to work towards "the formulation of an international bill of rights". When the Commission on Human Rights began its work in February 1947, this team was its first priority.

The members of the Commission were immediately divided over whether the Bill should take the form of a proclamation or a treaty. As a compromise, they decided that the Bill should have three parts: a declaration proclaiming general principles, a "covenant on covenants" embodying these principles in a form which would be binding on States which ratified them, and "measures of implementation" or provisions for review of the way in which States carried out their covenant obligations. In less than two years, the Commission sent to its superior bodies, the Economic and Social Council and the General Assembly, a completed draft of a Universal Declaration of Human Rights. On 10 December 1948, the General Assembly adopted the Universal Declaration of Human Rights by a vote of 48 in favour, eight abstentions and no dissensions.

The same day, the Assembly adopted a resolution urging that the Commission continue giving priority to drafting a treaty which would give legal force to the Declaration. In 1951, the Commission produced a draft covenant which it sent to its parent body, the Economic and Social Council. Seeing the difficulties in embodying in one covenant two different categories of rights, the Council urged the General Assembly to approve the drafting of two covenants. The Assembly agreed, and requested the Commission to proceed. The Commission compiled and produced two draft covenants—one on economic, social and cultural rights, the other on civil and political rights, the latter with an optional protocol, and providing also for measures of review of implementation of the Covenant provisions. On 16 December 1966, the Assembly voted unanimously to adopt the three instruments and open them for signature. The instruments, after their ratification by 35 United Nations Members States, entered into force in 1976.

On 15 December 1989, by a vote of 59 in favour to 26 against, with 48 abstentions, the General Assembly adopted the Second Optional Protocol to the International Covenant on Civil and Political Rights, aiming at the abolition of the death penalty. This Second Optional Protocol came into force in July 1991.

* * *

The *Universal Declaration Of Human Rights* is the basic international statement of the inalienable and inviolable rights of all members of the human family. It is intended to serve as "the common standards of achievement for all peoples and all nations" in the effort to secure universal and effective recognition and observance of the rights and freedoms it lists.

The two *Covenants* relating to human rights provide internal protection for specified rights and freedoms. Both Covenants recognise the right of peoples to self-determination. Both have provisions barring all forms of discrimination in the exercise of human rights. Both have the force of law for the countries which ratify them.

The first treaty, the *Covenant on Economic, Social and Cultural Rights*, recognises the right to work and to free choice of employment, to fair wages, to form and join unions, to social security, and to adequate standards of living conditions for their people. States' reports on their progress in promotion of these rights are reviewed by a committee of experts appointed by the Economic and Social Council.

The *Covenant on Civil and Political Rights* recognises the right of every human person to life, liberty and security of person, to privacy, to freedom from cruel, inhuman or degrading treatment and from torture, to freedom from slavery, to immunity from arbitrary arrest, to a fair trial, to recognition as a person before the law, to immunity from retroactive sentences, to freedom of thought, conscience and religion, to freedom of opinion and expression, to liberty of movement, including the right to emigrate, to peaceful assembly and to freedom of association.

The Covenant on Civil and Political Rights sets up a Human Rights Committee to consider progress reports from States which have ratified the Covenant. The Committee may also hear complaints by such States that other States which have ratified the Covenant have failed in upholding the obligations under the Covenant.

Under the *Optional Protocol* to the Civil and Political Covenant, individuals under certain circumstances may file complaints of human rights violations by ratifying States.

Under the *Second Optional Protocol* to the Civil and Political Covenant, States must take all necessary measures to abolish the death penalty.

The Declaration is accepted almost universally as a gauge by which Governments can measure their progress in the protection of human rights. In United Nations organs, the Declaration has an authority surpassed only by the Charter. It is invoked constantly not only in the General Assembly, but also in the Security Council and other organs. It is quoted in international legal instruments, including the Council of Europe's Convention for the Protection of Human Rights and Fundamental Freedoms (1950), the Japanese Peace Treaty (1951), the Special Statute for the status of Trieste (1954), the Constitution of the Organisation of African Unity (1963), and the Final Document of the Conference on Security and Co-operation in Europe (1975), signed at Helsinki by 35 States. It is invoked in a score of national constitutions. It has inspired and sometimes become part of many countries' national legislation, and has been cited with approval in national courts.

UNIVERSAL DECLARATION OF HUMAN RIGHTS

Preamble

Whereas recognition of the inherent dignity and of the equal and inalienable rights of all members of the human family is the foundation of freedom, justice and peace in the world.

Whereas disregard and contempt for human rights have resulted in barbarous acts which have outraged the conscience of mankind, and the advent of a world in which human beings shall enjoy freedom of speech and belief and freedom from fear and want has been proclaimed as the highest aspiration of the common people,

Whereas it is essential, if man is not to be compelled to have recourse, as a last resort, to rebellion against tyranny and oppression, that human rights should be protected by the rule of law,

Whereas it is essential to promote the development of friendly relations between nations,

Whereas the peoples of the United Nations have in the Charter reaffirmed their faith in fundamental human rights, in the dignity and worth of the human person and in the equal rights of men and women and have determined to promote social progress and better standards of life in larger freedom,

Whereas Member States have pledged themselves to achieve, in co-operation with the United Nations, the promotion of universal respect for and observance of human rights and fundamental freedoms,

Whereas a common understanding of these rights and freedoms is of the greatest importance for the full realisation of this pledge,

Now, therefore, The General Assembly *proclaims*

This Universal Declaration of Human Rights as a common standard of achievement for all peoples and all nations, to the end that every individual and every organ of society, keeping this Declaration constantly in mind, shall strive by teaching and education to promote respect for these rights and freedoms and by progressive measures, national and international to secure their universal and effective recognition and observance both among the peoples of Member States themselves and among the peoples of territories under their jurisdiction.

Article 1

All human beings are born free and equal in dignity and rights. They are endowed with reason and conscience and should act towards one another in a spirit of brotherhood.

Article 2

Everyone is entitled to all the rights and freedoms set forth in this Declaration, without distinction of any kind, such as race, colour, sex, language, religion, political or other opinion, national or social origin, property, birth or other status.

Furthermore, no distinction shall be made on the basis of the political, jurisdictional or international status of the country or territory to which a person belongs, whether it be independent, trust, non-self-governing or under any other limitation of sovereignty.

Article 3

Everyone has the right to life, liberty and security of person.

Article 4

No one shall be held in slavery or servitude; slavery and the slave trade shall be prohibited in all their forms.

Article 5

No one shall be subjected to torture or to cruel, inhuman or degrading treatment or punishment.

Article 6

Everyone has the right to recognition everywhere as a person before the law.

Article 7

All are equal before the law and are entitled without any discrimination to equal protection of the law. All are entitled to equal protection against any discrimination in violation of this Declaration and against any incitement to such discrimination.

Article 8

Everyone has the right to an effective remedy by the competent national tribunals for acts violating the fundamental rights granted him by the constitution or by law.

Article 9

No one shall be subjected to arbitrary arrest, detention or exile.

Article 10

Everyone is entitled in full equality to a fair and public hearing by an independent and impartial tribunal, in the determination of his rights and obligations and of any criminal charge against him.

Article 11

1. Everyone charged with a penal offence has the right to be presumed innocent until proved guilty according to law in a public trial at which he has had all the guarantees necessary for his defence.
2. No one shall be held guilty of any penal offence on account of any act or omission which did not constitute a penal offence, under national or international law, at the time when it was committed. Nor shall a heavier penalty be imposed that the one that was applicable at the time the penal offence was committed.

Article 12

No one shall be subjected to arbitrary interference with his privacy, family, home or correspondence, nor to attacks upon his honour and reputation. Everyone has the right to protection of the law against such interference or attacks.

Article 13

1. Everyone has the right to freedom of movement and residence within the borders of each state.
2. Everyone has the right to leave any country, including his own and to return to his country.

Article 14

1. Everyone has the right to seek and to enjoy in other countries asylum from persecution.
2. This right may not be invoked in the case of prosecutions genuinely arising from non-political crimes or form acts contrary to the purposes and principles of the United Nations.

Article 15

1. Everyone has the right to a nationality.
2. No one shall be arbitrarily deprived of his nationality nor denied the right to change his nationality.

Article 16

1. Men and women of full age, without any limitation due to race, nationality or religion, have the right to marry and to found a family. They are entitled to equal rights as to marriage, during marriage and at its dissolution.
2. Marriage shall be entered into only with the free and full consent of the intending spouses.
3. The family is the natural and fundamental group unit of society and is entitled to protection by society and the State.

Article 17

1. Everyone has the right to own property alone as well as in association with others.
2. No one shall be arbitrarily deprived of his property.

Article 18

Everyone has the right to freedom of thought, conscience and religion; this right includes freedom to change his religion or belief, and freedom, either alone or in community with others and in public or private, to manifest his religion or belief in teaching, practice, worship and observance.

Article 19

Everyone has the right to freedom of opinion and expression; this right includes freedom to hold opinions without interference and to seek, receive and impart information and ideas through any media and regardless of frontiers.

Article 20

1. Everyone has the right to freedom of peaceful assembly and association.
2. No one may be compelled to belong to an association.

Article 21

1. Everyone has the right to take part in the government of his country, directly or through freely chosen representatives.
2. Everyone has the right of equal access to public service in his country.
3. They will of the people shall be the basis of the authority of government; this will shall be expressed in periodic and genuine elections which shall be by universal and equal suffrage and shall be held by secret vote or by equivalent free voting procedures.

Article 22

Everyone, as a member of society, has the right to social security and is entitled to realisation, through national effort and international co-operation and in accordance with the organisation and resources of each State, of the economic, social and cultural rights indiscipline for his dignity and the free development of his personality.

Article 23

1. Everyone has the right to work, to free choice of employment, to just and favourable conditions of work and to protection against unemployment.
2. Everyone, without any discrimination, has the right to equal pay for equal work.

3. Everyone who works has the right to just and favourable remuneration ensuring for himself and his family an existence worthy of human dignity, and supplemented, if necessary, by other means of social protection.
4. Everyone has the right to form and to join trade unions for the protection of his interests.

Article 24

Everyone has the right to rest and leisure, including reasonable limitation of working hours and periodic holidays with pay.

Article 25

1. Everyone has the right to a standard of living adequate for the health and well-being of himself and of his family, including food, clothing, housing and medical care and necessary social services, and the right to security in the event of unemployment, sickness, disability, widowhood, old age or other lack of livelihood in circumstances beyond his control.
2. Motherhood and childhood are entitled to special care and assistance. All children, whether born in or out of wedlock, shall enjoy the same social protection.

Article 26

1. Everyone has the right to education. Education shall be free, at least in the elementary and fundamental stages. Elementary education shall be compulsory. Technical and professional education shall be made generally available and higher education shall be equally accessible to all on the basis of merit.
2. Education shall be directed to the full development of the human personality and to the strengthening of respect for human rights and fundamental freedoms. It shall promote understanding, tolerance and friendship among all nations, racial or religious groups, and shall further the activities of the United Nations for the maintenance of peace.
3. Parents have a prior right to choose the kind of education that shall be given to their children.

Article 27

1. Everyone has the right freely to participate in the cultural life of the community, to enjoy the arts and to share in scientific advancement and its benefits.
2. Everyone has the right to the protection of the moral and material interests resulting from any scientific, literary or artistic production of which he is the author.

Article 28

Everyone is entitled to a social and international order in which the rights and freedoms set forth in this Declaration can be fully realised.

Article 29

1. Everyone has duties to the community in which alone the free and full development of his personality is possible.
2. In the exercise of his right and freedoms, everyone shall be subject only to such limitations as are determined by law solely for the purpose of securing due recognition and respect for the rights and freedoms of others and of meetings the just requirements of morality, public order and the general welfare in a democratic society.
3. These rights and freedoms may in no case be exercised contrary to the purposes and principles of the United Nations.

Article 30

Nothing in this declaration may be interpreted as implying for any State, group or person any right to engage in any activity or to perform any act aimed at the destruction of any of the rights and freedoms set forth herein.

INTERNATIONAL COVENANT ON ECONOMIC SOCIAL AND CULTURAL RIGHTS

Preamble

The States Parties to the Present Covenant

Considering that, in accordance with the principles proclaimed in the Charter of the United Nations, recognition of the inherent dignity and of the equal and inalienable rights of all members of the humanity family is the foundation of freedom, justice and peace in the world,

Recognising that these rights derive from the inherent dignity of the human person,

Recognising that, in accordance with the Universal Declaration of Human Rights, the ideal of free human beings enjoying freedom from fear and want can only be achieved if conditions are created whereby everyone may enjoy his economic, social and cultural rights, as well as his civil and political rights,

Considering the obligation of States under the Charter of the United Nations to promote universal respect for, and observance of, human rights and freedoms,

Realising that the individual, having duties to other individuals and to the community to which he belongs, is under a responsibility to strive for the promotion and observance of the rights recognised in the present Covenant.

Agree upon the following articles:

PART I

Article 1

1. All peoples have the right of self-determination. By virtue of that right they freely determine their political status and freely pursue their economic, social and cultural development.

2. All peoples may, for their own ends, freely dispose of their natural wealth and resources without prejudice to any obligations arising out of international economic co-operation, based upon the principle of mutual benefit, and international law. In no case may a people be deprived of its own means of subsistence.

3. The State Parties to the present Covenant, including those having responsibility for the administration of Non-Governing and Trust Territories, shall promote the realisation of the right of self-determination, and shall respect that right, in conformity with the provisions of the Charter of the United Nations.

PART II

Article 2

1. Each State Party to the present Covenant undertakes to take steps, individually and through international assistance and co-operation, especially economic and technical, to the maximum of its available resources, with a view to achieving progressively the full realisation of the rights recognised in the present covenant by all appropriate means, including particularly the adoption of legislative measures.
2. The States Parties to the present Covenant undertake to guarantee that the rights enunciated in the present Covenant will be exercised without discrimination of any kind as to race, colour, sex, language, religion, political or other opinion, national or social origin, properly, birth or other status.
3. Developing countries, with due regard to human rights and their national economy, may determine to what extent they would guarantee the economic rights recognised in the present Covenant to non-nationals.

Article 3

The States Parties to the present Covenant undertake to ensure the equal right to men and women to the enjoyment of all economic, social and cultural rights set forth in the present Covenant.

Article 4

The States Parties to the present Covenant recognise that, in the enjoyment of those rights provided by the State in conformity with present Covenant, the State may subject such rights only to such limitations as are determined by law only in so far as this may be compatible with the nature of these rights and solely for the purpose of promoting the general welfare in a democratic society.

Article 5

1. Nothing in the present Covenant may be interpreted as implying for any State, group or person any right to engage in any activity or to perform any act aimed at the destruction

of any of the rights or freedoms recognised herein, or at their limitation to a greater extent than is provided for in the present Covenant.

2. No restriction upon or derogation from any of the fundamental human rights recognised or existing in any country in virtue of law, conventions, regulations or custom shall be admitted on the pretext that the present Covenant does not recognise such rights or that it recognises them to a lesser extent.

PART III

Article 6

1. The States Parties to the present Covenant recognise the right to work, which includes the right of everyone to the opportunity to gain his living by work which he freely chooses or accepts, and will take appropriate steps to safeguard this right.

2. The steps to be taken by a State Party to the present Covenant to achieve the full realisation of this right shall include technical and vocational guidance and training programmes, policies and techniques to achieve steady economic, social and cultural development and full and productive employment under conditions safeguarding fundamental political and economic freedoms to the individual.

Article 7

The States Parties to the present Covenant recognise the right of everyone to the enjoyment of just and favourable conditions of work which ensure, in particular:

(a) Remuneration which provides all workers, as a minimum, with:

   (i) Fair wages and equal remuneration for work of equal value without distinction of any kind, in particular of equal being guaranteed conditions of work not inferior to those enjoyed by men, with equal pay for equal work;

   (ii) A decent living for themselves and their families in accordance with the provisions of the present Covenant;

(*b*) Safe and healthy working conditions;

(*c*) Equal opportunity for everyone to the promoted in his employment to an appropriate higher level, subject to no considerations other than those of seniority and competence;

(*d*) Rest, leisure and reasonable limitations of working hours and periodic holidays with pay, as well as remuneration for public holidays.

Article 8

1. The States Parties to the present Covenant undertake to ensure:

   (*a*) The right of everyone to form trade unions and join the trade union of his choice, subject only to the rules of the organisation concerned, for the promotion and protection of his economic and social interests. No restrictions may be placed on the exercise of this right other than hose prescribed by law and which are necessary in a democratic society in the interests of national security or public order or for the protection of the rights and freedoms of others;

   (*b*) The right of trade unions to establish national federations or confederations and the right of the latter to form or join international trade-union organisations;

   (*c*) The right of trade unions to function freely subject to no limitations other than those prescribed by law and which are necessary in a democratic society in the interests of national security or public order or for the protection of the rights and freedoms of others;

   (*d*) The right to strike, provided that it is exercised in conformity with the laws of the particular country.

2. This article shall not prevent the imposition of lawful restrictions on the exercise of these rights by members of the armed forces or of the police or of the administration of the State.

3. Nothing in this article shall authorise States Parties to the International Labour Organisation Convention of 1948 concerning Freedom of Association and Protection of the

Right to Organise to take legislative measures which would prejudice, or apply the law in such a manner as would prejudice, the guarantees provided for in that Convention.

Article 9

The State Parties to the present Covenant recognise the right of everyone to social security, including social insurance.

Article 10

The States Parties to the present Covenant recognise that:

1. The widest possible protection and assistance should be accorded to the family, which is the natural and fundamental group unit of society, particularly for its establishment and while it is responsible for the care and education of dependent children. Marriage must be entered into with the free consent of the intending spouses.
2. Special protection should be accorded to mothers during a reasonable period before and after childbirth. During such period working mothers should be accorded paid leave or leave with adequate social security benefits.
3. Special measures of protection and assistance should be taken on behalf of all children and young persons without any discrimination for reasons of percentage or other conditions. Children and young persons should be protected from economic and social exploitation. Their employment in work harmful to their morals or health or dangerous to life or likely to hamper their normal development should be punishable by law. States should also set age limits below which the paid employment of child labour should be prohibited and punishable by law.

Article 11

1. The States Parties to the present Covenant recognise the right of everyone to an adequate standard of living for himself and his family, including adequate food, clothing and housing, and to the continuous improvement of living conditions. The States Parties will take appropriate steps to ensure the realisation of this right, recognising to this effect the essential importance of international co-operation based on free consent.

2. The States Parties to the present Covenant, recognising the fundamental right of everyone to be free from hunger, shall take, individually and through international co-operation, the measures, including specific programmes, which are needed.

   (a) To improve methods of production, conservation and distribution of food by making full use of technical and scientific knowledge, by disseminating knowledge of the principles of nutrition and by developing or reforming agrarian systems in such a way as to achieve the most efficient development and utilisation of natural resources;

   (b) Taking into account the problems of both food-importing and food-exporting countries to ensure an equitable distribution of world food supplies in relation to need.

Article 12

1. The States parties to the present Covenant recognise the right of everyone to the enjoyment of the highest attainable standard of physical and mental health.

2. The steps to be taken by the States Parties to the present Covenant to achieve the full realisation of this right shall include those necessary for:

   (a) The provision for the reduction of the stillbirth-rate and of infant mortality and for the healthy development of the child;

   (b) The improvement of all aspects of environmental and industrial hygiene;

   (c) The prevention, treatment and control of epidemic, endemic, occupational and other diseases;

   (d) The creation of conditions which would assure to all medical service and medical attention in the event of sickness.

Article 13

1. The States parties to the present Covenant recognise the right of everyone to education. They agree that education shall be directed to the full development of the human personality

and the sense of its dignity, and shall strengthen the respect for human rights and fundamental freedoms. They further agree that education shall enable all persons to participate effectively in a free society, promote understanding, tolerance and friendship among all nations and all racial, ethnic or religious groups and further the activities of the United Nations for the maintenance of peace.

2. The States Parties to the present Covenant recognise that with a view to achieving the full realisation of this right:

(*a*) Primary education shall be compulsory and available free to all;

(*b*) Secondary education in its different forms, including technical and vocational secondary education, shall be made generally available and accessible to all by every appropriate means, and in particular by the progressive introduction of free education;

(*c*) Higher education shall be made equally accessible to all, on the basis of capacity, by every appropriate means, and in particular by the progressive introduction of free education;

(*d*) Fundamental education shall be encouraged or intensified as far as possible for those persons who have not received or completed the whole period of their primary education;

(*e*) The development of a system of schools at all levels shall be actively pursued, an adequate fellowship system shall be established, and the material conditions of teaching staff shall be continuously improved.

3. The States parties to the present Covenant undertake to have respect for the liberty of parents, when applicable, legal guardians to choose for their children schools, other than those established by the public authorities, which conform to such minimum educational standards as may be laid down or approved by the State and to ensure the religious and moral education of their children in conformity with their own convictions.

4. No part of this article shall be constructed so as to interfere with the liberty of individuals and bodies to establish and direct educational institutions, subject always to the observance of the principles set forth in paragraph 1 of this article and to the requirement that the education given in such institutions shall conform to such minimum standards as may be laid down by the State.

Article 14

Each States party to the present Covenant which, at the time of becoming a Party, has not been able to secure in its metropolitan territory or other territories under its jurisdiction compulsory primary education, free of charge, undertakes, within two years, to work out and adopt a detailed plan of action for the progressive implementation, within a reasonable number of years, to be fixed in the plan, of the principle of compulsory education free of charge for all.

Article 15

1. The State parties to the present Covenant recognise the right of everyone:
   (a) To take part in cultural life;
   (b) To enjoy the benefits of scientific progress and its applications;
   (c) To benefit from the protection of the moral and material interests, resulting from any scientific, literary or artistic production of which he is the author.
2. The steps to be taken by the States Parties to the present Covenant to achieve the full realisation of this right shall include those necessary for the conservation, the development and the diffusion of science and culture.
3. The State Parties to the present Covenant undertake to respect the freedom indispensable for scientific research and creative activity.
4. The States Parties to the present Covenant recognise the benefits to be derived from the encouragement and development of international contacts and co-operation in the scientific and cultural fields.

PART IV

Article 16

1. The State Parties to the present Covenant undertake to submit in conformity with this part of the Covenant reports on the measures which they have adopted and the progress made in achieving the observance of the rights recognised herein.

2. *(a)* All reports shall be submitted to the Secretary-General of the United Nations, who shall transmit copies to the Economic, and Social Council for consideration in accordance with the provisions of the present Covenant.

   (b) The Secretary-General of the United Nations shall also transmit to the specialised agencies copies of the reports, or any relevant parts therefore, from States Parties to the present Covenant which are also members of these specialised agencies in so far as these reports, or parts thereform, relate to any matters which fall within the responsibilities of the said agencies in accordance with their constitutional instruments.

Article 17

1. The States Parties to the present Covenant shall furnish their reports in stages, in accordance with a programme to be established by the Economic and Social Council within one year of the entry into force of the present Covenant after consultation with the States Parties and the specialised agencies concerned.

2. Reports may indicate factors and difficulties affecting the degree of fulfillment of obligations under the present Covenant.

3. Whether relevant information has previously been furnished to the United Nations or to any specialised agency by any State Party to the present Covenant, it will not be necessary to reproduce that information, but a precise reference to the information so furnished will suffice.

Article 18

Pursuant to its responsibilities under the Charter of the United Nations in the field of human rights and fundamental freedoms, the Economic and Social Council may make arrangements with the specialised agencies in respect of their reporting to it on the progress made in achieving the observance of the provisions of the present Covenant falling within the scope of their activities. These reports may include particulars of decisions and recommendations on such implementation adopted by their competent organs.

Article 19

The Economic and Social Council may transmit to the Commission on Human Rights for study and general recommendations or, as appropriate, for information the reports concerning human rights submitted by States in accordance with articles 16 and 17, and those concerning human rights submitted by the specialised agencies in accordance with article 18.

Article 20

The States Parties to the present Covenant and the specialised agencies concerned may submit comments to the Economic and Social Council on any general recommendation under article 19 or reference to such general recommendation in any report of the Commission on Human Rights or any documentation referred to therein.

Article 21

The Economic and Social Council may submit from time to time to the General Assembly reports with recommendations of a general nature and a summary of the information received from the States Parties to the present Covenant and the specialised agencies on the measures taken and the progress made in achieving general observance of the rights recognised in the present Covenant.

Article 22

The Economic and Social Council may bring to the attainment of other organs of the United Nations, there subsidiary organs and specialised agencies concerned with furnishing technical assistance any matters arising out of the reports referred to in this part of the present Còvenant which may assist such bodies in deciding, each within its field of competence, on the advisability of international measures likely to contribute to the effective progressive implementation of the present Covenant.

Article 23

The States Parties to the present Covenant agree that international action for the achievement of the rights recognised in the present Covenant includes such methods as the conclusion of conventions, the adoption of recommendations, the furnishing of technical assistance and the holding of regional meetings and technical meetings for the purpose of consultation and study organised in conjunction with the Governments concerned.

Article 24

Nothing in the present Covenant shall be interpreted as imparting the provisions of the Charter of the United Nations and of the constitutions of the specialised agencies which define the respective responsibilities of the various organs of the United Nations and of the specialised agencies in regard to the matters dealt with in the present Covenant.

Article 25

Nothing in the present Covenant shall be interpreted as imparting the inherent right of all peoples to enjoy and utilise fully and freely their natural wealth and resources.

PART V

Article 26

1. The present Covenant is open for signature by any State Member of the United Nations or member of any of its specialised agencies, by any State Party to the Statute of the International Court of Justice, and by any other State which has been invited by the General Assembly of the United Nations to become a party to the present Covenant.
2. The present Covenant is subject to ratification. Instruments of ratification shall be deposited with the Secretary-General of the United Nations.

3. The present Covenant shall be open to accession by any State referred to in paragraph 1 of this article.

4. Accession shall be effected by the deposit of an instrument of accession with the Secretary-General of the United Nations.

5. The Secretary-General of the United Nations shall inform all States which have signed the present Covenant or acceded to it of the deposit of each instrument of ratification or accession.

Article 27

1. The present Covenant shall enter into force three months after the date of the deposit with the Secretary-General of the United Nations of the thirty-fifth instrument of ratification or instrument of accession.

2. For each State ratifying the present Covenant or acceding to it after the deposit of the thirty-fifth instrument of ratification or instrument of accession, the present Covenant shall enter into force three months after the date of the deposit of its own instrument of ratification or instrument of accession.

Article 28

The provision of the present Covenant shall extend to all parts of federal States without any limitations or exceptions.

Article 29

1. Any State Party to the present Covenant may propose an amendment and file it with the Secretary-General of the United Nations. The Secretary-General shall thereupon communicate any proposed amendments to the States Parties to the present Covenant with a request that they notify him whether they favour a conference of States Parties for the purpose of considering and voting upon the proposals. In the event that at least one third of the States Parties favours such a conference, the Secretary-General shall convene the conference under the auspices of the United Nations. Any amendment adopted by a majority of the States Parties present and voting at the conference shall be submitted to the General Assembly of the United Nations for approval.

2. Amendments shall come into force when they have been approved by the General Assembly of the United Nations and accepted by a two-thirds majority of the States Parties to the present Covenant in accordance with their respective constitutional processes.

3. When amendments come into force they shall be binding those States Parties which have accepted them, other States Parties still being bound by the provision of the present Covenant and any earlier amendment which they have accepted.

Article 30

Irrespective of the notifications made under article 26, paragraph 5, the Secretary-General of the United Nations shall inform all States referred to in paragraph 1 of the same article of the following particulars:

(a) Signatures, ratifications and accessions under article 26;

(b) The date of the entry into force of the present Covenant under article 27 and the date of the entry into force of any amendments under article 29.

Article 31

1. The present Covenant, of which the Chinese, English, French, Russian and Spanish texts are equally authentic, shall be deposited in the archives of the United Nations.

2. The Secretary-General of the United Nations shall transmit certified copies of the present Covenant to all States referred to in article 26.

INTERNATIONAL COVENANT ON CIVIL AND POLITICAL RIGHTS

Preamble

The States Parties to the Present Covenant,

Considering that, in accordance with the principles with the principles proclaimed in the Charter of the United Nations, recognition of the inherent dignity and of the equal and inalienable rights of all members of the human family is the foundation of freedom, justice and peace in the world,

Recognising that these rights derive from the inherent dignity of the human person,

Recognising that, in accordance with the Universal Declaration of Human Rights, the ideal of free human beings enjoying civil and political freedom and freedom from fear and want can only be achieved if conditions are created whereby everyone may enjoy his civil and political rights, as well as his economic, social and cultural rights,

Considering the obligation of States under the Charter of the United Nations to promote universal respect for, and observance of, human rights and freedoms,

Realising that the individual, having duties to other individuals and to the community to which he belongs, is under a responsibility to strive for the promotion and observance of the rights recognised in the present Covenant,

Agree upon the following articles:

PART I

Article 1

1. All peoples have the right of self-determination. By virtue of that right, they freely determine their political status and freely pursue their economic, social and cultural development.

2. All peoples may, for their own ends, freely dispose of their natural wealth and resources without prejudice to any obligations arising out of international economic co-peration, based upon the principle of mutual benefit, and international law. In no case may a people be deprived of its own means of subsistence.

3. The States Parties to the present Covenant, including those having responsibility for the administration of Non-Self-Governing and Trust Territories, shall promote the realisation of the right of self-determination, and shall respect that right, in conformity with the provisions of the Charter of the United Nations.

PART II

Article 2

1. Each State Party to the present Covenant undertakes to respect and to ensure to all individuals within its territory and subject to its jurisdiction the rights recognised in the present Covenant, without distinction of any kind, such as race, colour, sex, language, religion, political or other opinion, national or social origin, property, birth or other status.

2. Where not already provided for by existing legislative or other measures, each State Party to the present Covenant undertakes to take the necessary steps, in accordance with its constitutional processes and with the provisions of the present Covenant, to adopt such legislative or other measures as may be necessary to give effect to the rights recognised in the present Covenant.

3. Each State Party to the present Covenant undertakes:

    (a) To ensure that any person whose rights or freedoms as herein recognised are violated shall have an effective remedy, notwithstanding that the violation has been committed by persons acting in an official capacity;

    (b) To ensure that any person claiming such a remedy shall have high right thereto determined by competent judicial, administration or legislative authorities, or by any other competent, authority provided for by the legal system of the State, and to develop the possibilities of judicial remedy;

    (c) To ensure that the competent authorities shall enforce such remedies when granted.

Article 3

The State Parties to the present Covenant undertake to ensure the equal right of men and women to the enjoyment of all civil and political rights set forth in the present Covenant.

Article 4

1. In time of public emergency which threatens the life of the nation and the existence of which is officially proclaimed,

the States Parties to the present Covenant may take measures derogating from their obligations under the present Covenant to the extent strictly required by the exigencies of the situation, provided that such measures are not inconsistent with their other obligations under international law and do not involve discrimination solely on the ground of race, colour, sex, language, religion or social origin.

2. No derogation from articles 6, 7, 8 (paragraphs 1 and 2), 11, 15, 16 and 18 may be made under this provision.

3. Any State Party to the present covenant availing itself of the right of derogation shall immediately inform the other States Parties to the present Covenant, through the intermediary of the Secretary-General of the United Nations, of the provisions from which it has derogated and of the reasons by which it was actuated. A further communication shall be made, through the same intermediary, on the date on which it terminates such derogation.

Article 5

1. Nothing in the present Covenant may be interpreted as implying for any State, group or person any right to engage in any activity or perform any act aimed at the destruction of any of the rights and freedoms recognised herein or at their limitation to a greater extent than is provided for the present Covenant.

2. There shall be no restriction upon or derogation from any of the fundamental human rights recognised or existing in any State Party to the present Covenant pursuant to law, conventions, regulations or custom on the pretext that the present Covenant does not recognise such rights or that it recognises them to a lesser extent.

PART III

Article 6

1. Every human being has the inherent right to life. The right shall be protected by law. No one shall be arbitrarily deprived of his life.

2. In countries which have not abolished the death penalty, sentence of death, may be imposed only for the most serious crimes in accordance with the law in force at the time of the commission of the crime and not contrary to the provisions of the present Covenant and to the Convention of the Prevention and Punishment of the Crime of Genocide. This penalty can only be carried out pursuant to a final judgement rendered by a competent court.

3. When deprivation of life constitutes the crime of genocide, it is understood that nothing in this article shall authorise any State Party to the present Covenant to derogate in any way from any obligation assumed under the provisions of the Convention on the Prevention and Punishment of the Crime of Genocide.

4. Anyone sentenced to death shall have the right to seek pardon or commutation of the sentence. Amnesty, pardon or commutation of the sentence of death may be granted in all cases.

5. Sentence of death shall not be imposed for crimes committed by persons below eighteen years of age and shall not be carried out on pregnant women.

6. Nothing in this article shall be invoked to delay or to prevent the abolition of capital punishment by any State Party to the present Covenant.

Article 7

No one shall be subjected to torture or to cruel, inhuman or degrading treatment or punishment. In particular, no one shall be subjected without his free consent to medical or scientific experimentation.

Article 8

1. No one shall be held in slavery; and the slave-trade in all their forms shall be prohibited.

2. No one shall be held in servitude.

3. *(a)* No one shall be required to perform forced or compulsory labour;

(*b*) Paragraph 3 (*a*) shall not be held to preclude, in countries where imprisonment with hard labour may be imposed as a punishment for a crime, the performance of hard labour in pursuance of a sentence to such punishment by a competent court;

(*c*) For the purpose of this paragraph the term "forced or compulsory labour" shall not include:

(i) Any work or service, not referred to in sub-paragraph (*b*), normally required of a person who is under detention in consequence of a lawful order of a court, or of a person during conditional release from such detention;

(ii) Any service of a military character and, in countries where conscientious objection is recognised, any national service required by law of conscientious objectors;

(iii) Any service exacted in cases of emergency or calamity threatening the life or well-being of the community;

(iv) Any work or service which forms part of normal civil obligations.

Article 9

1. Everyone has the right to liberty and security of person. No one shall be subjected to arbitrary arrest or detention. No one shall be deprived of his liberty except on such grounds and in accordance with such procedure as are established by law.

2. Anyone who is arrested shall be informed, at the time of arrest, of the reasons for his arrest and shall be promptly informed of any charges against him.

3. Anyone arrest or detained on a criminal charge shall be brought promptly before a judge or other officer authorised by law to exercise judicial power and shall be entitled to trial within a reasonable time or to release. It shall not be general rule that persons awaiting trial shall be detained custody, but release may be subject to guarantees to appear for trial,

at any other stage of the judicial proceedings, and, should occasion arise, for execution of the judgement.

4. Anyone who is deprived of his liberty by arrest or detention shall be entitled to take proceedings before a court, in order that court may decide without delay on the lawfulness of his detention and order his release if the detention is not lawful.

5. Anyone who has been the victim of unlawful arrest or detention shall have an enforceable right to compensation.

Article 10

1. All persons deprived of their liberty shall be treated with humanity and with respect for the inherent dignity of the human person.

2. *(a)* Accused persons shall, save in exceptional circumstances, be segregated from convicted persons and shall be subject to separate treatment appropriate to their status as unconvinced persons;

   (b) Accused juvenile persons shall be separated from adults and brought as speedily as possible for adjudication.

3. The penitentiary system shall comprise treatment of prisoners the essential aim of which shall be their reformation and social rehabilitation. Juvenile offenders shall be segregated from adults and be accorded treatment appropriate to their age and legal status.

Article 11

No one shall be imprisoned merely on the ground of inability to fulfil a contractual obligation.

Article 12

1. Everyone lawfully within the territory of a State shall, within that territory, have the right to liberty of movement and freedom to choose his residence.

2. Everyone shall be free to leave any country, including his own.

3. The above-mentioned rights shall not be subject to any restrictions except those which are provided by law, are

necessary to protect national security, public order (*ordre public*), public health or morals or the rights and freedoms of others, and are consistent with the other rights recognised in the present Covenant.

4. No one shall be arbitrarily deprived of the right to enter his own country.

Article 13

An alien lawfully in the territory of a State Party to the present Covenant may be expelled therefrom only in pursuance of a decision reached in accordance with law and shall, except where compelling reasons of national security otherwise require, be allowed to submit the reasons against his expulsion and to have his case reviewed by, and be represented for the purpose before, the competent authority or a person or persons especially designated by the competent authority.

Article 14

1. All persons shall be equal before the courts and tribunals. In the determination of any criminal charge against him, or his rights and obligations in a suit at law, everyone shall be entitled to a fair and public hearing by a competent, independent and impartial tribunal established by law. The Press and the public may be excluded from all or part of a trial for reasons of morals, public order (*ordre public*) or national security in a democratic society, or when the interest of the private lives of the parties so requires, or to the extent strictly necessary in the opinion of the court in special circumstances where publicity would prejudice the interests of justice; but any judgement rendered in a criminal case or in a suit at law shall be made public except where the interest of juvenile persons otherwise requires or the proceedings concern matrimonial disputes or the guardianship of children.

2. Everyone charged with a criminal offence shall have the right to be presumed innocent until proved guilty according to law.

3. In the determination of any criminal charge against him, everyone shall be entitled to the following minimum guarantees, in full equality;

   (*a*) To be informed promptly and in detail in a language which he understands of the nature and cause of the charge against him;

   (*b*) To have adequate time and facilities for the preparation of his defence and to communicate with counsel of his own choosing;

   (*c*) To be tried without undue delay;

   (*d*) To be tried in his presence, and to defend himself in person or through legal assistance of his own choosing; to be informed, if he does not have legal assistance, of this right; and to have legal assistance assigned to him, in any case where the interests of justice so require, and without payment by him in any such case if he does not have sufficient means to pay for it;

   (*e*) To examine, or have examined, the witnesses against him and to obtain the attendance and examination of witnesses on his behalf under the same conditions as witnesses against him;

   (*f*) To have the free assistance of an interpreter if he cannot understand or speak the language used in court;

   (*g*) Not to be compelled to testify against himself or to confess guilt.

4. In the case of juvenile persons, the procedure shall be such as will take account of their age and the desirability of promoting their rehabilitation.

5. Everyone convicted of a crime shall have the right to his conviction and sentence being reviewed by a higher tribunal according to law.

6. When a person has by a final decision been convicted of a criminal offence and when subsequently his conviction has been reversed or he has been pardoned on the ground that a new or newly discovered fact shows conclusively that there has been a miscarriage of justice, the person who has suffered

punishment as a result of such conviction shall be compensated according to law, unless it is proved that the non-disclosure of the unknown fact in time is wholly or partly attributable to him.

7. No one shall be liable to be tried or punished again for an offence for which he has already been finally convicted or acquitted in accordance with the law and penal procedure of each country.

Article 15

1. No one shall be held guilty of any criminal offence on account of any act or omission which did not constitute a criminal offence, under national or international law, at the same time when it was committed. Nor shall a heavier penalty be imposed than the one that was applicable at the time when the criminal offence was committed. If, subsequent to the commission of the offence, provision is made by law for the imposition of a lighter penalty, the offender shall benefit thereby.

2. Nothing in this article shall prejudice the trial and punishment of any person for any act or omission which, at the time when it was committed, was criminal according to the general principles of law recognised by the community of nations.

Article 16

Everyone shall have the right to recognition everywhere as a person before the law.

Article 17

1. No one shall be subjected to arbitrary or unlawful interference with his privacy, family, home or correspondence, nor to unlawful attacks on his honour and reputation.

2. Everyone has the right to the protection of the law against such interference or attacks.

Article 18

1. Everyone shall have the right to freedom of thought, conscience and religion. This right shall include freedom to

have or to adopt a religion or belief of his choice, and freedom, either individually or in community with others and in public or private, to manifest his religion or belief in worship, observance, practice and teaching.

2. No one shall be subject to coercion which would impair his freedom to have or to adopt a religion or belief of his choice.

3. Freedom to manifest one's religion or beliefs may be subject only to such limitations as are prescribed by law and are necessary to protect public safety, order, health, or morals or the fundamental rights and freedoms of others.

4. The State Parties to the present Covenant undertake to have respect for the liberty of parents and, when applicable, legal guardians to ensure the religious and moral education of their children in conformity with their own convictions.

Article 19

1. Everyone shall have the right to hold opinions without interference.

2. Everyone shall have the right to freedom of expression; this right shall include freedom to seek, receive and impart information and ideas of all kinds, regardless of frontiers, either orally, in writing or in print, in the form of art, or through any other media of his choice.

3. The exercise of the rights provided for a paragraph 2 of this article carries with its special duties and responsibilities. It may therefore be subject to certain restrictions, but these shall only be such as are provided by law and are necessary:

   (a) For respect of the rights or reputations of others;

   (b) For the protection of national security or of public order (*ordre public*), or of public health or morals.

Article 20

1. Any propaganda for war shall be prohibited by law.

2. Any advocacy of national, racial or religious hatred that constitutes incitement to discrimination, hostility or violence shall be prohibited by law.

Article 21

The right of peaceful assembly shall be recognised. No restrictions may be placed on the exercise of this right other than those imposed in conformity with the law and which are necessary in a democratic society in the interests of national security or public safety, public order (*ordre public*), the protection of public, health or morals or the protection of the rights and freedoms of others.

Article 22

1. Everyone shall have the right to freedom of association with others, including the right to form and join trade unions for the protection of his interests.
2. No restrictions may be placed on the exercise of this right other than those which are prescribed by law and which are necessary in a democratic society in the interests of national security or public safety, public order (*ordre public*), the protection of public health or morals or the protection of the rights and freedoms of others. This article shall not prevent the imposition of lawful restrictions on members of the armed forces and of the police in their exercise of this right.
3. Nothing in this article shall authorise States Parties to the International Labour Organisation Convention of 1948 concerning Freedom of Association and Protection of the Right to Organise to take legislative measures which would prejudice, or to apply the law in such a manner as to prejudice, the guarantee provided for in that Convention.

Article 23

1. The family is a natural and fundamental group unit of society and is entitled to protection by society and the State.
2. The right of men and women of marriageable age to marry and to found a family shall be recognised.
3. No marriage shall be entered into without the free and full consent of the intending spouses.
4. States Parties to the present Covenant shall take appropriate steps to ensure equality of rights and responsibilities of spouses as to marriage, during marriage and at its dissolution. In the case of dissolution, provision shall be made for the necessary protection of any children.

Article 24

1. Every child shall have, without any discrimination as to race, colour, sex, language, religion, national or social origin, property or birth, the right to such measures of protection as are required by his status as a minor, on the part of his family, society and the State.
2. Every child shall be registered immediately after birth and shall have a name.
3. Every child has the right to acquire a nationality.

Article 25

Every citizen shall have the right and the opportunity, without any of the distinctions mentioned in article 2 and without unreasonable restrictions:

- *(a)* To take part in the conduct of public affairs, directly or through freely chosen representatives;
- *(b)* To vote and to be elected at genuine periodic elections which shall be by universal and equal suffrage and shall be held by secret ballot, guaranteeing the free expression of the will of the electors;
- *(c)* To have access, on general terms of equality, to public service in his country.

Article 26

All persons are equal before the law and are entitled without any discrimination to the equal protection of the law. In this respect, the law shall prohibit any discrimination and guarantee to all persons equal and effective protection against discrimination on any ground such as race, colour, sex, language, religion, political or other opinion, national or social origin, property, birth or other status.

Article 27

In those States in which ethnic, religious or linguistic minorities exist, persons belonging to such minorities shall not be denied the right, in community with the other members of their group, to enjoy their own culture, to profess and practise their own religion, or to use their own language.

PART IV

Article 28

1. There shall be established a Human Rights Committee (hereafter referred to in the present Covenant as the Committee). It shall consist of eighteen members and shall carry out the functions hereinafter provided.
2. The Committee shall be composed of nationals of the States Parties to the present Covenant who shall be persons of high moral character and recognised competence in the field of human rights, consideration being given to the usefulness of the participation of some persons having legal experience.
3. The members of the Committee shall be elected and shall serve in their personal capacity.

Article 29

1. The members of the Committee shall be elected by secret ballot from a list of persons possessing the qualifications prescribed in article 28 and nominated for the purpose by the States Parties to the present Covenant.
2. Each State Party to the present Covenant may nominate not more than two persons. These persons shall be nationals of the nominating State.
3. A person shall be eligible for renomination.

Article 30

1. The initial election shall be held no later than six months after the date of the entry into force of the present Covenant.
2. At least four months before the date of each election to the Committee, other than an election to fill a vacancy declared in accordance with article 34, the Secretary-General of the United Nations shall address a written invitation to the States Parties to the present Covenant to submit their nominations for membership of the Committee within three months.
3. The Secretary-General of the United Nations shall prepared a list in alphabetical order of all the persons thus nominated, with an indication of the States Parties which have nominated them, and shall submit it to the States Parties to the present

Covenant no later than one months before the date of each election.

4. Elections of the members of the Committee shall be held at a meeting of the States Parties to the present Covenant convened by the Secretary-General of the United Nations at the Headquarters of the United Nations. At the meeting, for which two thirds of the States Parties to the present Covenant shall constitute a quorum, the persons elected to the Committee shall be those nominees who obtain the largest number of votes and an absolute majority of the votes of the representatives of States Parties present and voting.

Article 31

1. The Committee may not include more than one national of the same State.

2. In the election of the Committee, consideration shall be given to equitable geographical distribution of membership and to the representation of the different forms of civilisation of the principal legal system.

Article 32

1. The members of the Committee shall be elected for a term of four years. They shall be eligible for re-election if renominated. However, the terms of nine of the members elected at the first election shall expire at the end of two years; immediately after the first election, the names of these nine members shall be chosen by lot by the Chairman of the meeting referred to in article 30, paragraph 4.

2. Elections at the expiry of office shall be held in accordance with the preceding articles of this part of the present Covenant.

Article 33

1. If, in the unanimous opinion of the other members, a member of the Committee has ceased to carry out his functions, for any cause other than absence of a temporary character, the Chairman of the Committee shall notify the Secretary-General of the United Nation, who shall then declare the seat of that member to be vacant.

2. In the event of the death or the registration of a member of the Committee, the Chairman shall immediately notify the Secretary-General of the United Nations, who shall declare the seat vacant from the date of death or the date on which the registration takes effect.

Article 34

1. When a vacancy is declared in accordance with article 33 and if the term of office of the member to be replaced does not expire within six months of the declaration of the vacancy, the Secretary-General of the United Nations shall notify each of the States Parties to the present Covenant, which may within two months submit nominations in accordance with article 29 for the purpose of filling the vacancy.
2. The Secretary-General of the United Nations shall prepare a list in alphabetical order of the persons thus nominated and shall submit it to the States Parties to the present Covenant. The election to fill the vacancy shall then take place in accordance with the relevant provisions of this part of the present Covenant.
3. A member of the Committee elected to fill a vacancy declared in accordance with article 33 shall hold office, for the remainder of the term of the member who vacated the seat on the Committee under the provision of that article.

Article 35

The members of the Committee shall, with the approval of the General Assembly of the United Nations, receive emoluments from United Nations resources on such terms and conditions as the General Assembly may decide, having regard to the importance of the Committee's responsibilities.

Article 36

The Secretary-General of the United Nations shall provide the necessary staff and facilities for the effective performance of the functions of the Committee under the present Covenant.

Article 37

1. The Secretary-General of the United Nations shall convene the initial meeting of the Committee at the Headquarters of the United Nations.

2. After its initial meetings, the Committee shall meet at such times as shall be provided in its rules of procedure.

3. The Committee shall normally meet at the Headquarters of the United Nations or at the United Nations Office at Geneva.

Article 38

Every member of the Committee shall, before taking up his duties, make a solemn declaration in open committee that he will perform his functions impartially and conscientiously.

Article 39

1. The Committee shall elect its officers for a term of two years. They may be re-elected.

2. The Committee shall establish its own rules of procedure, but these rules shall provide, *inter alia*, that:

   (a) Twelve members shall constitute a quorum;

   (b) Decisions of the Committee shall be made by a majority vote of the member present.

Article 40

1. The States Parties to the present Covenant undertake to submit reports on the measures they have adopted which give effect to the rights recognised herein and on the progress made in the enjoyment of those rights:

   (a) Within one year of the entry into force of the present Covenant for the States Parties concerned;

   (b) Thereafter whenever the Committee so requests.

2. All reports shall be submitted to the Secretary-General of the United Nations, who shall transmit them to the Committee for consideration. Reports shall indicate the factors and difficulties, if any, affecting the implementation of the present Covenant.

3. The Secretary-General of the United Nations may, after consultation with the Committee, transmit to the specialised agencies concerned copies of such parts of the reports as may fall within their field of competence.

4. The Committee shall study the reports submitted by the States Parties to the present Covenant. It shall transmit its reports, and such general comments as it may consider appropriate, to the States Parties. The Committee may also transmit to the Economic and Social Council these comments along with the copies of the reports it has received from States Parties to the present Covenant.

5. The States Parties to the present Covenant may submit to the Committee observations on any comments that may be made in accordance with paragraph 4 of this article.

Article 41

1. A State Party to the present Covenant may at any time declare under this article that it recognises the competence of the Committee to receive and consider communications to the effect that a State Party claims that another State Party is not fulfilling its obligations under the present Covenant. Communications under this article may be received and considered only if submitted by a State Party which has made a declaration recognising in regard to itself the competence of the Committee. No communication shall be received by the Committee if it concerns a State Party which has not made such a declaration. Communications received under this article shall be dealt with in accordance with the following procedure:

   (*a*) If a State Party to the present Covenant considers that another State Party is not giving effect to the provisions of the present Covenant, it may, by written communication, bring the matter to the attention of that State Party. Within three months after the receipt of the communication, the receiving State shall afford the State which sent the communication an explanation or any other statement in writing clarifying the matter, which should include, to the extent possible and pertinent, reference to domestic procedures and remedies taken, pending, or available in the matter.

   (*b*) If a matter is not adjusted to the satisfaction of both States Parties concerned within six months after the receipt by the receiving State of the initial communication, either State shall have the right to refer the matter to the Committee, by notice given to the Committee and to the other State.

(c) The Committee shall deal with the matter referred to it only after it has ascertained that all available domestic remedies have been involved and exhausted in the matter, in conformity with the generally recognised principles of international law. This shall not be the rule where the application of the remedies is unreasonably prolonged.

(d) The Committee shall hold closed meetings when examining communications under this article.

(e) Subject to the provisions of sub-paragraph *(c)*, the Committee shall make available its good offices to the States Parties concerned with a view to a friendly solution of the matter on the basis of respect for human rights and fundamental freedoms as recognised in the present Covenant.

(f) In any matter referred to it, the Committee may call upon the States Parties concerned, referred to in sub-paragraph *(b)*, to supply any relevant information.

(g) The State Parties concerned, referred to in sub-paragraph *(b)*, shall have the right to be represented when the matter is being considered in the Committee and to make submissions orally and/or in writing.

(h) The Committee shall, within twelve months after the date of receipt of notice under sub-paragraph *(b)*, submit a report:

(i) If a solution within the terms of sub-paragraph *(e)* is reached, the Committee shall confine its report to a brief statement of the facts and of the solution reached;

(ii) If a solution within the terms of sub-paragraph *(e)* is not reached, the Committee shall confine its report to a brief statement of the facts; the written submissions and record of the oral submissions made by the States parties concerned shall be attached to the report.

In every matter, the report shall be communicated to the States Parties concerned.

2. The provisions of this article shall come into force when ten States Parties to the present Covenant have made declarations under paragraph 1 of this article. Such declarations shall be deposited by the States Parties with the Secretary-General of the United Nations, who shall transmit copies thereof to the other States Parties. A declaration may be withdrawn at any time by notification to the Secretary-General. Such a withdrawal shall not prejudice the consideration of any matter which is the subject of a communication already transmitted under this article; no further communication by any State Party shall be received after the notification of withdrawal of the declaration has been received by the Secretary-General, unless the State Party concerned had made a new declaration.

Article 42

1. *(a)* It a matter referred to the Committee in accordance with article 41 is not resolved to the satisfaction of the States Parties concerned, the Committee may, with the prior consent of the State Parties concerned, appoint an *ad hoc* Conciliation Commission (hereinafter referred to as the Commission). The good offices of the Commission shall be made available to the States Parties concerned with a view to an amicable solution of the matter on the basis of respect for the present Covenant;

   (b) The Commission shall consist of five persons acceptable to the State Parties concerned. If the States Parties concerned fail to reach agreement within three months on all or part of the composition of the Commission, the members of the Commission concerning whom no agreement has been reached shall be elected by secret ballot by a two-thirds majority vote of the Committee from among its members.

2. The members of the Commission shall serve in their personal capacity. They shall not be nationals of the States Parties concerned, or of a State not party to the present Covenant, or of a State Party which has not made a declaration under article 41.

3. The Commission shall elect its own Chairman and adopt its own rules of procedure.

4. The meetings of the Commission shall normally be held at the Headquarters of the United Nations or at the United Nations Office at Geneva. However, they may be held at such other convenient places as the Commission may determine in consultation with the Secretary-General of the United Nations and the States Parties concerned.

5. The secretariat provided in accordance with article 36 shall also service the commissions appointed under this article.

6. The information received and collated by the Committee shall be made available to the Commission and the Commission may call upon the States Parties concerned to supply any other relevant information.

7. When the Commission has fully considered the matter, but in any event not later than twelve months after having been sized of the matter, it shall submit to the Chairman of the Committee a report for communication to the States Parties concerned:

   (a) If the Commission is unable to complete its consideration of the matter within twelve months, it shall confine its report to a brief statement of the status of its consideration of the matter;

   (b) If an amicable solution to the matter on the basis of respect for human rights as recognised in the present Covenant is reached, the Commission shall confine its report to a brief statement of the facts and of the solution reached;

   (c) If a solution within the terms of sub-paragraph *(b)* is not reached, the Commission's report shall embody its findings on all questions of fact relevant to the issues between the States Parties concerned, and its views on

the possibilities of an amicable solution of the matter. This report shall also contain the written submissions and a record of the oral submissions made by the States parties concerned;

(d) If the Commission's report is submitted under sub-paragraph *(c)*, the State Parties concerned shall, within three months of the receipt of the report, notify the Chairman of the Committee whether or not they accept the contents of the report of the Commission.

8. The provisions of this article are without prejudice to the responsibilities of the Committee under article 41.

9. The States Parties concerned shall share equally all the expenses of the members of the Commission in accordance with estimates to be provided by the Secretary-General of the United Nations.

10. The Secretary-General of the United Nations shall be empowered to pay the expenses of the members of the Commission, if necessary, before reimbursement by the States Parties concerned, in accordance with paragraph 9 of this article.

Article 43

The members of the Committee, and of the *ad hoc* conciliation commissions which may be appointed under article 42, shall be entitled to the facilities, privileges and immunities of experts omission for the United Nations as laid down in the relevant sections of the Convention on the Privileges and Immunities of the United Nations.

Article 44

The provisions for the implementation of the present Covenant shall apply without prejudice to the procedures prescribed in the field of human rights by or under the constituent instruments and the conventions of the United Nations and of the specialised agencies and shall not prevent the States Parties to the present Covenant from having recourse to other procedures for settling a dispute in accordance with general or special international agreements in force between them.

Article 45

The Committee shall submit to the General Assembly of the United Nations, through the Economic and Social Council, an annual report on its activities.

PART V

Article 46

Nothing in the present Covenant shall be interpreted as imparting the provisions of the Charter of the United Nations and of the constitutions of the specialised agencies which define the respective responsibilities of the various organs of the United Nations and of the specialised agencies in regard to the matters dealt with in the present Covenant.

Article 47

Nothing in the present Covenant shall be interpreted as impairing the inherent right of all peoples to enjoy and utilise fully and freely their natural wealth and resources.

PART VI

Article 48

1. The present Covenant is open for signature by any State Member of the United Nations or member of any of its specialised agencies, by any State Party to the Statute of the International Court of Justice, and by any other State which has most invited by the General Assembly of the United Nations to become a party to the present Covenant.
2. The present Covenant is subject to ratification. Instruments of ratification shall be deposited with the Secretary-General of the United Nations.
3. The present Covenant shall be open to accession by any State referred to in paragraph 1 of this article.
4. Accession shall be effected by the deposit of an instrument of accession with the Secretary-General of the United Nations.
5. The Secretary-General of the United Nations shall inform all States which have signed this Covenant or acceded to it of the deposit of each instrument of ratification or accession.

Article 49

1. The present Covenant shall enter into force three months after the date of the deposit with the Secretary-General of the United Nations of the thirty-fifth instrument of ratification or instrument of accession.

2. For each State ratifying the present Covenant or acceding to it after the deposit of the thirty-fifth instrument of ratification or instrument of accession, the present Covenant shall enter into force three months after the date of the deposit of its own instrument of ratification or instrument of accession.

Article 50

The provision of the present Covenant shall extent to all parts of federal States without any limitations or exceptions.

Article 51

1. Any State Party to the present Covenant may propose an amendment and file it with the Secretary-General of the United Nations. The Secretary-General of the United Nations shall thereupon communicate any proposed amendments to the States Parties to the present Covenant with a request that they notify him whether they favour a conference of State Parties for the purpose of considering and voting upon the proposals. In the event that at least one third of the State Parties favours such a conference, the Secretary-General shall convene the conference under the auspices of the United Nations. Any amendment adopted by a majority of the States Parties present and voting at the conference shall be submitted to the General Assembly of the United Nations for approval.

2. Amendments shall come into force when they have been approved by the General Assembly of the United Nations and accepted by a two-thirds majority of the States Parties to the present Covenant in accordance with their respective constitutional processes.

3. When amendments come into force, they shall be binding on those State Parties which have accepted them, other States Parties still being bound by the provisions of the present Covenant and any earlier amendments which they have accepted.

Article 52

Irrespective of the notification made under article 48, paragraph 5, the Secretary-General of the United Nations shall inform all States referred to in paragraph 1 of the same article of the following particulars:

(a) Signatures, ratifications and accessions under article 48;

(b) The date of the entry into force of the present Covenant under article 49 and the date of the entry into force of any amendments under article 51.

Article 53

1. The present Covenant, of which, the Chinese, English, French, Russian and Spanish texts are equally authentic, shall be deposited in the archives of the United Nations.
2. The Secretary-General of the United Nations shall transmit certified copies of the present Covenant to all States referred to in article 48.

OPTIONAL PROTOCOL TO THE INTERNATIONAL COVENANT ON CIVIL AND POLITICAL RIGHTS

The States Parties to the Present Protocol

Considering that in order further to achieve the purposes of the covenant on Civil and Political rights (hereinafter referred to as the Covenant) and the implementation of its provisions it would be appropriate to enable the Human Rights Committee set up in part IV of the Covenant (hereinafter referred to as the Committee) to receive and consider, as provided in the present Protocol, communications from individuals claiming to be victims of violations of any of the rights set forth in the Covenant,

Have agreed as follows:

Article 1

A State Party to the Covenant that becomes a party to the present protocol recognises the competence of the Committee to receive and consider communications from individuals subject to its jurisdiction who claim to be victims of a violation by that State Party of any of the rights set forth in the Covenant. No communication shall be received by the Committee if it concerns a State Party to the Covenant which is not a party to the present Protocol.

Article 2

Subject to the provisions of article 1, individuals who claim that any of their rights enumerated in the Covenant have been violated and two have exhausted all available domestic remedies may submit a written communication to the Committee for consideration.

Article 3

The Committee shall consider inadmissible any communication under the present Protocol which is anonymous, or which it considers to be an abuse of the rights of submission of such communications or to be incompatible with the provisions of the Covenant.

Article 4

1. Subject to the provision of article 3, the Committee shall bring any communications submitted to it under the present Protocol to the attention of the State Party to the present Protocol alleged to be violating any provisions of the Covenant.
2. Within six months, the receiving State shall submit to the Committee written explanations or statements clarifying the matter and the remedy, if any, that may have been taken by that State.

Article 5

1. The Committee shall consider communications received under the present Protocol in the light of all written information made available to it by the individual and by the State Party concerned.
2. The Committee shall not consider any communication from an individual unless it has ascertained that:
   (a) The same matter is not being examined under another procedure of international investigation or settlement;
   (b) The individual has exhausted all available domestic remedies. This shall not be the rule where the application of the remedies is unreasonably prolonged.

3. The Committee shall hold closed meetings when examining communications under the present Protocol.

4. The Committee shall forward its views to the State Party concerned and to the individual.

Article 6

The Committee shall include in its annual report under article 45 of the Covenant a summary of its activities under the present Protocol.

Article 7

Pending the achievement of the objectives of resolution 1514 (XV) adopted by the General Assembly of the United Nations on 14 December 1960 concerning the Declaration on the Granting of Independence to Colonial Countries and Peoples, the provisions of the present Protocol shall in no way limit the right of petition granted to these peoples by the Charter of the United Nations and other international conventions and instruments under the United Nations and its specialised agencies.

Article 8

1. The present Protocol is open for signature by any State which has signed the Covenant.

2. The present Protocol is subject to ratification by any State which has ratified or acceded to the Covenant. Instruments of ratification shall be deposited with the Secretary-General of the United Nations.

3. The present Protocol shall be open to accession by any State which has ratified or acceded to the Covenant.

4. Accession shall be effected by the deposit of an instrument of accession with the Secretary-General of the United Nations.

5. The Secretary-General of the United Nations shall inform all States which have signed the present Protocol or acceded to it of the deposit of each instrument of ratification or accession.

Article 9

1. Subject to the entry into force of the Covenant, the present Protocol shall enter into force three months after the date of

the deposit with the Secretary-General of the United Nations of the tenth instrument of ratification or instrument of accession.

2. For each State ratifying the present Protocol or acceding to it after the deposit of the tenth instrument of ratification or instrument of accession, the present Protocol shall enter into force three months after the date of the deposit of its own instrument of ratification or instrument of accession.

Article 10

The provisions of the present Protocol shall extend to all parts of federal States without any limitations or expectations.

Article 11

1. Any State Party to the present Protocol may propose an amendment and file it with the Secretary-General of the United Nations. The Secretary-General shall thereupon communicate any proposed amendments to the States Parties to the present Protocol with a request that they notify him whether they favour a conference of States Parties for the purpose of considering and voting upon the proposal. In the event that at least one third of the States Parties favours such a conference, the Secretary-General shall convene the conference under the auspices of the United Nations. Any amendment adopted by a majority of the States Parties present and voting at the conference shall be submitted to the General Assembly of the United Nations for approval.

2. Amendments shall come into force when they have been approved by the General Assembly of the United Nations and accepted by a two-thirds majority of the States Parties to the present Protocol in accordance with their respective constitutional processes.

3. When amendments come into force, they shall be binding on those States Parties which have accepted them, other States Parties still being bound by the provisions of the present Protocol and any earlier amendment which they have accepted.

Article 12

1. Any State Party may denounce the present Protocol at any time by written notification addressed to the Secretary-General of the United Nations. Denunciation shall take effect three months after the date of receipt of the notification by the Secretary-General.
2. Denunciation shall be without prejudice to the continued application of the provisions of the present Protocol to any communication submitted under article 2 before the effective date of denunciation.

Article 13

Irrespective of the notification made under article 8, paragraph 5, of the present Protocol, the Secretary-General of the United Nations shall inform all States referred to in article 48, paragraph 1, of the Covenant of the following particulars:

(*a*) Signatures, ratifications and accessions under article 8;

(*b*) The date of the entry into force of any amendments under article 11;

(*c*) Denunciations under article 12.

Article 14

1. The present Protocol, of which the Chinese, English, French, Russian and Spanish texts are equally authentic, shall be deposited in the archieves of the United Nations.
2. The Secretary-General of the United Nations shall transmit certified copies of the present Protocol to all States to in article 48 of the Covenant.

SECOND OPTIONAL PROTOCOL TO THE INTERNATIONAL COVENANT ON CIVIL AND POLITICAL RIGHTS AIMING AT THE ABOLITION OF THE DEATH PENALTY

The States Parties to the Present Protocol

Believing that abolition of the death penalty contributes to enhancement of human dignity and progressive development of human rights,

Recalling article 3 of the Universal Declaration of Human Rights adopted on 10 December 1948 and article 6 of the International Covenant on Civil and Political Rights adopted on 16 December 1966,

Noting that article 6 of the International Covenant on Civil and Political Rights refers to abolition of the death penalty in terms that strongly suggest that abolition is desirable,

Convinced that all measures of abolition of the death penalty should be considered as progress in the enjoyment of the right to life,

Desirous to undertake hereby an international commitment to abolish the death penalty,

Have agree as follows:

Article 1

1. No one within the jurisdiction of the State Party to the present Protocol shall be executed.
2. Each State Party shall take all necessary measures to abolish the death penalty within its jurisdiction.

Article 2

1. No reservation is admissible to the present Protocol, except for a reservation made at the time of ratification or accession that provides for the application of the death penalty in time of war pursuant to a conviction for a most serious crime of a military nature committed during wartime.
2. The State Party making such a reservation shall at the time of ratification or accession communicate to the Secretary-General of the United Nations the relevant provisions of its national legislation applicable during wartime.
3. The State Party having made such a reservation shall notify the Secretary-General of the United Nations of any beginning or ending of a state of war applicable to its territory.

Article 3

The State Parties to the present Protocol shall include in the reports they submit to the Human Rights Committee, in accordance with article 40 of the Covenant, information on the measures that they have adopted to give effect to the present Protocol.

Article 4

With respect to the States to the Covenant that have made a declaration under article 41, the competence of the Human Rights Committee to receive and consider communications when a State Party claims that another State Party is not fulfilling its obligations shall extend to the provisions of the present Protocol, unless the State Party concerned has made a statement to the contrary at the moment of ratification or accession.

Article 5

With respect to the States Parties to the first Optional Protocol to the International Covenant on Civil and Political Rights adopted on 16 December 1966, the competence of the Human Rights Committee to receive and consider communications from individuals subject to its jurisdiction shall extend to the provisions of the present Protocol, unless the State Party concerned has made a state to the contrary at the moment of ratification or accession.

Article 6

1. The provisions of the present Protocol shall apply as additional provisions to the Covenant.
2. Without prejudice to the possibility of a reservation under article 2 of the present Protocol, the right guaranteed in article 1, paragraph 1, of the present Protocol shall not be subject to any derogation under article 4 of the Covenant.

Article 7

1. The present Protocol is open for signature by any State that has signed the Covenant.
2. The present Protocol is subject to ratification by any State that has ratified the Covenant or acceded to it. Instruments of ratification shall be deposited with the Secretary-General of the United Nations.
3. The present Protocol shall be open to accession by any State that has ratified the Covenant or acceded to it.
4. Accession shall be effected by the deposit of an instrument of accession with the Secretary-General of the United Nations.

5. The Secretary-General of the United Nations shall inform all States that have signed the present Protocol or acceded to it of the deposit of each instrument of ratification or accession.

Article 8

1. The present Protocol shall enter into force three months after the date of the deposit with the Secretary-General of the United Nations of the tenth instrument of ratification or accession.

2. For each State ratifying the present Protocol or acceding to it after the deposit of the tenth instrument of ratification or accession, the present Protocol shall enter into force three months after the date of the deposit of its own instrument of ratification or accession.

Article 9

The provision of the present Protocol shall extend to all parts of federal States without any limitations or exceptions.

Article 10

The Secretary-General of the United Nations shall inform all States referred to in article 48, paragraph 1, of the Covenant of the following particulars:

(a) Reservations, communications and notifications under article 2 of the present Protocol.

(b) Statements made under articles 4 or 5 of the present Protocol;

(c) Signatures, ratifications and accessions under article 7 of the present Protocol;

(d) The date of the entry into force of the present Protocol under article 8 thereof.

Article 11

1. The present Protocol, of which the Arabic, Chinese, English, French, Russian and Spanish texts are equally authentic, shall be deposited in the archives of the United Nations.

2. The Secretary-General of the United Nations shall transmit certified copies of the present Protocol to all States referred to in article 48 of the Covenant.

9

Human Rights: A United Nations Priority

Introduction

We are living in an era of dramatic change and transition, in a world that is being transformed by complex financial systems and revolutionary information technologies into a vast globalmarket place. Globalisation is creating new patterns of interaction among people and States, promising unprecedented opportunities for material progress in larger freedom, but also threatening to compound many existing challenges before the international community while deepening the economic marginalisation of those most vulnerable. In this complex scenario, human rights, which were embedded formally at the United Nations as a great international priority 50 years ago—through the December 1948 Universal Declaration of Human Rights—have gained prominence as a universally recognised set of norms and standards that increasingly inform all aspects of our relations as individuals and as collective members of groups, within communities and among nations. There is now near-universal recognition that respect for human rights—the rights of political choice and association, of opinion and expression, and of culture, the freedom from fear and from all forms of discrimination and prejudice; from want and the right to employment and well-being

---

Data Presented in this Chapter is as on October 1998.

and, collectively, to development—is essential to the sustainable achievement of the three agreed global priorities of peace, development and democracy.

Given their centrality, the United Nations has made the strengthening of human rights a cross-cutting focus in all its work. But assuring human rights for all people remains a daunting challenge, especially given the impunity with which they continue to be violated in all parts of the world. Billions continue to live in extreme poverty, and the huge disparity between rich and poor countries continues to grow. Violent conflicts, increasingly ethnic in nature, have proliferated, uprooting entire communities, forcing millions of people from their homes. Political extremism and terrorism continue to target countless innocent civilians. Unemployment, discrimination and social exclusion bedevil all societies. And although globalisation has brought the world closer together, it has also benefited elements of unveil society, reflected in the increase in corruption, organised crime and transnational trafficking in illicit drugs, arms, toxic materials, even in human beings, particularly of women for sexual exploitation.

The revitalisation of the United Nations that has become another priority in recent years will be judged in large part by its success in meeting these challenges—old and new—and in extending not merely the theory but the practice of human rights. The first-ever judgements and sentencing for the crime of genocide—50 years after the Convention on Genocide was concluded—by the International Criminal Tribunal for Rwanda in September 1998, and the agreement in Rome two months previously, on the establishment of an International Criminal Court, are concrete examples of a deepened resolve by the international community to ensure respect for all human rights, and of the centrality of the United Nations and its effectiveness in the realisation of this goal.

Today's United Nations human rights programme has evolved in over 50 years of difficult but steady progress in the fact of numerous challenges and frequent disappointments (*see chronology in Annex 1*). Since its creation in 1945, the United Nations has overseen the codification of human rights in a major effort to move them from the realm of ethical guidelines to that of binding law. Especially, the Universal Declaration of Human Rights, adopted in 1948, continues to guide the United Nations through the simplicity of its language and the clarity of its purpose. The Universal Declaration, an eloquent inspiration for the worldwide struggle for human dignity and freedom, had become the correspondence of an increasingly cohesive body of international human rights standards and laws. The enhanced focus on human rights is, in turn, having a direct impact on all aspects of the work of the United Nations, in many cases, such as the role and rights of women, driving action in crucial areas.

The *Briefing Paper* describes the manifold aspects of United Nations work in the area of human rights today, and the challenges that lie ahead in realising the objectives of the body of human rights law now in place. The Organisation bases its work on the principle that human rights are universal and indivisible. In practical terms, this means that all rights and freedoms—economic rights, as well as political and civil freedoms—are interrelated and interdependent, and need to be promoted and protected in equal manner. If one set of rights is promoted at the expense of another, then all rights are undermined. For this reason, the United Nations has sought a balanced and comprehensive approach to the effective promotion of all human rights, including the right to development. Overcoming the artificial split between two "kinds" of rights is the key to an overall promotion of human rights.

Another common thread in United Nations human rights action is to challenge discrimination in all its forms. It has a long history of fighting racism and racial discrimination and, in recent years, it has increasingly focused on the widespread discrimination against ethnic, religious or linguistic minorities, as well as on the basis of gender. It has stepped up efforts to protect vulnerable groups, such as indigenous people, migrant workers and especially children, who are the most vulnerable to physical and sexual exploitation, particularly in times of armed conflict. The United Nations also continues to work for the advancement and empowerment of women in society, and combats all forms of discrimination and violence against women and girls, whether in private or in public life.

The United Nations is increasingly integrating a human rights component into its peacekeeping operations and into its humanitarian activities, as well as advocating a rights-based approach to peace-building in the aftermath of conflicts. For the United Nations, conflict prevention also means fighting impunity, ensuring that the perpetrators of the most atrocious violations of human rights—genocide, war, crimes and crimes against humanity—are held accountable for their offences. This is the main rationale for the international criminal tribunals for Rwanda and the former Yugoslavia and for the recent decision to establish a permanent International Criminal Court, which will have its seat at The Hague in the Netherlands.

With the standard-setting work in international human rights law nearly complete, the United Nations is now concerning efforts and marshalling resources to implement the legislation. The Organisation seeks to ensure the compliance of Member States and to effectively promote a global culture of human rights through a number of practical strategies:

- *Various working groups and experts advance human rights research, establishing standards, codifying the content of human rights, identifying obstacles to their implementation and developing ways to realise these rights;*
- *An evolving human rights monitoring system of commissions and committees responds to growing demands to prevent or remedy human rights violations, pressing for the universal ratification of international human rights treaties and assisting Governments in conforming to the provision of these treaties; and*
- *A growing number of technical cooperation and training programmes in the administration of justice, implemented through human rights field operations and office, assist States and civil society worldwide in building national networks supporting and strengthening human rights and the rule of law at regional and local levels.*

The United Nations continues to reorient its human rights programme to respond more effectively to today's challenges, whether they arise as a massive human rights violations or systematic political oppression or persist in more complex and pervasive forms of discrimination—affecting the right to development or the right to a healthy environment, for example. However, it is internationally recognised that the prime responsibility for the promotion and protection of human rights remains with Member States. For this reason, in order to strengthen human rights at the national level, the United Nations has greatly expanded its human rights work in the field. Through the Office of the United Nations High Commissioner for Human Rights, the focal point of all system-wide integration of human rights activities, the United Nations assists Governments and other national and international partners in their promotion and protection of human rights. Strengthening international human rights law and increasing accountability of individuals and Members States in the area of human rights are crucial steps towards an effective implementation of human rights standards. All these complementary approaches advance and enhance United Nations efforts to create a global culture of human rights.

1. Universal Declaration of Human Rights

Fifty years ago, the United Nations General Assembly adopted the Universal Declaration of Human Rights as a bulwark against oppression and discrimination. In the wake of a devastating world war, which had witnessed some of the most barbarous crimes in human history, the Universal Declaration marked the first time that the rights and freedoms of individual were set forth in such detail. It also represented the first international recognition that human rights and fundamental freedoms are applicable to every person, everywhere. In this sense, the Universal Declaration was a landmark achievement in world history. Today, it continues to affect people's lives and inspire human rights activism and legislation all over the world.

The Universal Declaration is remarkable in two fundamental aspects. In 1948, the then 58 Member States of the United Nations represented a range of ideologies, political system and religious and cultural backgrounds, as well as different stages of economic development. The authors of the declaration, themselves from different regions of the world, sought to ensure that the draft text would reflect these different cultural traditions and incorporate common values inherent in the world's principal legal systems and religious and philosophical traditions. Most important, the Universal Declaration was to be a common statement of mutual aspirations—a shared vision of a more equitable and just world.

The success of their endeavour is demonstrated by the virtually universal acceptance of the Declaration. Today, the Universal Declaration, translated into nearly 250 national and local languages, is the best known and most cited human rights document in the world. The foundation of international human rights law, the Universal Declaration serves as a model for numerous international treaties and declarations and is incorporated in the constitutions and laws of many countries.

For the first time in history, the international community embraced a document considered to have universal value—"a common standard of achievement for all peoples and all nations". Its Preamble acknowledges the importance of a human rights legal framework to maintaining international peace and security, stating that recognition of the inherent dignity and equal and inalienable rights of all individuals is the foundation of freedom, justice and peace in the world. Elaborating the United Nations Charter's declared purpose of promoting social progress and well-being in larger freedom, the Declaration gives equal importance to economic, social and cultural rights and to civil rights and political liberties, and affords them the same degree or protection. The Declaration has inspired more than 60 international human rights instruments, with together constitute a comprehensive system of legally binding treaties for the promotion and protection of human rights.

Article 1: Right to Freedom and Equality in Dignity and Rights

The Universal Declaration covers the range of human rights in 30 clear and concise articles. The first two articles lay the universal foundation of human rights human beings are equal because of their shared essence of human dignity; human rights are universal, not because of any State or international organisation, but because they belong to all of humanity. The two articles assures that human rights are the birthright of everyone, not privileges of a select few, nor privileges to be granted or denied Article 1 declares that "all human beings are born equal in dignity and rights. They are endowed with reason and conscience and should act towards one another in a spirit of brotherhood". Article 2 recognises the universal dignity of a life free from discrimination. "Everyone is entitled to all the rights and freedoms set forth in this Declaration, without distinction of any kind such as race, colour, sex, language, religion, political or other opinion, national or social origin, property, birth or other status".

The first cluster of articles, 3 to 21, sets forth civil and political rights to which everyone is entitled. The right to life, liberty and personal security, recognised in Article 3, sets the base for all following political rights and civil liberties, including freedom from slavery, torture and arbitrary arrest, as well as the rights to a fair trial free speech and free movement and privacy (*for a list of all articles, see Annex* 2).

The second cluster of article 22 to 27, sets forth the economic, social and cultural rights to which all human beings are entitled. The cornerstone of these rights is Article 22, acknowledging that, as a member of society, everyone has the right to social security and is therefore entitled to the realisation of the economic, social and cultural rights "indispensable" for his or her dignity and free and full personal development. Five article elaborate the rights necessary for the enjoyment of the fundamental rights to social security, including economic rights related to work, fair remuneration and leisure, social rights concerning an adequate standard of living for health, well-being and education, and the right to participate in the cultural life of the community.

The third and final cluster of articles 28 to 30, provides a large protective framework in which all human rights are to be universally enjoyed. Article 28 recognises the right to a social and international order that enables the realisation of human rights and fundamental freedoms. Article 29 acknowledges that, along with rights, human beings also have obligations to the community which also enable them to develop their individual potential freely and fully. Article 30, finally, protects the interpretation of the articles of the Declaration from any outside interference contrary to the purposes and principles of the United Nations. It explicitly states that no State, group or person can claim, on the basis of the Declaration, to have the right to engage in any activity or to perform any act aimed at the destruction of any of the right and freedoms set forth in the Universal Declaration.

International Bill of Human Rights

Once the Universal Declaration of Human Rights was adopted, the Commission on Human Rights, the premier human rights intergovernmental body within the United Nations, set out to translate its principles into international treaties that protected specific rights. Given the unprecedented nature of the task, the General Assembly decided to draft two Covenant codifying the two sets of rights outlined in the Universal Declaration: Civil and Political Rights and Economic, Social and Cultural Rights. The Member States debated the individual provisions for two decades, seeking to give explicit endorsement to certain aspects of the universality of human rights only implicitly referred to in the Universal Declaration, such as the right of all peoples to self-determination, as well as reference to certain vulnerable groups, such as indigenous people and minorities.

Consensus was reached in 1966, and the United Nations General Assembly adopted the *International Covenant on Economic, Social and Cultural Rights* and the *International Covenant on Civil and Political Rights* that year. The preambles and articles 1, 2, 3 and 5 are virtually identical in both International Covenants. Both preamble recognise that human rights derive from the inherent dignity of human beings. Article 1 of each Covenant affirms that all peoples have the right of self-determination and that by virtue of that right they are free to determine their political status and to pursue their economic, social and cultural development. Article 2, in both cases, reaffirms the principle of non-discrimination, echoing the Universal Declaration, while Article 3 stresses that States should ensure the equal right of men and women to the enjoyment of all human rights, Article 5 of both Covenants echoes the final provision of the Universal Declaration, providing safeguards against the destruction or undue limitation of any human rights or fundamental freedom. Two *Optional Protocol* elaborate certain provisions of the Covenant on Civil and Political Rights, one providing for complaints by individuals, the other advocating the abolition of the death penalty.

When they entered into force in 1976, the two International Covenants made may of the provisions of the Universal Declaration effectively binding for States that ratified them. These two International Covenants, together with the Universal Declaration and the Optional Protocols, comprise the International Bill of Human Rights.

Drafting the Universal Declaration

The preparatory work for the Universal Declaration of Human Rights is a remarkable and early example of the Organisation's capacity to bring about international cooperation and consensus. The text was drafted in two years—between January 1947, when the Commission on Human Rights first met to prepare an International Bill of Human Rights, and December 1948, when the General Assembly adopted the Universal Declaration. An eight-member drafting committee prepared the preliminary text of the Universal Declaration. The Committee, chaired by Mrs. Eleanor Roosevelt, widow of the former United States President, agreed on the central importance of affirming universal respect for human rights and fundamental freedoms, including the principles of non-discrimination and civil and political rights, as well as social, cultural and economic rights. The Commission then revised the draft declaration, in the light of replies from Member States, before submitting it to the General Assembly.

The General Assembly, in turn, scrutinized the document, with the 58 Member States voting a total of 1,400 times on practically every word and every clause of the text. There were many debates. Some Islamic States objected to the articles on equal marriage rights and on the right to change religious belief, for example, while several Western countries criticised the inclusion of economic, social and cultural rights. On 10 December 1948, the United Nations General Assembly unanimously adopted the Universal Declaration of Human Rights, with 8 abstentions. Since then, 10 December is celebrated every year worldwide as Human Rights Day. The adoption of the Declaration was immediately hailed as a triumph, uniting very diverse and even conflicting political regimes, religious systems and cultural traditions. During 1998, the fiftieth anniversary of the Universal Declaration is being commemorated all over the world as Human Rights Year.

Article 2: Freedoms from Discrimination

Over 60 human rights treaties elaborate fundamental rights and freedoms contained in the International Bill of Human Rights, addressing concerns such as slavery, genocide, humanitarian law, the administration of justice, social development, religious tolerance, cultural cooperation, discrimination, violence against women, and the status of refugees and minorities (*for a listing of major international instruments, see Annex* 3). The following four Conventions, relating to racial discrimination torture, women and children, are considered core human rights treaties, together with the two International Covenants:

- *The International Convention on the Elimination of All Forms of Racial Discrimination (adopted in 1965/entry into force 1969) was a ground-breaking treaty defining and condemning racial discrimination. Calling for national measures towards the advancement of specific racial or ethnic groups, the Convention also makes the dissemination of ideas based on racial superiority or inspiring racial hatred punishable by law.*
- *The Convention on the Elimination of all Forms of Discrimination against Women (1979/1981) specific measures for the advancement and empowerment of women in private and public life, particularly in the areas of education, employment, health, marriage and the family.*
- *The Convention against Torture and Other Cruel, Inhuman or Degrading Treatment or Punishment (1984/1987) bans torture and rape as weapons of war. In 1998, in a major effort to help torture victims and to step up international attempts to end torture, the United Nations declared 26 June as the annual International Day in Support of Victims of Torture.*
- *The Convention on the Rights of the Child (1989/1990) is the most universally ratified human rights Convention. Only two Member States, the United States and Somalia, are not yet parties to the Convention, which protects children, among other things, from economic and sexual exploitation.*

Some 14 States have incorporated provisions of the Convention on the Rights of the Child into their constitutions, while 35 have passed new laws conforming to the Convention or amended laws related to child abuse, child labour and adoption. Other Member States have extended the length of compulsory education, guaranteed child refugees and minority children special protection or reformed juvenile justice systems, as stipulated by the Convention.

World Conference on Human Rights

The United Nations designated 1968 as the International Year for Human Rights to mark the twentieth anniversary of the Universal Declaration on Human Rights, and convened an International Conference on Human Rights in Tehran, Iran, to enhance, national and international human rights efforts and initiatives. After evaluating the impact of the Universal Declaration on national legislation and judicial decisions, the Conference approved the Proclamation of Tehran, which formulated a programme for the future, addressing the problems of colonialism, racial discrimination, illiteracy and the protection of the family. The Tehran Proclamation emphasised particularly the principle, of non-discrimination, condemning the policy of apartheid as a "crime against humanity", and urged the international community to ratify the International Covenants on Civil and Political Rights and on Economic, Social and Cultural Rights adopted by the United Nations two years earlier.

The *World Conference on Human Rights in Vienna* reassessed the progress of United Nations human rights work over the years. The Vienna Conference was marked by an unprecedented degree of support by the international human rights community. Some 7,000 participants, including delegations from 171 States and representatives of more than 840 non-governmental organisations, gathered for two weeks to set out a revitalised programme for global human rights action. There was broad consensus that, with fundamental rights codified and the essential machinery in place, it was time to implement the established human rights standards and norms with greater vigilance.

In adopting the *Vienna Declaration and Programme of Action* by consensus, the World Conference reaffirmed the centrality of the Universal Declaration for human rights protection, and recognised, for the first time unanimously, the right to development as an inalienable right and an integral part of international human rights law. The Conference also emphasised that, as human rights are universal and indivisible as well as interrelated and interdependent, they should be promoted in equal manner. The delegates rejected arguments that some human rights were optional or subordinate to cultural traditions and practices. The Vienna Conference thus gave high priority to preserving the integrity of the Universal Declaration. Giving new impetus to the worldwide implementation of human rights norms, the Conference emphasised that most violations could be addressed by forcefully implementing existing norms through the mechanisms already available.

Article 3: Right to Life, Liberty and Security of Person

Stating that the protection and promotion of human rights are the "first responsibility" of Governments, the Vienna Declaration recognised democracy as a human right, thus strengthening the promotion of democracy and the rule of law. Also, giving high priority to the universal ratification of international human rights treaties, the World Conference urged States especially to ratify promptly the Convention on the Rights of the Child and the Convention on the Elimination of All Forms of Discrimination against Women. Similarly, the Conference took innovative steps to protect the rights of vulnerable groups and to bring women's rights into the mainstream of United Nations human rights work, supporting the establishment of a Special Rapporteur on violence against women and calling for an international decade of the world's indigenous peoples.

The World Conference had a catalytic role in revitalising the human rights programme of the United Nations. The Vienna Declaration and Programme of Action provides the international community with a new framework of planning, dialogue and cooperation that enables an integrated approach to promoting human rights. The recognition of the interdependence between democracy, development and human rights, for example, laid the groundwork for increased cooperation among international development agencies and national organisations in promoting human rights. The Vienna Declaration states, for the first time explicitly, that all organs, programmes and specialised agencies of the United Nations should have a central role in strengthening human rights. Its key institutional recommendation, however, was the establishment of the post of United Nations High Commissioner for Human Rights to coordinate all human rights activities system-wide. The World Conference also called for a comprehensive five-year review of the progress made in the implementation of the Vienna Declaration and Programme of Action in 1998. This review coincides with the fiftieth anniversary of the adoption of the Universal Declaration of Human Rights.

2. Human Right in Action

The United Nations has been adapting its human rights machinery in order to better respond to the changing demands of the international community. During the cold war, the United Nations created the normative and institutional structures for international human rights protection, steadily broadening its competence in this area. At the same time, it supported the vast process of decolonisation, which led to the birth of over 80 new independent nations. Landmark United Nations actions, such as the Declaration on the Granting of Independence to Colonial Countries and Peoples (1960), provided the blueprint for universally establishing the collective right to self-determination. The United Nations also concentrated its efforts on the human rights abuses resulting from the policy of apartheid in South Africa, over-seeing international action which eventually helped to end this grass abrogation of fundamental rights. Despite these successes, however, the effectiveness of the United Nations was severely restricted by the cold war, both in terms of the range of human rights to be defended and in terms of ensuring their respect in practice. The world political situation did not allow for much concerted human rights activism in the field. Doctrines of national security and sovereignty were often invoked to conceal, excuse or justify human rights abuses.

Today, there is widespread recognition that the 50-year investment in development and human rights promotion requires new impetus to secure broader realisation of economic and social rights. Extreme poverty and exclusion from economic, political and cultural life continue to be the fate of millions in both developing and developed countries. Currently, there are 48 countries where more than one fifth of the population live in "absolute poverty", with little prospect of dramatic change in the short term. Breaking the cycle of poverty thus continues to be a formidable task for the international community. For this reason, the United Nations has increasingly emphasised the right to development, which can provide the basis for a strategy for the more comprehensive human rights programme.

Strengthening the Human Rights Machinery

In the wake of the Vienna Conference, the United Nations has intensified efforts to refocus its human rights programme, shifting its main concern from standards setting to implementation. This efforts was led by the main intergovernmental body in this area, the United Nations Commission on Human Rights, supported by the secretariat of the United Nations for Human Rights. In 1993, the General Assembly significantly strengthened the Organisational's human rights machinery by creating the post of United Nations High Commissioner for Human Rights.

Mandated to coordinate all United Nations human rights programmes and improve their impact and overall efficiency, the High Commissioner is the chief official responsible for human rights. Operating under the direction and authority of the Secretary-General as his representative in the field of human rights, the High Commissioner also reports to the General Assembly, the Economic and Social Council and the Commission on Human Rights. The *Office of the United Nations High Commissioner for Human Rights* (OHCHR) serves as the secretariat of the Commission on Human Rights, the treaty bodies and other United Nations human rights organs, and is the focal point for all United Nations human rights activities.

The first High Commissioner was Mr. José Ayala Lasso, who served from 1994 to 1997. Having assumed office only one day before the outbreak of genocidal killing in Rwanda. Mr. Ayala Lasso called for the convening of an emergency session of the Commission on Human Rights to address the human rights situation in that country. The Rwandan tragedy made clear the need to strengthen the range of human rights instruments at the disposal of the United Nations.

In 1997, as part of wide-ranging reforms, to enhance the effectiveness of the United Nations, Secretary-General Kofi Annan placed human rights at the heart of all the work of the Organisation. The Secretary-General organised the work of the United Nations into four substantive fields—peace and security, economic and social affairs, development cooperation, and humanitarian affairs —with human rights as the issue fifth priority area across each of these four programme fields. The United Nations is thus enhancing its human rights programme by integrating a human rights focus into the entire range of the Organisation's activities. In addition, the High Commissioner's Office and the Centre for Human Rights were consolidated into a single Office of the United Nations High Commissioner for Human Rights. This merger gave the new High Commissioner a solid institutional basis from which to lead, as the focal point of all system-wide integration of human rights activities, the Organisation's mission in the domain of human rights.

Article 4: Freedom from Slavery and Servitude

Office of the United Nations High Commissioner for Human Rights

Ms. Mary Robinson, the former President of Ireland, assumed her post as the second High Commissioner for Human Rights in September 1997. The High Commissioner's mandate has four essential components:

- *Building global partnerships for human rights;*
- *Preventing human rights violations and responding to emergencies;*
- *Promoting human rights, together with democracy and development, as the guiding principles for lasting peace; and*
- *Coordinating the system-wide strengthening of the United Nations human rights programme.*

The Office of the High Commissioner, based in Geneva with country office around the world, has a staff of some 200; its three main components deal with activities and programmes, research and right to development, and support services. The Office has a limited annual budget of about $20 million, about 1.7 per cent of the United Nations regular budget. However, the growing number of human rights activities in the field has led to a sharp increase in costs. Overall funding requirements for 1998 were $54 million. The High Commissioner's broadened mandate supports the work of the Commission on Human Rights and the treaty bodies, focusing, among other things, on advancing the rights of women and children, combating racial discrimination in all its forms and protecting vulnerable groups and minorities such as indigenous people, migrants and disabled people.

In order to carry out these expanded mandates, the office increasingly relies on voluntary contributions to finance its activities. The Human Rights Field Operation in Rwanda, for example, was funded entirely by voluntary contributions from Governments. Several voluntary funds support the High Commissioner's initiatives on indigenous people, the rights of the child, economic rights, victims of torture and contemporary forms of slavery, as well as combating racism and racial discrimination.

Especially through the expansion of its technical cooperation programme. OHCHR has been able to provide human rights support to virtually all programmes and agencies within the United Nations system. In the area of peacekeeping, for example, the programme has provided various forms of assistance to major United Nations missions in Angola, Cambodia, Mozambique, Haiti and the countries of the former Yugoslavia. It has also advised the United Nations electoral missions in Ertrea and South Africa. Such advisory services often entail the provision of human rights expertise, legislative analysis and training for personnel. The increased focus on joint operations has made it possible to fund a presence in the field through the regular budgets of the wider United Nations system.

Today, virtually every United Nations body and specialised agency, including the World Bank and the International Monetary Fund, is making efforts to incorporate the promotion or protection of human rights into its programmes and activities, including a gender perspective and an emphasis on the right to development. OHCHR is taking other steps to strengthen the United Nations human rights machinery by supporting the human rights bodies and monitoring mechanisms in their efforts to streamline their work.

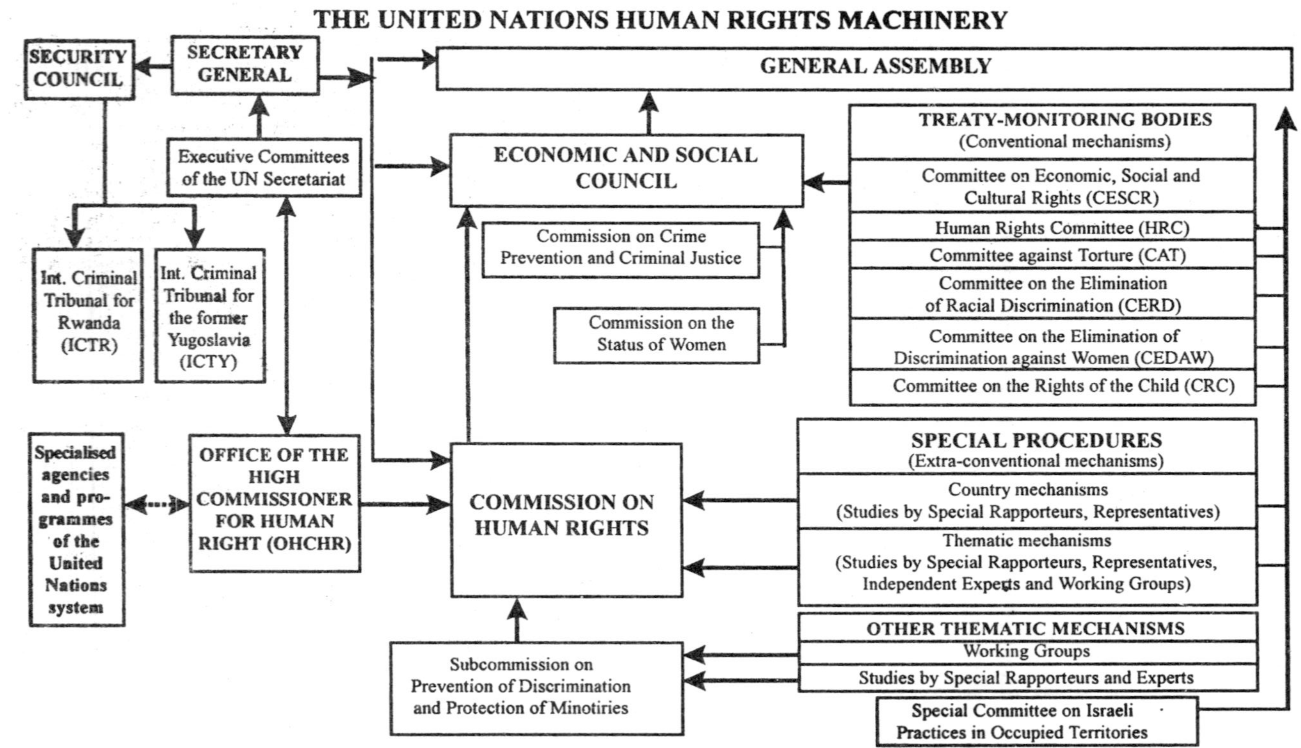
THE UNITED NATIONS HUMAN RIGHTS MACHINERY
SECURITY COUNCIL
SECRETARY GENERAL
GENERAL ASSEMBLY
Executive Committees of the UN Secretariat
ECONOMIC AND SOCIAL COUNCIL
TREATY-MONITORING BODIES
(Conventional mechanisms)
Committee on Economic, Social and Cultural Rights (CESCR)
Human Rights Committee (HRC)
Committee against Torture (CAT)
Committee on the Elimination of Racial Discrimination (CERD)
Committee on the Elimination of Discrimination against Women (CEDAW)
Committee on the Rights of the Child (CRC)
Commission on Crime Prevention and Criminal Justice
Commission on the Status of Women
Int. Criminal Tribunal for Rwanda (ICTR)
Int. Criminal Tribunal for the former Yugoslavia (ICTY)
Specialised agencies and programmes of the United Nations system
OFFICE OF THE HIGH COMMISSIONER FOR HUMAN RIGHT (OHCHR)
COMMISSION ON HUMAN RIGHTS
SPECIAL PROCEDURES
(Extra-conventional mechanisms)
Country mechanisms
(Studies by Special Rapporteurs, Representatives)
Thematic mechanisms
(Studies by Special Rapporteurs, Representatives, Independent Experts and Working Groups)
OTHER THEMATIC MECHANISMS
Working Groups
Studies by Special Rapporteurs and Experts
Subcommission on Prevention of Discrimination and Protection of Minotiries
Special Committee on Israeli Practices in Occupied Territories

Commission on Human Rights

United Nations policy on human rights is governed, through the General Assembly, by a number of intergovernmental bodies, which also provide guidance to OHCHR. The main intergovernmental policy-making body concerned with human rights issues is the Commission on Human Rights. Established in 1946 by the Economic and Social Council, the Commission provides overall policy guidance, studies human rights problems, develops and codifies new international norms, and monitors the observance of human rights around the world. Made up of 53 Member States elected for three-year terms, the Commission provides a forum for States and intergovernmental and non-governmental organisations (NGOs) to voice their concerns about human rights issues.

Article 5: Freedom from Torture or Degrading Treatment

The Commission originally concerned its efforts on defining and codifying international human rights standards. In the past two decades, however, the Commission has set up a system of special procedures to investigate alleged violations of human rights, and routinely dispatches fact-finding missions to countries in all parts of the world. Today, the Commission's annual six-week session in Geneva provides a unique global forum for raising, discussing and clarifying allegations of a wide range of violations. States as well as NGOs present information on situations of concern to them; the Governments involved often submit replies. In the light of the examination of such situations, fact-finding groups of experts may be designated, on-the-spot visits may be organised, discussions with Governments pursued, assistance provided and violations condemned.

In recent years, the Commission has increasingly turned its attention to the promotion of economic, social and cultural rights, including the right to development. It has established a number of subsidiary bodies to assist its work in this area, such as the working groups on the effects of foreign-debt burdens and the impact or extreme poverty on the enjoyment of human rights.

High on the Commission's agenda are the promotion of women's rights and the protection of the rights of the child. Special attention is given to children in situations of armed conflict, to violence against women, including against women migrant workers, and to trafficking in women and girls. The Commission has further sought to protect the rights of vulnerable groups, particularly ethnic, religious and linguistic minorities and indigenous people. For this reason, it is seeking to create a permanent forum for indigenous people within the United Nations system.

Since 1948, the Commission has been assisted by the 26-member *Subcommission on Prevention of Discrimination and Protection of Minorities*, composed of independent experts from all regions of the world. The Subcommission, in turn, has established several working groups, which serve as forums for interaction between Governments and civil society concerning the rights of indigenous people, minorities and groups vulnerable to contemporary forms of slavery (*see Annex 5*). Among other issues, the Subcommission focuses on contemporary forms of slavery, including forced labour, illegal and pseudo-legal adoptions aiming at the exploitation of children, and sexual slavery during wartime. It also considers human rights issues concerning domestic and migrant workers and examines preventive measures for the elimination of violence against women, in particular in situations of armed conflict.

Monitoring Human Rights Violations

All integral part of the body of human rights law provides for a monitoring role for the United Nations. At the heart of the United Nations monitoring system are two types of human rights mechanisms—conventional and extra-conventional—which respond to individual human rights abuses and to the systematic abrogation of rights by Member States.

Six core human rights treaties provide for so-called conventional monitoring mechanisms consisting of six treaty bodies or committees, which monitor States parties' adherence to the international standards established in the treaties. However, States parties must ratify these treaties before their principles and standards apply to them.

The *Human Rights Committee* monitors implementation of the International Covenant on Civil and Political Rights.

The *Committee on Economic, Social and Cultural Rights* monitors implementation of the International Covenant on Economic, Social and Cultural Rights.

The *Committee on the Elimination of Racial Discrimination* monitors implementation of the International Convention on the Elimination of All Forms of Racial Discrimination.

The *Committee on the Elimination of Discrimination against Women* monitors implementation of the Convention on the Elimination of All Forms of Discrimination against Women.

The *Committee against Torture* monitors implementation of the Convention against Torture and Other Cruel, Inhuman or Degrading Treatment or Punishment.

The *Committee on the Rights of the Child* monitors implementation of the Convention on the Rights of the Child.

In periodic reports to the committees, States parties outline the legislative, judicial and administrative measures taken to ensure that government policies and practices conform to treaty principles. The Human Rights committee, for example, has considered over 800 reports with respect to 56 countries and published 270 decisions. While, the committees' views are not legally binding, they possess significant weight. States have frequently followed their decisions and made constitutional changes or adjusted their policies as a result of their recommendations.

Three human rights treaties allow for communications from individuals. The Human Rights Committee, the Committee against Torture and the Committee on the Elimination of Racial Discrimination are authorised to accept individual complaints from citizens of States that have ratified the respective provisions concerning individual communications. Two specialised agencies, the *United Nations Educational, Scientific and Cultural Organisation (UNESCO)* and the *International Labour Organisation (ILO)*, also examine alleged discrimination in their respective fields of competence.

In 1967, the Economic and Social Council adopted resolution 1235 (XLII), authorising the Commission on Human Rights and its Subcommission on Prevention of Discrimination and Protection of Minorities to extreme information relevant to gross violations of human rights and fundamental freedoms. In 1970, the Council adopted resolution 1503 (XLVIII), establishing a mechanism to respond to complaints by individuals, now commonly known as the "1503 procedure". The allegations are summarised in confidential documents sent to the Commission on Human Rights for review. If a consistent pattern of verified and serious human rights abuse is evident, the Commission can investigate the situation through its system of "special procedures".

The Office of the High Commissioner for Human Rights maintains a 24-hour fax "hot line" (0041-22-917-0092) for reporting alleged human rights violations. Each year, it receives nearly 200,000 communications reporting violations.

Article 6: Right to Recognition as a Person Before the Law

Special Procedures

The United Nations human rights programme relies increasingly on an independent system of fact-finding outside the treaty framework, which permits a more flexible approach to individual violations. This system of so-called extra-conventional mechanisms refers to the special procedures of the Commission on Human Rights. The Commission can appoint independent experts international stature to examine, monitor and publicly report either on the situation of human rights in specific countries or, in the case of a thematic mandate, on serious human rights violations related to certain phenomena in various parts of the world, such as religious intolerance or the use of mercenaries. These experts, acting in their personal capacity, are designated, as special rapporteurs, representatives, independent experts or, when several experts share a mandate, working group (*see Annex 5*).

The special rapporteurs are free to use all reliable sources available to them to prepare their reports, and much of their research is done in the field, where they conduct interviews with authorities, NGOs and victims, gathering on-site evidence whenever possible. In 1997, there were fact-finding missions to 14 countries; and inquiries regarding more than 5,000 cases were transmitted to Governments. The special rapporteurs report annually to the Commission on Human Rights, with recommendations for action. Their findings are also used by the treaty bodies in their work, especially in evaluating States' reports.

As of mid-1998, there were over 20 country mandates on the human rights situation in specific religions. Country rapporteurs generally monitor the complex human rights situation in regions where massive violations have occurred, often in the aftermath of large-scale violence or conflict, as in Cambodia, Rawanda and the former Yogoslavia. They make recommendations on how human rights can be strengthen at the national level. The Commission on Human Rights appointed a Special Rapporteur on the human rights situation in Rwanda in May 1994, while the genocide was still ongoing, to examine all human rights aspects of the situation, including root causes and responsibility for the atrocities. In 1997, the Commission followed up on that three-year mandate by appointing a Special Representative to facilitate the creation and effective functioning of an independent national human rights commission in Rwanda.

Emergency Measures

Special Rapporteurs sometimes submit urgent appeals to Governments it they learn of serious human rights violations about to be committed against individuals or vulnerable groups, such as refugees or indigenous communities. In 1997, close to 400 urgent interventions were made to prevent possible violations, particularly in cases of threatened or actual disappearances, possible torture and imminent executions. In 1995, the Special Rapporteur on torture sent 68 letters to 61 Governments regarding 669 cases, as well as 130 urgent appeals on behalf of nearly 500 people. Some 42 countries responded in 459 of those cases. Between 1992 and 1996, the Special Rapporteur on extrajudicial, summary or arbitrary executions made 818 urgent appeals on behalf of more than 6,500 persons to 91 different countries and received replies in roughly half of the instances. In his 1997 report, the Special Rapporteur noted that violations of the rights to life were still on the rise. That year, the Special Rapporteur acted on more than 960 cases or alleged violations of the right to life, submitting 122 urgent appeals on behalf of 3,720 persons.

The General Assembly also requested the Secretary-Assembly also requested the Secretary-General to investigate the systematic rape and abuse of women and children during the armed conflict in the former Yugoslavia, particularly in the Republic of Bosnia and Herzegovina.

The experts entrusted with thematic mandates cover a range of specific human rights issues of worldwide significance. The right to life, for instance, is recognised as the most fundamental rights, and its violation by States is an issue of international concern. The *Working Group on Enforced and Involuntary Disappearances*, established in 1980, was the first to take up individual complaints and visit States. In 1995, one of the experts of the Working Group began to examine the problem of missing persons in the former Yugoslavia. In his final report of 1997, the expert reported that in Bosnia and Herzegovina, some 20,000 persons were still missing, the great majority of whom—Bosnian men of Muslim origin—were victims of systematic "ethnic cleansing" operations carried out by Bosnian Serb forces between 1992 and 1995.

In 1997, the *Special Rapporteur on violence against women* visited Rwanda to study the issue of violence against women in wartime and in post-conflict situations and met with numerous women survivors. The Special Rapporteur also visited the International Criminal Tribunal for Rwanda in Tanzania, where she observed the trial of Jean-Paul Akayesu—the first such trial which included charges of sexual violence in the indictment.

Since 1982, the *Special Rapporteur on extrajudicial, summary or arbitrary executions* has been entrusted with the investigation of violations of the right to life committed by State authorities or armed groups. Working closely with Governments, United Nations bodies and NGOs, the Special Rapporteur appeals to Governments to prevent executions, particularly when the right to a fair trial seems to have been violated. The Rapporteur responds to information on death threats against individual and death in custody, calling for public inquiries or submitting urgent appeals.

Civil Society—Partners in Human Rights Action

The United Nations believes that creating a pervasive culture of human rights requires a dynamic network of partnerships worldwide. The High Commissioner for Human Rights implements her broad mandate in partnership with a variety of actors, including the programmes and agencies within the United Nations system, Governments, regional organisations, academic communities, committed individuals and the NGO community. New types of partnerships are being developed with civil society. In the field of child rights, NGOs have participated in discussions relating to the preparation of government groups. With the help of the United Nations Children's Fund (UNICEF), they have submitted their own information to the Committee on the Rights of the Child, attended the Committee's sessions and monitored, at the national level, the implementation of its recommendations.

NGOs and other representatives of civil, such as academic institutions and citizens' groups, have been crucial to the United Nations human rights work since its inception—from the inclusion of human rights clauses in the Charter to the establishment of the Office of the High Commissioner for Human Rights. NGOs have also been key to developing human rights priorities in the major world conferences of this decade—particularly the agreements achieved on human rights in Vienna (1993), on population and development in Cairo (1994), on social development in Copenhagen (1995), on women's rights in Beijing (1995) and on food security in Rome (1996).

NGOs provide leadership in other areas, too. In the preparation of the Rome Conference, which approved the establishment of an International Criminal Court in July 1998, a well-informed and vocal NGO coalition was instrumental in pushing for a strong mandate for the Court. The coalition often led the debate on contentious issues such as the need for an independent prosecutor and the inclusion of the crime of aggression as one of the core crimes under the Court's jurisdiction. The strong NGO partnership with Governments and the United Nations ensured that the International Criminal Court, the last institution expected to be created in this century, possesses the capacity to exercise its dual purpose of prosecuting individuals responsible for atrocities and deterring future barbarities.

The strength of non-governmental human rights organisations lies in their ability to mobilise public opinion, disseminate information and pressure Governments to conform to international human rights standards. There is great diversity among these NGOs. Some defend all human rights in general, while others protect the specific rights of particular vulnerable groups, such as women and children, or deal with urgent human rights issues, such as torture, enforced disappearances or the treatment of prisoners.

Article 7: Right to Equal Consideration Before the Law

NGOs are vital actors in human rights advocacy: representing and protecting victims, providing expertise, collecting and disseminating information and encouraging human rights education. Among human rights NGOs women's groups are among the most active in the world today, playing a vital role in the advancement and empowerment of women by increasing awareness of women's issues, as well as educating women in their human rights. Many other NGOs have an indirect role in defending human rights. They focus primarily on other issues but have incorporated human rights into their activities and, by offering legal assistance to vulnerable groups, advance the cause of human rights.

Defending Human Rights Defenders

Around the World, there is a small but vital community of human rights defenders, comprising representatives of NGOs and other individuals or associations, all involved in the "front-line" struggle for human rights. Some are non-governmental organisation volunteers, lawyers or journalists; others are peasant leaders, students or relatives of victims. Often they are part of local organisations, which do not benefit from the protection of a large international association and are vulnerable to attacks. Their work is especially important in countries recovering from armed conflict, suffering the consequences of dictatorship or undergoing major social and political transformations.

Watching that Governments live up to their promises and obligations to protect and promote the rights of their citizens, human rights defenders are often at considerable risk of becoming themselves victims of serious violations, facing death threats, arrest and detention or suffering abduction and torture. Many have lost their lives while defending human rights.

In 1985, to protect human rights activities and NGOs, the Commission on Human Rights established a working group to draft a declaration aimed at guaranteeing individuals the right to publicly denounce violations, to form and participate in human rights NGOs and to communicate with international human rights organisations. In 1998, after more than 13 years of discussion, the Commission adopted the draft Declaration on the Right and Responsibility of Individuals, Groups and Organs of Society to Promote and Protect Universally Recognised Human Rights and Fundamental Freedoms, also known as the Declaration on Human Rights Defenders. The Declaration is not a legally binding treaty but clarifies and reinforces rights that are already recognised in existing international instruments.

Some human rights organisations, such as Human Rights Watch and the International Federation for Human Rights, have a large international reach, and conduct independent surveys, publish newsletters and disseminate detailed reports. Today, there are hundreds of NGOs whose human rights work has taken on a transnational character. Amnesty International, for example, the largest human rights NGO, with 1.2 million members in 160 countries, recently launched a world-wide petition drive to secure the commitment of over 6 million people to the Universal Declaration of Human Rights. The pledges will be handed over to the United Nations General Assembly on Human Rights Day, 10 December, on the occasion of the fiftieth anniversary of the Universal Declaration.

3. A Comprehensive Approach to Human Rights

The International Human Rights standards and norms adopted through the United Nations represent the hard-won consensus of the international community, not the hegemony of any particular region or set of traditions. The international human rights instruments establish minimum standards for the range of economic, social, cultural, civil and political rights. But they do not impose a single cultural standard; rather, they promote a common legal standard of respect for human dignity. Within this international framework, States have sovereign power to adapt human rights to their national settings, as long as they do not contradict the norms established through international human rights treaties.

A fundamental tenet of international human rights law is that all human rights are of equal importance. In practical terms, this means that they must be viewed collectively and that a comprehensive and balanced approach in promoting these rights must be found. No set of rights—say, cultural rights—can be given pre-eminence over other human rights without distorting the principles of indivisibility and interdependence. Every human being, for example, has the right to participate in the cultural life of his or her community. The right to practise one's cultural belief, however, is limited at the point at which it infringes on another human rights. This means that cultural rights cannot be invoked or interpreted in such a way as to justify any act leading to the denial of violation of other human rights and fundamental freedoms.

Despite its commitment to protect all human rights, the United Nations in reality has promoted civil and political rights much more than economic, social and cultural rights in the past decades. This imbalance is reflected in the Universal Declaration itself. Eighteen articles deal in great detail with civil and political rights, while only six articles deal with economic, social and cultural rights. Since 1993, guided by the Vienna Declaration and Programme of Action, the United Nations has been addressing this imbalance by giving economic, social and cultural rights the same priority as civil and political rights within a human rights framework based on a unifying set of standards. The Organisation also emphasises the right to development as a human rights, for it offers an integrated approach to all human rights, an approach which promises to overcome this artificial split between two sets of rights, thus allowing for a cohesive strategy to strengthen human rights.

Civil and Political Rights

The United Nations protects the civil and political rights of individuals and groups through a number of international treaties, but particularly through the International Covenant on Civil and Political Rights. The Covenant deals with such rights as freedom of movement; equality before the law; the right to a fair trial and presumption of innocence; freedom of thought, conscience and religion; freedom of opinion and expression; freedom of association, participation in public affairs and elections; and protection of minority rights.

The Human Rights Committee plays a central role in monitoring its implementation, clarifying contentious issues concerning individual rights. Indeed, civil and political rights, including those concerning free speech, assembly and religion, have become so entrenched in international human rights law that States can no longer claim to violate them unknowingly. However, the need for protection has not diminished. Even though states of emergency can no longer be inconsistent with obligations under international law, Governments frequently use national security concerns as a pretext for infringing on civil and political rights, especially in their treatment of dissident groups and critical members of the press.

Serious violations of the fundamental rights to life, liberty and personal security have not abated. Hundreds of persons disappear every year or are the victims of torture or extra-judicial killings. The United Nations investigates gross human rights violations through the working groups on arbitrary detention and enforced or involuntary disappearance, as well as the special rapporteurs on extra-judicial, summary or arbitrary executions and on torture.

The Special Rapporteur on torture, for example, plays a key role in the international fight against cruel and inhuman punishment by responding to complaints from individuals and groups. In 1981, the United Nations set up a Voluntary Fund for Victims of Torture. Since its inception, the Fund has finance over 300 projects, giving priority to those providing direct medical or physiological assistance to torture victims. The United Nations also urges all States to provide for compensation and rehabilitation of torture victims in their domestic law.

Economic, Social and Cultural Rights

With the success of decolonization and the increase in the number of newly independent States, the membership of the United Nations underwent a significant change. By the 1970s, developing countries represented a majority in the General Assembly, and their concerns and priorities became increasingly reflected in the work of the General Assembly—particularly the issue of economic and social development. Reflecting this overall change of emphasis, the main thrust of United Nations work in the area of human rights today has been to strengthen the promotion of economic, social and cultural rights, particularly the right to development.

The United Nations has provided leadership in articulating the inherent relationship between human rights and economic and social development, providing a framework in which they reinforce each other. Beginning in the 1970s, the Commission on Human Rights turned its attention to the obstacles hindering the full realisation of economic, social and cultural rights, particularly in developing countries. The landmark achievement of the Commission was the drafting of the Declaration on the Right to Development, adopted by the General Assembly in 1986. It was the first time that the international community explicitly recognised the right to development as an inalienable and fundamental human rights.

Article 8: Right to Remedy through a Competent Tribunal

The *Committee on Economic, Social and Cultural Rights* has increasingly concentrated its efforts in establishing benchmarks for economic and social rights so that these rights can be more effectively implemented and monitored. At the national level, the strengthening of economic, social and cultural rights is being achieved through the provision of basic social services to all sectors of society, in agrarian economies, this is achieved by giving clear legal rights of ownership of land. But also crucial is the effective functioning of a free and fair legal system, protecting civil and political rights, such as freedom of expression, eliminating discrimination and, in particular, advancing the human rights of women. Benchmarks are crucial to improving accountability and to ensuring that standards and norms regarding economic, social and cultural rights are progressively raised to the same level as civil and political rights.

In recent years, a great deal of effort has been devoted to further elaborating the rights to adequate food, health care, housing and primary education. The right to food, for example, was affirmed by the 186 countries at the 1996 World Food Summit.

The right to adequate housing was the focus of the 1996 Habitat Conference in Istanbul. The United Nations estimates that 100 million people are homeless and 1 billion people inadequately housed worldwide. Due to the recommendations of the Committee on Economic, Social and Cultural rights, several Governments have agreed to stop forced evictions and are now focusing on ways to guarantee housing. The Dominican Republic, after being criticized for inadequate housing, invited the committee to carry out a survey mission and meet with non-governmental organisations. The Government of the Philippines recently reported to the Committee that it would increase its spending on new housing and had developed programmes to relocate and shelter homeless persons who had been evicted. Advancing the universal recognition of the right to education, the Committee recently persuaded Zimbabwe to abandon the charging of fees for primary education, a policy incompatible with the promotion of education as a human right.

Right to Development: Eradicating Poverty

Poverty is a Condition that reflects the disregard for a wide range of human rights. Accordingly, the eradication of poverty remains one of the most important goals for United Nations activities in development and is a central theme of the right to development. A quarter of the population in the developing world lives in extreme poverty, while in many parts of the developed world the percentage of those living in poverty is increasing. Poverty affects society in many ways. Since 70 per cent of the 1.6 billion people living in extreme poverty worldwide are women, United Nations efforts to eradicate poverty increasingly give special consideration to its female dimension. Women work two thirds of the world's working hours, but earn only one tenth of the world's income and own less than one tenth of the world's property. In addition, two thirds of the world's illiterate are women. A women's right to development still encounters many barriers, rooted in domestic laws, cultural traditions, practices and gender-based stereotypes that are extremely difficult to eradicate.

A rights-based approach to development provides the ethical foundation for concerted action against poverty and empowers the poor in their struggle for social justice. The United Nations helps Governments set targets and measures progress in poverty reduction. Crucial to the success of these initiatives is the close involvement of NGOs representing the poor, and, at the local level, the people themselves, in planning, implementing and evaluating development projects. Key to eradicating poverty is the sustained cooperation between developed and developing countries. One of the most promising recent initiatives, embraced by several United Nations agencies and funds, is the 20/20 Compact, which calls for developed and developing countries to allocate, on average, 20 per cent of official development assistance (ODA) and 20 per cent of national budgets to basic social programmes. In 1995, the World Summit for Social Development in Copenhagen and the World Conference on Women in Beijing endorsee the 20/20 Compact, recognising that one of the most effective and efficient methods for poverty alleviation is the universal provision of basic social services.

The Right to Development

The right to development is the result of a conceptual evolution within the United Nations, shaped first by the experience of decolonization and later by the recognition that developing countries need sustained assistance in order to create the conditions necessary for the universal enjoyment of human rights. The emphasis on the right to development reflects the conviction that a narrowly defined notion of economic development is not enough to create these conditions. Development that occurs without respect for human rights and rule of law remains incomplete. Development leads to the strengthening of human rights to the same degree that the promotion and protection of human rights provide the basis for sustainable development. In 1997, Secretary-General Kofi Annan stressed the crucial importance of the right to development for the international community.

"Truly sustainable development is possible only when the political, economic and social rights of all people are fully respect. They help to create the social equilibrium which is vital if a society is to evolve in peace. The right to development is the measure of respect of all other human rights. They should be our aim: a situation in which all individuals are enabled to maximise their potential, and to contribute to the evolution of society as a whole".

The universal right of peoples to self-determination in all its dimensions lies at the heart of the right to development. The 1986 *Declaration on the Right to Development* sees development as a complex, comperhensive and dynamic process, involving cultural, economic, political and social aspects, by which the well-being of all individuals and society as a whole is steadily improved. The individual is recognised as the central subject of development, with rights as well as responsibilities regarding his or her participation in development. States have "primary responsibility" for creating the conditions enabling the realisation of the right to development, as both an individual and a collective right.

Participation is given special emphasis in the right to development, entailing the active, free and meaningful participation of individuals in the process and in the fair distribution of the resulting social benefits. The Declaration also provides for an international dimension in its implementation: developed countries should assist developing countries in creating the necessary conditions for development by reducing the negative aspects of international terms of trade, of foreign-debt repayments and of structural adjustment programmes.

The right to development has the potential to provide the integration of human rights that the international community has been striving to achieve for over five decades. This right not only encompasses all civil, cultural, economic, political and social rights, but it also promotes the recognition of interdependent and indivisible ties between various human rights, permitting the individuals full participation and involvement in economically durable, politically free and socially just development. These are long-term goals that they yet to be realised and will require the commitment and efforts of all development actors—from local and regional NGOs and national Government to international organisations and global financial institutions.

In today's age of globalisation, where national economies become more and more interdependent, the United Nations recognises the need for closer partnerships with the private sector. There is a growing awareness that many decisions originating in the private sector have a direct or indirect impact on the global respect for human rights. Constructive cooperation between the

United Nations and the business community is crucial in meeting the pressing challenge of implementing the right to development, promoting good governance and improving health and education.

Article 9: Freedom from Arbitrary Arrest or Exile

A milestone in this direction was the establishment of the United Nations Foundation in 1998, as a result of United States businessman Ted Turner's commitment to support the Organisation with $1 billion over a 10-year period. Also, Rotary Clubs worldwide have donated more than $400 million to the World Health Organisation (WHO). Major airlines have been working together with UNICEF by collecting over $18 million from passengers' donations of spare change in foreign currency. An Italian fashion group has launched a global campaign promoting the fiftieth anniversary of the Universal Declaration of Human Rights. International banks are contributing to the United Nations Development Programmes's programme of offering micro-credits to poor people to start their own business and create sustainable livelihoods.

Realising the Right to Development

The 1993 World Conference on Human Rights dealt extensively with the right to development, linking it inextricably with democracy and peace. It recommended that the High Commissioner for Human Rights be given a specific mandate to promote the right to development, as well as to coordinate support from relevant bodies of the United Nations system for that purpose. Currently, the High Commissioner is reorienting the human rights programme to improve the implementation of economic, social and cultural rights by giving special attention to the right to development.

The agencies and programmes of the United Nations system are also incorporating the right to development into their activities, on the basis of a comprehensive rights-based approach to development. A rights-based approach not only defines beneficiaries according to their needs, but also recognises that the individuals receiving assistance are autonomous subjects with legitimate claims to the right to development. This rights-based framework introduces an important element of accountability, which promises to improve effectiveness and transparency of action.

Article 10: Right to a Fair Trial or Public Hearing

In response to the Secretary-General's reform efforts to integrate human rights into all aspects of the Organisation's work, the *United Nations Development Programme (UNDP)* issued in 1998 a policy document, "Integrating human rights with sustainable human development", which out-lines of UNDP's right-based approach to development. The document takes the realisation of the right to development as its starting point. It deals with the human rights implications for sustainable human development and the effectiveness UNDP support for human rights, and indicates ways of implementing the strategy, including working closely with the Office of the High Commissioner for Human Rights. UNDP's human rights commitment provides a promising model for system-wide cooperation in human rights.

The promotion and protection of labour rights have been a central mandate of the *International Labour Organisation (ILO)* since its establishment in 1919. ILO, through its unique tripartite structure of government, business and labour representatives, formulates international policies and programmes to promote basic human rights, improve working conditions and expand employment. ILO develops and monitors labour standards in the workplace, through conventions and guidelines that have been incorporated in the national legislation of virtually all countries.

Other members of the United Nations system have also taken measures to advance human rights. The *United Nations Children's Fund (UNICEF)* uses the Convention on the Rights of the Child as a basis for dialogue with Governments. UNICEF strongly supports the work of the Committee on the Rights of the Child and other child rights initiatives. Promoting and protecting the right to food have led to cooperation between the Office of the High Commissioner and the *Food and Agriculture Organisation of the United Nations (FAO)*. Similarly, the High Commissioner is developing close contacts with the *United Nations Conference on Trade and Development (UNCTAD)* and the *United Nations Population Fund (UNFPA)* to share expertise in areas relating to economic development and human rights.

4. Strengthening Human Rights at the National Level

In Recent Years, the United Nations has concentrated its efforts on strengthening the promotion of human rights at the national and local levels. There is a strong rationale for this. Human rights are best secured when they have taken root in the local culture. The International human rights standards can only be effective when they have been incorporated into national legislation and are promoted through national institutions. Still, many obstacles continue to impede the universal enjoyment of human rights at the national level. A number of Member States do not have adequate infrastructure to promote and protect their citizens' rights effectively. This is especially the case when they have recently emerged from bloody civil conflicts, as in Burundi, Cambodia, Rwanda, Sierra Leone and the former Yugoslavia.

There is another important reason for encouraging capacities at the national level. In the absence of sufficient resources, the United Nations human rights programme cannot routinely carry out comprehensive human rights field operations at the national level. The United Nations has therefore intensified its advisory services to Governments and greatly expanded its technical cooperation programmes within the larger framework of promoting democracy, development and human rights, strengthening the capacity of States to promote and protect human rights within their jurisdictions.

Technical Cooperation for Human Rights

The number of United Nations technical cooperation programmes in the field of human rights has risen from two projects in 1984 to nearly 200 annually now. The programmes, supervised by the Office of the High Commissioner for Human Rights (OHCHR), focus on countries in transition to democracy and on developing countries which request technical expertise in establishing national human rights structures. Human Rights monitoring often takes place in conjunction with advisory services, complementing the technical assistance projects by identifying problems and providing feedback on their effectiveness.

The *Human Rights Technical Cooperation Programme* is financed from the regular budget of the United Nations and through the

Voluntary Fund for Technical Cooperation in the Field of Human Rights. Established in 1987, the Fund has received more than $19 million in voluntary contributions and pledges. The budgetary resources of the Technical Cooperation Programme for 1998 and 1999 total nearly $3.4 million. The allocations by region are Africa 31 per cent, Latin America and the Caribbean 20 per cent, Asia and the Pacific 18 Per cen and Europe 9 Per cent. Besides country-specific projects requested by States, OHCHR also undertakes technical cooperation projects with a global or thematic emphasis. Twenty per cent of the funds for technical cooperation are devoted to global projects, such as human rights education and training initiatives for the military and for peacekeeping operations. During 1997, a total of 43 technical cooperation projects were carried out, of which 25 were at the national level, 9 at the regional level and 9 at the international level. By the beginning of 1998, there were ongoing projects in 58 countries.

OHCHR provides guidance in drafting legislative reforms, that effect, directly or indirectly, the realisation of human rights. Legislation includes penal codes and prison regulations, codes of criminal procedure, laws affecting freedom of expression, association and assembly, immigration and nationality laws, minority protection, the judiciary and legal practice, and security legislation. The cooperation programme provides comprehensive technical assistance in the incorporation of international human rights standards and norms into national laws and policies, and helps in the establishment of national institutions capable of protecting human rights and promoting democracy and the rule of law.

OHCHR also helps Governments identify human rights issues and define policies, particularly through the formulation and implementation of comprehensive national plans of action. These plans, which can be relatively simple or prepared in great detail, identify national priorities in the promotion and protection of human rights and set targets and benchmarks, and often involve a wide range of human rights actors from both governmental institutions and civil society.

Article 11: Right to be Considered Innocent Until Proven Guilty

Electoral Assistance

Various parts of the United Nations system provide assistance in the preparation and holding of elections. The *Electoral Assistance Division of the United Nations Department of Political Affairs* is the main Secretariat body assisting States in holding free and fair elections, it has provided various forms of electoral assistance to over 80 countries, ranging from advisory services to election verification. The *United Nations Development Programme (UNDP)* provides technical support to electoral processes, helps countries to build electoral bodies and coordinates electoral assistance at election time. Since 1990, the technical cooperation programmes now under the coordination of OHCHR have provided electoral assistance by training electoral officials, preparing guidelines for electoral laws and procedures, publishing a handbook on human rights and elections and carrying out public information activities relating to human rights and elections. Countries that have received technical electoral assistance from OHCHR include Albania (1991), Angola (1992), Cambodia (1992), Eritrea (1992), Lesotho (1991-1993), Malawi (1992-1993), Romania (1990-1992) and South Africa (1993).

Human Rights and the Administration of Justice

Technical cooperation is vital in building and strengthening national infrastructures that have a direct impact on the rule of law and the overall respect for human rights. Such infrastructure work proceeds slowly, particularly where war or military rule has undermined the administration of justice. Crucial to rebuilding institutions of governance is an effective system of justice, as due process is almost always a casualty of military dictatorships and armed conflicts. In situations where the police and armed forces inspite fear and suspicion, citizens cease to rely on them for protection. For this reason. OHCHR provides training in the administration of justice and law enforcement, so that lawmakers and law enforcement officers develop and enhance their role as human rights defenders.

Training courses for judges, lawyers, prosecutors, police officers and prison personnel aim at developing effective techniques for the ethical performance of penal and judicial functions and law enforcement in a democratic society. Areas covered in these human rights courses include the independence of judges and lawyers, elements of a fair trial, juvenile justice, special protection of the rights of women and human rights under states of emergency. Law enforcement courses cover principles of ethnical police conduct in democracies, the use of force in law enforcement, the human rights suspect during criminal investigations, arrest and pre-trial detention, effective methods of ethical interrogation and the legal status and rights of the accused. Prison officials are instructed in the minimum standards for prisons and detention camps, in prison health issues, including AIDS/HIV, and in the treatment of special categories of delinquents, such as juveniles and women. Military personnel are trained in the principles of humanrights and humanitarian law guiding their legitimate functions in society.

National Human Rights Institutions

The establishment and strengthening of national human rights institutions is perhaps the single most important component in the United Nations Technical Cooperation Programme. National human rights institutions are the primary mechanisms for translating international concepts and norms into a local culture of human rights. Two valuable bodies for human rights protection are the *ombudsman,* who serves as a focal point for complaints by individuals, and *truth and reconciliation commissions,* which are able to minitor the work of Governments from within and assist them in carrying out their treaty obligations under the human rights conventions. Their main functions are:

- *Providing human rights expertise to Governments and praliaments;*
- *Investigating individual human rights violations;*
- *Conducting public inquiries into systematic or structural violations;*
- *Fostering human rights education.*

Because these institutions are rooted in their local cultures, they can protect vulnerable groups and uphold international human rights standards without seeming alien to the national consensus. They can provide effective protection in a more informed manner and with greater attention to local cultural sensitivities than international or even regional organisation possibly could.

While most national human rights institutions can purpose necessary legislative reforms or suggest changes in government policy, some ombudsmen also have the authority to conduct public inquiries on their own initiatives to bring systematic and structural violations against vulnerable groups to public attention. One of the more important functions of a national human rights institution is, in fact, a side effect of its investigatory powers. As seen with the Truth and Reconciliation Commission in South Africa, the existence of a national mechanism with the power to investigate abuses and to provide compensation to victims may, it itself, figure as a deterrent to future abuse. Another important role a national institution can perform is fostering human rights education with a strategic focus on preventive strategies.

Since the new emphasis on national institutions, beginning in 1995, the United Nations has been assisting an increasing number of States in establishing such institutions. During 1997, 18 States received advice or assistance: Armenia, Bangladesh, Cambodia, Fiji, Georgia, Liberia, Malawi, Madagascar, Mauritius, Mongolia, Nepal, Papua, New Guinea, Rwanda, South Africa, Sri Lanka, Thailand, Uganda and Zambia. OHCHR has begun to work closely with UNDP to implement joint projects on national institutions, such as the recently established human rights institutions for southern Africa.

The United Nations also assists in developing human rights structures at the national level. It supported the first Regional Conference of African National Human Rights Institutions, held in 1996. Other regional forums that have received assistance are the African Commission on Human and Peoples' Rights, the African Centre for Democracy and Human Rights Studies in the Gambia and the Arab Institute for Human Rights in Tunis. There are now regional associations or periodic meetings of national institutions in Africa, the Asian-Pacific region, Latin America and Europe. In 1997, the national institutions in the Asian-Pacific region met in New Delhi and the Fourth International Workshop of National Institutions was held in Mexico.

Human Rights in Rwanda

For Four Years (1994-1998), the Human Rights Field Operation in Rwanda (HRFOR) provided technical assistance and monitored the critical human rights situation in that country. Financed entirely through voluntary contributions, HRFOR was the first human rights field operation to be run under the authority of the High Commissioner for Human Rights. At its peak, the operation had over 137 international staff members deployed in the country, with 58 observers still in Rwanda when it was shut down at the end of July 1998.

In assisting Rwanda in its continuing efforts to rebuild its shattered judiciary, the Human Rights Field Operation concentrated on building an effective judicial system, training judges, prosecutors and other court personnel at all levels of the new justice system. Another strong component of the technical assistance programme was training and human rights education for prison officials and civilian police, including judicial police inspectors, gendarmes and communal police constables.

As of January 1998, an estimated 126,000 detainees were being held in Rwandan prisons or local detention centres, whose combined estimated capacity, according to official sources, was 30,000. With one third of the detainees still waiting to be charged with genocide, the dangerously overcrowded prisons pose a large threat to health, sanitation and security. Armed Hutu extremists have repeatedly targeted detention centres in order to persuade detainees to join them. In May 1998, the Rwandan Government requested that the Field Operation be suspended until a new agreement revised the mandate, greatly reducing the monitoring functions of HRFOR. The United Nations rejected the limitation and decided to withdraw its observers by the end of July.

Human Rights in the Field

As human rights fieldwork is a relatively new area, it is still being shaped by the different needs of the individual countries and the experiences specific to each project. Some field operations derive from Security Council resolutions, as in the former Yugoslavia; others are authorised by the Commission on Human Rights or are the result of agreements between the High

Commissioner and the country concerned. Some field offices are set up in cooperation with other multilateral institutions, such as the Organisation for Security and Cooperation in Europe, or directly established by the Office of the High Commissioner for Human Rights. In all cases, the field offices are supervised by the High Commissioner's Office and cooperate closely with other United Nations agencies and programmes. Today, human rights field activities are being carried out in 22 countries staffed by over 200 individuals, a significant increase in the programme, which began with one presence in 1992.

Human rights field offices often combine technical assistance with a monitoring functions, such as gathering information, analysing the general human rights situation or reporting violations. In certain instance, these monitoring and protection activities in the field help create the conditions for ensuring the safe return of refugees or displaced persons in the aftermath of conflicts. Some field offices, such as those in Gaza, Malawi, Mongolia and South Africa, assist in development programmes building national capacity in the areas of legislation, the administration of justice and education. The field office for Gaza and the West Bank forms an integral part of a concerted international effort aimed at advancing the peace process and furthering the social and ecnomic development of Palestine. The fieldwork in Gaza is based on a multidimensional strategy that focuses on establishing a legal framework consistent with human rights standards, developing a plan of action for an official human rights policy and strengtheing structures to protect and promote human rights.

Human rights field operation priorities are clearly oriented towards technical cooperation, but monitoring continues to be necessary in order to assist Governments in introducing corrective measures when necessary. Monitoring is also useful in identifying human rights initiatives than can be implemented by non-governmental institutions. The *Human Rights Field Operation in the Former Yugoslavia* (HRFOFY), for example, assist in the establishment of multi-ethnic police forces, monitors personal security and freedom of returnees, supervises exhumations and coordinates the search for mising persons. The former *Human*

Rights Field Operation in Rwanda (HRFOR) integrated the spectrum of civil, political, economic, social and cultural rights into all reconstruction activities, which required close coordination between United Nations agencies and donor Governments sponsoring economic and social development programmes. The United Nations is exploring the possibility of creating an intergovernmental body to coordinate all activities in support of Rwandan genocide survivors, especially in the areas of comprehension laws and their role as claimants in genocide trials.

Promoting Human Rights Education

The United Nations sees education as a fundamental human rights and as a prime means for the promotion of human rights. Human rights education aims at teaching skills, offering knowledge and shaping attitudes, that advance a universal cultural of human rights. While human rights education is a global issue, it is effective primarily at the national and local levels. It is through human rights education that the standards established in international human rights law take rot in the everyday life of individuals and the local culture of nations. The 1993 Vienna Conference confirmed that human rights education, training and public information were essential for fostering mutual understanding, tolerance and peace among communities.

Article 12: Freedom from Interference with Privacy, Including Home, Family and Correspondence

United Nations human rights education campaigns operate at three levels. At the local level, education in hman rights provides individuals with practical knowledge about human rights and mechanisms for their protection and the development of their individual potential. At the national and international levels, human rights education promotes values, beliefs and attitudes that inspire action in upholding human rights. Human rights education thus encourages all—from the individual to the international community—to take action to defend human rights and prevent abuses.

The United Nations proclaimed the period 1995-2004 the *Decade for Human Rights Education* in order to raise awareness of human rights worldwide and to foster a universal culture for human rights. The Decade has been a catalyst for initiatives in some 30 countries to revise school curricula to promote human rights education. To assist States in developing national agendas for human rights education, the United Nations developed, a Plan of Action for the Decade and urged governmental and non-governmental authorities to implement the recommendations contained in the plan. The *Plan of Action for the Decade for Human Rights Education* aims at building effective human rights education programmes and strengthening the role of the mass media. It also encourages the identification of needs and the formulation of educational strategies, the development of educational materials, and the worldwide dissemination of the Universal Declaration.

The United Nations has urged Member States to draw up national plans, with the involvement, of a wide range of civil society actors, in order to strengthen human rights education programmes at the national and local levels. To help States set up national committees for human rights education, the Office of the High Commissioner for Human Rights prepared guidelines for national plans of action for human rights education. In this context, national human rights institutions are considered good focal points for all kinds of local education strategies. They can support school and community teaching, as well as training in the administration of justice, in particular for members of the armed forces and for law enforcement and prison officials. They can also be instrumental in human rights information campaigns and in the creation of documentation centres. United Nations fellowships and training programmes are available to members and staff of national human rights institutions, providing advice on the domestic implementation of international human rights instruments, in the effective investigation of human rights violations and in conflict resolution.

5. Combating Discrimination

The Horrors of the Mass Examination of people during the Second World War because of their ethnic origins made it clear to the founders of the United Nations how important it is to protect the human rights of vulnerable groups and to eliminate discrimination. Fifty years later, incidents of genocide and ethnic strife still occur in all parts of the world. Recent violence in

Cambodia, Rwanda and the former Yugoslavia, to name only the most notorious conflicts, reminds us, that, more than ever, the rights of vulnerable groups need to be protected. Nations face an alarming upsurge of xenophobia and attacks on migrant workers and minorities of all kinds. These are grave dangers not only for the direct victims, but also for societies as a whole, as racism and discrimination engender serious conflict and undermine the overall freedom and prosperity of a community.

Discrimination countries to focus on arbitrarily emphasised differences between individuals and groups. Unfavourable treatment due to ethnic, origin, skin colour, gender, language, religion, nationality, class status, political opinion or sexual orientation is a marker of discrimination identified in the Universal Declaration. This marker is applicable today as it was 50 years ago. Widespread discrimination still persists women. However, recent global trends have also led to new forms of discrimination, particularly directed against immigrant workers. Despite affirmative and punitive legislative measures, there are no quick solutions. Discrimination can be eliminated only through long-term strategies in eradicating poverty, fostering education, empowering women and strengthening accountability—making certain that, worldwide, discrimination will not be tolerated. Until then, groups most vulnerable to discrimination will need special protection.

United Nations efforts to combat discrimination are concentrated in the following areas:

- *Eliminating racism and racial discrimination;*
- *Safeguarding the rights of indigenous people;*
- *Defending the special rights of all minorities;*
- *Promoting the human rights of women;*
- *Protecting the rights of children.*

Racism

Distinctions and restrictions, preferences and exclusions based on racial prejudice continue to create animosity among people and cause immense suffering and even loss of life. The United Nations combats racial discrimination because of its fundamental injustice. But racial discrimination also represents a serious danger to international peace and security—most contemporary armed conflicts are not of international, but of internal, origin. Just as political doctrines of superiority based on racial differentiation are not only scientifically false but also morally condemnable, the existence of racial barriers in contrary to the notion of open and free societies, harming not only those who are its victims, but also who discriminate. The United Nations therefore provides leadership in drafting legislation, outlawing discrimination and developing policies to combat it effectively. *The Office of the United Nations High Commissioner for Human Rights* (OHCHR), after reviewing existing national laws against racial discrimination, has drawn up model anti-discrimination legislation concentrating on the following areas:

- *Guaranteeing the equality of persons before the law, irrespective of their race, colour, nationality or ethnic origin;*
- *Punishing the dissemination of ideas based on racial superiority and incitement to racial discrimination, as well as racist activities;*
- *Prohibiting organisation which promote and incite racial discrimination;*
- *Assuring protection and remedies against acts of racial discrimination.*

Article 13: Right to Freedom of Movement and Residence in One's Own Country and to Leave and Return at will

The United Nations also provides leadership in coordinating international action against discrimination in the fields of education, culture and information. Since 1973, the Organisation has instituted three successive Decades for Action to Combat Racism and Racial Discrimination. The *Third Decade to Combat Racism and Racial Discrimination*, which began in 1993, provides an important framework for present action against racism. A third *World Conference against Racism, Racial Discrimination, Xenophobia and Related Intolerance* is planned for the year 2000, offering an opportunity to review progress in the fight against racism and to mobilise effective support at all levels to confront racism and racial discrimination.

In 1993, the Commission on Human Rights appointed a *Special Rapporteur on contemporary forms of racism, racial discrimination, xenophobia and related intolerance.* In his 1998 report, the Special Rapporteur stated that discrimination against foreigners persisted throughout the world, and was directed particularly against blacks, Arabs and other Muslims, Jews and the Rome, or Gypsies. Also, studies indicate that discrimination against migrant workers in host countries is on the rise worldwide. The globalisation of international economic relations has promoted many countries to take discriminatory legislative and regulatory measures to protect their domestic labour force, effectively excluding certain categories of immigrants.

One of the most disturbing recent phenomena of racial prejudice, the Special Rapporteur reported, is the upsurge of racist and xenophobic activities on the Internet, with over 100 extremist, especially neo-Nazi, sites advocating white supremacy and inciting racial hatred. Germany and Switzerland have already adopted legislation against the electronic dissemination of racist propaganda. In 1997, a United Nations seminar focused on the role of the Internet in contemporary forms of racism. Reviewing possible responses, such as blocking certain material and prohibiting propaganda on the Internet, participants highlighted the difficulty of finding an effective way to block racist material while protecting the right to free speech.

Indigenous People

Spread across the world from the Arctic to the South Pacific, indigenous people number at a rough estimate, some 300 million, about 5 per cent of the world's population. Still living on the lands of their ancestors, indigenous people are the descendants of the aboriginal populations that inhibited a geographical region at the time when settlers to different cultures or ethnic origins arrived. The new arrivals later came to dominate the region through conquest, occupation or settlement. Retaining social, cultural, economic and political characteristics clearly distinct from those of the other segments of the national populations, indigenous people have become threatened minorities and are perhaps the most vulnerable groups in the world today.

The main threats to the survival of indigenous people arise from the uniqueness of their cultures, the ownership of their lands and their legal status. Although some groups have been relatively successful in retaining their culture, in most parts of the world indigenous people are struggling to maintain their cultural identities and their ways of life. Since 1982, when the United Nations began to formally consider the situation of indigenous people with the establishment of the *Working Group on Indigenous Populations*, a wide range of activities have been undertaken by the Organisation's human rights programme and by the United Nations system as a whole.

The main areas of concern regarding the human rights of indigenous people are:

- *Land rights and indigenous treaties with national Governments;*
- *Forced displacement and cultural genocide;*
- *Economic and social marginalisation, including a lack of political representation at the national level;*
- *Disproportionate impact of unemployment and poverty on indigenous communities;*
- *Lack of basic health infrastructures and inadequate level of education, with little consideration for indigenous traditional culture in national education programmes;*
- *Lack of production for indigenous people's intellectual and cultural property, such as knowledge of medicinal plants and preservation of their unique cultural artifacts.*

Article 14: Right to Asylum

The Working Group on Indigenous populations, a subsidiary organ of *Subcommission on Prevention of Discrimination and Protection of Minorities*, consists of five independent experts representing each of the geopolitical regions of the world. Today, the Working Group, whose sessions are open to representatives of indigenous people as well as Governments, United Nations agencies and non-governmental organisations (NGOs), is one of the main international forums in the field of human rights, in charge of reviewing the development of international standards concerning indigenous rights.

The decision that the issue of indigenous rights should be given special consideration led to the long process of drafting a *Declaration on the Rights of Indigenous People,* beginning in 1985. The draft declaration, concluded in 1993, acknowledges the human rights and fundamental freedoms of indigenous people, including equality, self-determination and non-discrimination. The Declaration, adopted by the Subcommission on Prevention of Discrimination and Protection of Minorities, is now being reviewed by an inter-sessional working group of the Commission on Human Rights.

The General Assembly proclaimed 1993 the *International Year of the World's Indigenous People* to raise public awareness of indigenous issues and to increase Member States' efforts to protect their rights. Some States with significant indigenous communities, such as Bolivia, Colombia, Norway and Canada, have adopted legislation ensuring that indigenous people become fully involved in their nations' political and economic life. The World Conference on Human Rights further recommended the establishment of a permanent forum for indigenous people within the United Nations system, a proposal which is still being discussed by the Commission on Human Rights. In recent years, however, the concerns of indigenous people have entered the discussions of other forums, particularly their role in sustainable development and the application of their knowledge to biological diversity, desertification and sustainable ecology.

The inauguration of the *International Decade of the World's Indigenous People (1995-2004)* marked the beginning of a series of promotional activities aimed at strengthening international cooperation for the solution of problems faced by indigenous people in such areas as human rights, the environment, development, education and health. The General Assembly is working towards the adoption of the Declaration on the Rights of Indigenous People as the most important action of the Decade.

Article 15: Right to a Nationality and Freedom to Change it

OHCHR has created two voluntary funds to assist indigenous people who want to participate in the activities of the Working Group on Indigenous Populations. The Office has also established an Indigenous Fellowship Programme, which offers six months' training on human rights issues and the United Nations system. The programme gives indigenous individuals the opportunity to gain knowledge and skills in the field of international human rights in general, and on indigenous rights in particular, enabling them to assist their local organisations and communities.

Many Governments are aware of the serious problems faced by indigenous people living in their territories and of the factors that make them one of the most vulnerable groups in national societies. In some parts of the world, an ongoing dialogue is taking place. In other places, direct negotiations between indigenous people and Governments have been instituted and are moving forward with the aim of improving relations and guaranteeing better protection of indigenous people's rights.

Minorities

Almost every country has one or more minority groups within its territory, characterised by their own ethnic, linguistic or religious, distinct from the majority of the population. Through respect for each group's identity is a great asset to the multicultural diversity of our global society, relations between the majority and a minority as well as among different minorities often cause tensions and violence. In recent years, ethnic, racial and religious tensions have escalated, threatening the economic, social and political fabrics of States, as well as their territorial integrity. For this reason, the United Nations is greatly concerned with human rights issues affecting minorities. Some issues—for instance, demands for independence or autonomy—present a challenge to States that is not always resolved by eliminating discrimination. But meeting the aspirations of various ethnic, religious or linguistic communities and ensuring the rights of minorities significantly lesson tensions among groups and individuals and help to further participatory development, thus contributing to stability and peace.

In the wake of rising discrimination and violence against majority groups, many of whom are demanding greater autonomy, the protection of minorities' rights has attracted the same level of attention as other rights. In 1992, the United Nations adopted the *Declaration on the Rights of Persons Belonging to National or Ethnic,*

Religious and Linguistic Minorities. Because there is no specific reference to minorities in the Universal Declaration of Human Rights, the Declaration emphasises the special status and rights of minority groups, recognising the value of preserving their identity, traditions and language. The Declaration spells out the responsibility of States to protect and promote the rights of their minorities by creating favourable conditions for their cultural expression and participation in the economic development of each nation. The Secretary-General has entrusted the High Commissioner for Human Rights with promoting the principles of the Declaration by engaging in continuous dialogue with Governments on behalf of national or ethnic, religious and linguistic minorities. Contrary visits and reports by Special Rapporteurs are also essential in the implementation of minority-related resolutions.

The tremendous variety of situations among minorities—some are linked by a common cultural heritage, other by geographical closeness—often complicates matters. But it has not precluded United Nations activities promoting human rights standards concerning these vulnerable groups. In 1995, the Subcommission on Prevention of Discrimination and Protection of Minorities established a *Working Group on Minorities*. The sessions of the Working Group, which are open to representatives of Governments and NGOs involved with the protection of these vulnerable groups, have become the focal point of United Nations activities in the field of minority rights.

Migrant Workers

In recent years, the phenomenon of migration, in the wake of increasing globalisation, has affected a large number of States in all regions of the world. Millions of people are now earning their livelihood or looking for paid employment as immigrants in another State. Migrant workers and their families face economic exploitation and discrimination related to labour, as well as low income, poor working, standards and lack of job security. In their quest to cope psychologically and adjust culturally to the host country, they also often suffer from hostile attitudes from the Government, local prejudices and other human rights abuses. These human problems involved in migration are even more serious in cases of irregular or illegal immigration, fulled by clandestine trafficking in migrant workers.

The number of women migrant workers who have left their country to escape poverty and who suffer inhuman treatment and sexual abuse at the hands of their employers is on the rise. The phenomenon is increasingly recognised as a new form of slavery related to the increase in the transnational sex trade and trafficking in women and girls. This has promoted the United Nations and the international community to give special attention to the plight of female migrant workers.

Article 16: Right to Marriage and Protection of Family

In 1990, the General Assembly strengthened efforts to recognise the human rights of migrant workers by adopting the *International Convention on the Protection of the Rights of All Migrant Workers and Members of Their Families*. Besides the core human rights treaties and relevant international labour standards, the Convention takes into account the Slavery Conventions and the United Nations Educational, Scientific and Cultural Organisation's Convention against Discrimination in Education. At present, the Convention has been ratified by only nine countries and is not yet in force. In 1997, the Commission on Human Rights established a working group of intergovernmental experts on the human rights of minorities to study the status of migrant workers.

Human Rights of Women

Although women constitute a majority of the world's population, there is still no society in which women enjoy full equality with men. In 1996, for example, women held only 7 per cent of ministerial level posts in Governments worldwide. Figures for the number of women in high-level positions in business and in higher education are similar. Women are still subject to widespread discrimination in everyday life and often lack adequate representation in the public life of developing, as well as developed countries. The United Nations has always affirmed that the promotion of the human rights of women must eliminate all forms of gender-based discrimination and enable them to participate fully in all spheres of civil, political, economic, social and cultural life.

Article 17: Right to Own Property

Recognising the important contribution of women to development and peace, and concerned that in many parts of the world women still did not enjoy equal rights, the United Nations General Assembly proclaimed the period 1976-1985 the *United Nations Decade for Women* in support of national women's movements around the world. The most significant achievement during the Decade for Women was the adoption (1979) and quick entry into force (1981) of the *Convention on the Elimination of All Forms of Discrimination against Women*, which established the *Committee on the Elimination of Discrimination against Women* to oversee the implementation of all principles of gender equality and empowerment of women *(see Annex 5)*.

National women's movements, in turn, have had a profound impact on the world conferences in this past decade: emphasising the special needs of the girl child at the Children's Summit in New York (1990); the central role of women in sustainable development at the Earth Summit in Rio de Janeiro (1992); women's reproductive rights at the Population Conference in Cairo (1994); and the special focus on women in the eradication of poverty at the Social Summit in Copenhagen (1995).

Women's movements have also been instrumental in effecting a conceptual shift in emphasis concerning the advancement and empowerment of women. Until the 1980s, the United Nations stressed the recognition of women's rights without women's rights in order to ensure their full participation in development and to realise non-discrimination. But women's groups advocated, with increasing persuasiveness, that there are no human rights without women's rights, thus grounding the promotion and protection of the rights of women in the universality and indivisibility of all human rights.

This new emphasis, in turn, become the central, cross-cutting theme of the *Fourth World Conference on Women in Beijing* (1995) . Attended by nearly 50,000 participants, the Beijing Conference on Women significantly strengthened the empowerment of women by elaborating the crucial links between the universal advancement of women and social progress around the world. The *Beijing Declaration and Platform for Action*, adopted by consensus, highlighted the global nature of human rights issues concerning women and signalled a clear commitment to international norms in gender equality. The Platform for Action advanced a number of forward-looking strategies to integrate a gender perspective into all policies and programmes at all levels and to enhance women's participation in political, civil, economic, social and cultural life. Its multidimentional strategy aims at enabling women to act as autonomous subjects in development and participate in society on their own terms.

The Beijing Declaration elaborates on themes of the Convention on the Elimination of All Forms of Discrimination against Women by recognising that:

- *Women's rights are human rights, which need to be protected particularly in relation to violence, sexuality and reproductive health;*
- *Women should have equal rights in inheriting land and property;*
- *Women have a special role in the family an in society, but maternity should not impede the full participation of women in society nor should they be penalised for illegal abortions;*
- *Rape is a war crime, and in some cases an act of genocide, under international humanitarian law.*

In the past decade, the United Nations has moved to coordinate its actions in advancing the equal status of women by strengthening women's rights throughout the United Nations system, a principle first explicitly expressed at the 1993 Vienna Conference. Its main thrust is to integrate women's concerns into the mainstream of the Organisation so that the protection of women becomes a central concern in all human rights activities and economic and social development programmes.

The 45-member *Commission on the Status of Women (CSW)*, established in 1946, is the leading United Nations policy-making body concerned with women's rights and issues affecting the equal status of women. CSW has recently cooperated with the Commission on Human Rights on issues concerning women's human rights. A recent joint project, examining the impact of discrimination against women on their socio-economic status, revealed how gender-specific denial of economic rights directly reduces women's opportunities for social advancement.

Other United Nations programmes are specifically dedicated to the advancement and empowerment of women. The *International Research and Training Institute for the Advancement of Women (INSTRAW)*, established by the Economic and Social Council in 1976, provides training and advisory services for women, especially in developing countries. INSTRAW is currently promoting the training of women in computer-related communications, and also fostering a more gender-sensitive media.

Article 18: Freedom of Belief and Religion

The *United Nations Development Programme (UNDP)* has also increasingly focused on the inclusion of women in its development projects, and in 1984 established a fund aimed at strengthening women's economic, capacity, the *United Nations Development Fund for Women* (UNIFEM). UNIFEM offers technical and financial support to women in cooperation with Governments and NGOs and works closely with other United Nations programmes to ensure women's participation in decision-making at all levels of development planning and practice.

Within the United Nations Secretariat, the *Division for the Advancement of Women (DAW)* and the Secretary-General's *Special Adviser on Gender Issues and the Advancement of Women* monitor the progress in women's full enjoyment of their rights in the light of the goals set by the Beijing Platform for Action. The Division also plays an important role in supporting the Committee on the Elimination of Discrimination against Women. DAW, UNIFEM and INSTRAW have jointly set up an important UN Internet gateway on the advancement and empowerment of women titled "Women Watch".

Within the United Nations system, the *Office of the United Nations High Commissioner for Refugees (UNHCR)*, the *World Health Organisation (WHO)* and the *International Labour Organisation (ILO)* have also taken significant steps towards integrating women rights issues and a gender perspective into their activities. The mandate of the *United Nations Children's Fund (UNICEF)* has always been oriented to the well-being of women in their role as mothers, with activities to combat malnutrition, maternal mortality, gender-based violence and unequal access to education. One important UNICEF programme aims at eliminating the sexual exploitation of girls by providing basic education and employment counselling for girls at risk.

Violence Against Women

According to the 1997 UNICEF report *The Progress of Nations*, violence against women and girls is the most pervasive violation of human rights in the world today. Cutting across economic, social, cultural and religious barriers, violence against women is an insidious phenomenon affecting the lives of millions of women and taking a dismaying variety of forms. The international community did not take concrete action against the alarming global dimensions of gender-based violence until 1993, when, the Gender Assembly adopted the *Declaration on the Elimination of Violence against Women*. Until that point, most Governments tended to regard violence against women largely as a private matter between individuals, and not as a pervasive human rights problem requiring active State intervention.

The Declaration defines violence against women as "any act of gender-based violence that results in, or is likely to result in, physical, sexual or psychological harm or suffering to women, including threats of such acts, coercion or arbitrary deprivation of liberty, whether, occurring in public or in private life". It also identifies systematic rape, sexual slavery and forced pregnancy of women in situations of armed conflicts as extremely grave violations of the fundamental principles of human rights and international humanitarian law. The Declaration identifies three areas in which women are particularly vulnerable:

- *Violence in the family;*
- *Violence within the community;*
- *Violence perpetrated or condoned by the State.*

Article 19: Freedom of Opinion and Information

In the family, domestic violence is on the increase, according to a World Bank study, which found that, worldwide, 25 to 50 per cent of all women suffer physical abuse by their partner. An estimated 60 million females die because of son-preference; many parents, hoping for sons, kill or neglect their daughters before or shortly after birth. Each year, an estimated 2 million girls in at least 28 countries are subjected to the traumatising traditional practice of female genital mutilation. In some societies, girls are completed to marry at an early age before they are physically, mentally or emotionally mature.

In the community, rape continues to be widespread offence that still brings shame and blame onto the innocent victims. Women who are victims of rape and sexual harassment often suffer trauma, physical handicap or even death. The extent of trafficking in women and girls, within and across borders, has reached alarming proportions, especially, in Asian and Eastern European countries. At the same time, sex tourism to developing countries is well-organised industry in several Western and other developed countries.

In cases of State-perpetrated or condoned violence, police or prison officials, who supposedly protect women from violence, are often perpetrators of sexual abuse. Thousands of women held in custody are routinely raped in police detention centres worldwide and cruelly tortured by security forces. In virtually all armed conflicts, rape continuous to be widely used as a cynical tactic to subjugate and terrify entire communities. Women and girl children are frequently victims of gang rape and sexual slavery at the hands of soldiers, as seen during the conflicts in Rwanda and the former Yugoslavia and in many other conflicts around the world.

Article 20: Right to Peaceful Assembly and Association

The United Nations is committed to combating violence against women by addressing the root causes of the problem as well as treating its manifestations, challenging the ways in which gender roles and unequal power relations are articulated in society. Because most always fail to protect victims or to punish perpetrators, it is crucial to enforce laws that redefine the limits of acceptable behaviour and to eliminate the prevailing culture of impunity by applying standards of "due diligence" for Governments. At the same time, information campaigns emphasising the equal rights of women must address society at large, educating judges and police officers, as well as boys and men in general, in order to change the social attitudes and beliefs that tolerate violence against women.

Changing people's attitudes and mentality towards women will take a long time. But raising awareness of the issue of violence against women and educating boys and men to view women as equal partners in private and public life are crucial to democratising society and are as important as taking legal steps to ensure the protection of women's rights. This will require sustained collaboration between governmental and non-governmental actors, including educators, health-care authorities, legislators, the judiciary and the mass media.

The United Nations is mobilising concerted international initiatives to protect women from violence at the local and national levels. The 1993 World Conference on Human Rights urged Governments and the United Nations system to work together towards banning all forms of sexual harassment and exploitation. The Vienna Declaration highlighted as areas of critical concern international trafficking, cultural prejudices and religious extremism, as well as gender bias in the administration of justice and in all aspects of political, civil, economic, social and cultural life. Since 1994, the *Special Rapporteur on violence against women*, in concert with other special rapporteurs of the Commission on Human Rights, has been drawing increasing political attention to the causes and consequences of gender-related violence, recommending measures to eliminate its occurrence and to remedy its consequences. The Special Rapporteur has carried out missions on military and sexual slavery in wartime in Korea and Japan; trafficking in women and girls in Poland; domestic violence in Brazil; rape in South Africa; violence against women in armed conflicts in Rwanda; and violence against women in prisons in the United States.

Monitoring and reporting on violations are essential tools for protecting women's rights. The experts of the Commission on Human Rights and the treaty bodies are increasingly integrating a gender perspective into their work and now generally devote a separate section of their reports to the analysis of discrimination that women still face. Besides the Special Rapporteur on violence against women, some of the thematic mandates, such as executions, torture, religious intolerance, freedom of opinion and expression, racial discrimination and independence of the judiciary, are also concerned with women's rights and are required to fully integrate these concerns in their reports.

Protecting the Rights of Children

Two billion people in the world today are under the age of 18. As the most vulnerable members of a society, children are often victims of serious human rights violations. The extent of systematic abuses against children is disturbing, ranging from malnutrition to military recruitment, from labour exploitation to lack of education, with lifelong implications for their well-being as adults.

Article 21: Right to Participate in Government and in Free Elections and to Equal Access to Public Service

Malnutrition is by far the most pernicious abuse against children in the world. Each year, more than 12 million children under the age of five die in developing countries. More than 55 per cent of all child deaths worldwide can be attributed to malnutrition. Some 40 million babies, one out of three born each year, are at risk simply because they are not registered at birth. Without a birth certificate, a child is not officially recognised as a citizen and is often denied adequate access to basic health services and primary education. At least 120 million children between the ages of 5 and 14 work full time, according to ILO, and for about 250 million children work is a secondary activity. Other threats to children's lives and development throughout the world include murder of street children, sale of organs, child pornography and prostitution. More than 2 million children are believed to be involved in prostitution, including some 1 million in Asia and 300,000 in the United States.

Protection and promotion of the rights of children have always been a central issues on the agenda of the United Nations. Slow but steady progress has been made towards the affirmation that children, like adults, are the subjects of rights, and not only helpless objects of concern or beneficiaries of services. In 1959, the Declaration of the Rights of the Child represented the first concrete affirmation by the international community that children needed special protection and, for the first time, defined a child as a person below the age of 18.

The *International Year of the Child* in 1979 marked the starting point of the debates that led to the formulation of the *Convention on the rights of the Child*, which was adopted unanimously in 1989.

Setting common standards for the protection of the rights of children within different cultural settings, the Convention is today the most widely ratified instrument in the field of human rights, with a total of 191 States parties. Reaffirming the principles of the International Bill of Human Rights, the Convention emphasises particularly the right to life, survival and development of children. The main principles outlined in the Convention are non-discrimination, the child's best interests and the views of the child. These last two concepts reflect recent awareness of the importance of recognising a child's own needs and opinions within a society.

The Convention provides the framework that serves as a catalyst and guideline for action at the national level. Its sets universal standards to which each country should conform its laws with respect to its specific cultural situation. The *Committee on the Rights of the Child*, composed of 10 international experts, was convened for the first time in 1991. Its main role is to monitor the implementation of the Convention by examining regular mandatory reports submitted by States Parties. While some countries leg behind in submitting their reports and others provide insufficient data, there has been great progress in the implementation of the national plans of action.

In 1990, the *World Summit for Children* in New York reaffirmed the standards established by the Convention and adopted the World Declaration on the Survival, Protection and Development of Children, setting the year 2000 as the deadline for the successful implementation of benchmarks benefiting the lives and development of children:

- *Reduction of the infant mortality rate by one third or at least to under 50 per 1,000 live births and reduction of the maternal mortality rate by half;*
- *Reduction of serve and moderate malnutrition among under-five children by half;*
- *Universal access to safe drinking water and to adequate sanitation;*
- *Universal access to basic education and completion of primary education by at least 80 per cent of primary-school-age children;*
- *Reduction of the adult illiteracy rate to no more than half its 1990 level, with emphasis on female literacy.*

The summit developed a Plan of Action that called for various activities on behalf of the well-being of children and mobilised international among Governments, NGOs the media and civil society. At the national level, each country is urged to review its budget to ensure that programmes aimed at the protection of children's rights receive priority when resources are allocated.

Guided by the Convention on the Rights of the Child, UNICEF promoted sustainable development for children and strives to establish children's rights as enduring ethical principles and international standards of behaviour towards children. Working together with other United Nations agencies, Governments and NGOs, UNICEF provides low-cost, community-based services in primary health care, nutrition, basic education and sanitation as a way to protect the rights of the child in the developing world UNICEF's annual reports *The State of the World Children* and *The Progress of Nations* review steps undertaken by States parties to meet the goals of the Convention and promote the well-being of children.

Article 22: Right to Social Security

The United Nations machinery in the field of children's rights comprises a variety of bodies, among which the Committee on the Rights of the Child plays a central role. The *Special Rapporteur on the sale of children, child prostitution and child pornography* analysis instances of sexual exploitation of children in various countries. A working group of the Commission on Human Rights is drafting an optional protocol to the Convention on the Rights of the Child on the sale of children, child prostitution and child pornography.

Children and Armed Conflicts

Children all over the world continue to the victims of the wars of adults—losing parents, families and homes, losing their childhood and the opportunity for education, losing limbs and their lives to armed conflicts. In the past decade alone, as estimated 2 million children have been killed in armed conflicts. Three times as many have been seriously injured or permanently disabled. One million have been orphaned. Countless other have been forced to witness or even take part in horrifying acts of violence. A 1995 UNICEF survey of more than 3,000 children in Rwanda, in the aftermath of the genocidal killings of the previous year, found that more than 80 per cent had lost immediate family members, and more than one third had actually witnessed the murders.

The direct physical effects and the collateral psychosocial damage endured by children during armed conflicts are devastating to their future development. One of the most alarming trends in armed conflicts is the forced recruitment of young children as active soldiers. Some are conscripted, others kidnapped or forced to join armed groups to defend their families. They are sometimes used as advance scouts or mine detectors. In cases of acute hunger and poverty, parents sometimes offer their children for service or, if marriage prospects are poor, encourage their daughters to become soldiers. An estimated 500,000 children are currently involved in armed conflicts around the world.

Article 23: Right to Work and Fair Pay for Work

Modern warfare often brutally uproots children because their families are forced to flee to neighbouring States or are internally displaced within their own countries. Of the world's estimated 22 million refugees and 30 million displaced people, half are children. Displacement has a profound physical, emotional and development impact on children and sharply increases their vulnerability. Wandering around as refugees, often separated from their families, these children are continually threatened by sudden attacks, shelling and landmines.

Rape and sexual exploitation are a continual threat in armed conflicts. Girls, in particular, are subjected to gender-based violence, such as sexual abuse and multilation, prostitution and trafficking. The widespread practice of rape by armed forces often has a tragic ripple effect that extends far beyond the immediate pain and degradation. Sexual abuse can lead to sexually transmitted diseases and HIV/AIDS infection. Rape victims who become pregnant are often ostracized by their families and communities and forced to abandon their unwanted babies. In such unbearable circumstances, many of these girls commit suicide out of despair.

In addition to the fragmenting of family and community, the breakdown of infrastructure and disruption of education due to armed conflicts have devastating long-term effects on the future of children. The destruction of schools and education networks represents one of the greatest development setbacks for countries affected by armed conflict. Missed education and most vocational skills take years to replace, making the overall task of post-conflict recovery even more difficult.

Since the 1990 World Summit on Children, the United Nations has been placed the plight of children affected by armed conflicts high on the international agenda. The United Nations report *Impact of Armed Conflict on Children* (1996) provided the first comprehensive assessment of the multiple ways in which children are abused and brutalised in the context of war. In 1997, in response to the urgent need for a public advocate on behalf of children's rights in situations of armed conflict, the Secretary-General appointed a *Special Representative for Children in Armed Conflict*. A working group is also drafting, an *Optional Protocol to the Convention on the Rights of the Child on Involvement of Children in Armed Conflicts*, which seeks to raise the minimum age of recruitment into armed forces to 18 and to specify measures for demobilisation and reintegration of child soldiers into society.

6. Human Rights and Conflicts

Today, some of the most serious threats to international peace and security are armed conflicts that arise, not among nations, but among warring factions within a State. Although situations of internal violence, they often spill over borders, endangering the security of other States and resulting in complex humanitarian emergencies. The human rights, abuses prevalent in internal conflicts are now among the most atrocious in the world. In 1996, there were 19 ongoing situations of internal violence around the world in which 1,000 people or more were killed. These so-called "high-intensity conflicts" cumulatively led to between 6.5 million and 8.5 million deaths. In the same year, there were also 40 "low-intensity conflicts", each causing between 100 and 1,000 deaths. Another 2 million deaths can be added to these figures if one includes situations of internal violence that had de-escalated in 1996.

The number of conflict-related is only a small indication of the tremendous amount of suffering, displacement and devastation caused by conflicts. Assaults on the fundamental rights to life are widespread—massacres, indiscriminate attacks on civilians, executions of prisoners, starvation of entire populations. Torture is common in internal conflicts, as are measures restricting people's freedom of movement—forcible relocations, mass expulsions, denial of the right to seek asylum or the right to return to one's home. Women and girls are raped by soldiers and forced into prostitution, and children are abducted to serve as soldiers. Tens of thousands of people detained in connection with conflicts "disappear" each year, usually killed and buried in secret, leaving their families with the torment of not knowing their fate. Thousands of others are arbitrarily imprisoned and never brought to trial or, if they are, are subject to grossly unfair procedures. Homes, schools and hospitals are deliberately destroyed. Relief convoys, which try to assist civilians by providing humanitarian aid, are attacked.

The denial of fundamental rights relating to employment, housing, food or the respect for cultural life and large-scale discrimination and exclusion from the decision-making processes of society are the root causes of many grave crises today. Armed conflicts clearly illustrate the indivisibility and interdependence of all human rights. The collapse of infrastructure and civic institutions under-mines the range of civil, economic, political and social rights. The rights to adequate health, housing, education, freedom of movement and expression, privacy and fair trial are only some of the fundamental rights and freedoms affected when hospitals and schools are closed, water and sanitation polluted, local administrations unable to function, and police and judicial systems shattered or corrupted. Government institutions often become increasingly militarised, with the armed forces assuming civilian policing functions and military courts trying civilians. Prolonged conflicts also affect rural areas; crops are destroyed, crippling productivity in subsistence farming and agriculture and leading to chronic food shortages, malnutrition and families. Ill health and poverty are often the most devastating long-term consequences of conflicts.

Human Rights and the Transition to Peace

The 1993 World Conference on Human Rights affirmed the crucial connection between international peace and security and the rule of law and human rights, placing them all within the larger context of democratisation and development. The need to reinforce these vital links has been highlighted by the sharp increase in bloody conflicts and man-made calamities in this decade.

The United Nations is increasingly combining efforts to prevent or end conflicts with measures aimed at reducing human rights abuses in situations of internal violence. Special emphasis is placed on ensuring the protection of minorities, strengthening democratic institutions, realising the right to development and securing universal respect for human rights. Preventing massive human rights violations from arising, responding to violations before they escalate into conflicts and controlling and resolving conflicts before they escalate further are central concerns of preventive action. In the context of preventive action and peacemaking, the Security Council and the Secretary-General, in carrying out his "good offices", are also assisted by the *Department of Political Affairs (DPA)*.

Recognising that human rights violations are frequently the root causes of conflict and humanitarian crises, the United Nations is making efforts towards strengthening its early warning capacity and response to conflicts by integrating human rights monitoring into peacekeeping operations, thus enhancing its ability to deal with allegations of human rights violations. The Office of the High Commissioner for Human Rights is developing close contacts with the United Nations departments, offices and programmes responsible for peacekeeping and for humanitarian assistance, in particular the *Department of Peacekeeping Operations (DPKO)*, DPA, the *Office for the Coordination of Humanitarian Affairs (OCHA)* and the *Office of the United Nations High Commissioner for Refugees (UNHCR)*.

The human rights programme is performing a crucial role not only in the United Nations early warning system, but also in post-conflict reconstruction, building mutual confidence and helping to re-establish a climate of understanding. The international community has recognised that protecting human rights in the aftermath of conflicts cannot be isolated from how the conflict is brought to an end. Experience in assisting countries in transition to democracy has shown how important the inclusion of human rights provision in peace or transitional agreements can be.

Article 24: Right to Rest and Leisure

In recent years, beginning with the El Salvador mission in 1990, a number of peacekeeping and other political operations have included a human rights component. A human rights field presence was part of the peace processes in Cambodia, El Salvador, Guatemala and Haiti. The International Civilian Mission in Haiti, for example, has been dedicated to verifying the respect for human rights since its inception in February 1993. After the return to constitutional order in October 1994, the Mission expanded its work to include the promotion of human rights, civic education. Commission and assists in the strengthening of the Haitian judicial and penal system.

The human rights missions in El Salvador and Guatemala demonstrate the crucial role of human rights in rebuilding trust and fostering a climate of reconciliation after armed conflict. In Guatemala, the *Human Rights Verification Mission (MINUGUA)* was deployed in 1994, two years in advance of the final peace agreement signed by the Government and the opposition front. The largest United Nations human rights verification mission ever mounted, with 13 regional and sub-regional offices and 245 international staff, MINUGUA's field presence is more extensive than that of many national institutions in Guatemala. In the past two years, the Mission has successively reported dramatic declines in verified complaints of torture, forced disappearances and arbitrary detention.

The High Commissioner for Human Rights has deployed human rights field operations in Burundi, Rwanda, the former Yugoslavia and the Democratic Republic of the Congo (formerly Zaire). In each case, following up allegations of violations and establishing a framework of respect for human rights were seen as part and parcel of the work of creating an atmosphere of trust in a post-conflict situation. This has been a vital lesson for the United Nations in the 1990s.

Article 25: Right to Adequate Standard of Living for Health and Well-being

Developing Fundamental Humanitarian Standards

Just as human rights are a key element in peacekeeping and peace-building efforts, the protection of human rights is also recognised as a priority in humanitarian operations. The United Nations is currently leading efforts to establish minimum humanitarian standards, seeking to identify fundamental rules of human rights and humanitarian standards, seeking to identify fundamental rules of human rights and humanitarian law that can be applied in all circumstances, in times of conflict, as well as in situations of mass exodus, for the protection of human rights. These efforts aim to provide the human rights framework necessary to find long-term solutions to the root causes of conflict and to prevent the excesses that make reconciliation so difficult. The United Nations urges national authorities to respect international human rights standards in such situations. But one of the most pressing, problems now in enforcing accountability of non-State actors committing crimes against humanity. For these reasons, the United Nations is incorporating human rights concerns into all aspects of its response to conflicts—from preventive action to humanitarian assistance.

For the United Nations, providing assistance to the victims of conflict is the supreme humanitarian task. Though not traditionally considered a human rights function, there is no doubt that the provision of food, medical care and basic education is a direct and tangible means of supporting the human dignity of the affected population. The human rights framework can also help to set the parameters and rules for the delivery of humanitarian assistance—ensuring the non-discriminatory treatment of those in need, and paying due regard to the special needs of women and children.

Refugees are particularly vulnerable to the loss of human right. The violation of fundamental rights is almost always the root cause of refugees flows. Displacement and forced migrant are intrinsically human rights issues, underlying related questions such as mass exoduses, the status of internally displaced persons and the right to return to their homes and communities. Since it began its work in 1951, UNHCR has always incorporated a human rights dimension into humanitarian action, particularly concerning the rights to asylum and non-forced repatriation. Its work has been used in the 1951 *Convention relating to the Status of Refugees* and its 1967 *Protocol*, which define the rights and duties of refugees. Durable solutions to these man-made catastrophes require sustained and concerted efforts towards reconstruction and reconciliation. The challenges of ensuring the sustainability of return extends far beyond the capacities of any single organisation and requires the creative collaboration of a variety of actors. For this reason, the High Commissioner for Human Rights and the High Commissioner for Refugees are expanding the cooperation of their offices, on both an informal and a formal basis, through the day-to-day contacts among the staff, at Headquarters and in the field. Their interaction, guided by a Memorandum of Understanding, includes joint meetings and projects, as well as facilitating the sharing of responsibilities by exchanging personnel and co-sponsoring staff training.

The Office of the United Nations High Commissioner for Human Rights also works closely with OCHA, the central Secretariat body responsible for coordinating United Nations humanitarian action. The increased collaboration between the two offices seeks to provide relief for victims of humanitarian disasters within an integrated framework of human rights law and humanitarian law. In order to ensure that their work is harmonised, the High Commissioner for Human Rights participates in the meetings of the Executive Committee on Humanitarian Affairs and the Inter-Agency Standing Committee, the main coordinating forums for developing humanitarian programmes and formulating strategies policies.

Article 26: Right to Education

A right-based Approach to Peace-building

Just as human rights forge vital links between peace, democracy and development, bringing the full weight of the United Nations human rights programme to bear can also facilitate the successful transition between peacekeeping operations and humanitarian emergency assistance to long-term peace-building and sustainable development. Societies that are emerging from civil conflict have particular needs in the area of human rights and economic development. The complexities of post-conflict situations require that special attention be given to repairing the large-scale damage inflicted on economic, health and educational infrastructures. But international development programmes can also contribute to healing the psychological scars of conflict. Strengthening respect for human rights through development contributes to a climate of confidence that helps a society regain its equilibrium.

Such a human rights framework is most effectively realised when United Nations operations oversees or implementing peace agreements incorporate human rights specialists, both in their monitoring capacity as human rights observers and as technical advisers, to help strengthen the administration of justice. The United Nations is developing a two-track approach in which immediate humanitarian assistance and long-term development assistance eventually converge, with human rights a crucial binding element in both. This means that the various actors, from international institutions developing projects to individuals operating in the field, must work together, aware of the common goals and mutual needs of the parallel programmes. As demonstrated in Cambodia, El Salvador, Haiti and Rwanda, work in the field demands a delicate mix of standard-setting, training, advice on laws and procedures, and funding. United Nations human rights experts assist in building an independent judiciary and in training police and security personnel in human rights standards for law enforcement. They also provide guidance in drafting press freedom laws, minority legislation or laws securing women's equality.

Without prescribing for any one society a preferred model of economic development or cultural organisation, the right-based approach to peace-building facilitates the growth of civil society. Human rights standards provide the impartial means through which reconciliation can be achieved. A human rights framework provides certain guarantees for justice and also protects against random retribution, establishing the parameters within which democratic societies can legitimately balance the interests of the victims against larger concerns for social harmony.

Breaking the Cycle of Impunity

Solving conflicts also means addressing past abuses, especially against the civilian population. A recurring theme that applies to all human rights abuses in conflicts is that again and again the members of armed groups kills, torture, rape or attack civilians with virtual impunity, apparently confident that they will never be called to account for their crimes. Impunity is a relatively new concept for an age-old phenomenon of injustice, namely, the absence of penalties or inadequacy of compensation for massive and grace violations of human rights. The manner in which a Government reacts to human rights violations committed by its agents, through action or omission, clearly shows the degree of its willingness to ensure effective protection of human rights. Very often, a Government's declared commitment to respect human rights is contradicted in practice by an alternating cycle of violations and impunity. In some cases, impunity is inscribed in legislation that examples perpetrators of human rights abuses from prosecution. In other cases, despite the existence of legal provisions for the prosecution of human rights violators, impunity continues in practice. Authorities often do not react to complaints filed by victims, their families or representatives, or to urgent appeals by United Nations special rapporteurs.

Problems related to the independent and impartial functioning of the judiciary have also encouraged impunity. Although Governments are under an obligation to initiate inquiries into allegations as soon as they are brought to their attention, in some countries impartial investigations are rarely conducted. In other cases, public inquiries are compromised, with light sentences imposed on perpetrators despite the gravity of the crimes committed. In particular, trials of members of the security forced before military courts are sometimes undermined by an ill-conceived *esprit de corps*. There are also instances where low-ranking officials are convicted of human rights violations or crimes, while those in positions of command escape responsibility. Often victims—and sometimes witnesses who assist in investigate efforts—are subjected to intimidation and death threats.

For this reason, the United Nations has intensified efforts to bring the perpetrators of such crimes to justice and break the cycle of impunity. Ensuring that individuals are held criminally responsible and published for committing serious human rights abuses is one of the most effective means of dealing with grave injustice and fostering necessary reconciliation. In countries where the justice system does not function properly, legislative reforms are required first, before the judiciary can effectively undertake investigations. In cases where violations warrant particular treatment because of their special nature or gravity, as with apartheid in South Africa, for example, Governments may establish special truth commissions adhering to the same requirements of independence, impartiality and competence as ordinary courts. The results of their investigations can be made public, and sometimes their recommendations are binding on the authorities.

Article 27: Right to Participate in the Cultural Life of the Community

The history of impunity parallels the struggle of civil society against authoritarian States. During the 1970s, the United Nations began to take action in the campaign against impunity after non-governmental organisations and human rights groups pioneered the creation of an international strategy to address the widespread problem. In the absence of an international criminal court, prominent "courts of opinion" sometimes filled an institutional gap in international human rights law. In the 1980s, the proliferation of "amnesty" laws proclaimed by military dictatorships anxious to arrange their own permanent impunity while still in power provoked a strong reaction from victims, who undertook legal campaigns to ensure that justice was done.

In the 1990s, with the end of the cold war and the restoration of democracy in many parts of the world, thc question of question of impunity within the context of national reconciliation became a matter of international concern. When, in the course of democratisation, the former victims took over the responsibility of the State, they often found themselves forced to moderate their initial commitment against impunity in the name of national reconciliation. But Inter-American Court of Human Rights, in a recent ground-breaking ruling, found that amnesty for the perpetrators of serious human rights violations was incompatible with the right of every individual to a fair hearing before an impartial and independent court.

Crimes Against Humanity

Genocide Refers to acts committed with intent to destroy, in whole or in part, a national, ethnical, racial or religious groups, by either killing or causing serious bodily or mental harm to members of the group. Genocide also includes deliberately imposing living conditions calculated to bring about the group's physical destruction, such as imposing measures intended to prevent births or forcibly transferring children of the group.

Crimes against humanity are acts deliberately committed as part of a widespread or systematic attack directed against any civilian population. Crimes include murder and extermination (the international deprivation of access to food and medicine, calculated to bring about the destruction of part of a population). Crimes against humanity also include the deportation or forcible transfer of people and inhumane imprisonment in violation of fundamental rules of international law. Persecution of any identifiable group or collectivity on political, racial, national, ethnic, cultural, religious, gender or other grounds is also universality, recognised as impermissible under international law. This applies also to the enforced disappearance of persons, the crime of apartheid and other inhumane acts accusing serious physical injury or great suffering.

War crimes are grave breaches of the 1949 Geneva Conventions. Serious violations of the laws and customs of war include intentionally directing attacks against the civilian population not taking direct part in hostilities or deporting the population, of an occupied territory; employing weapons, material and methods of warfare which cause superfluous injury or unnecessary suffering or which are inherently indiscriminate in violation of the international law of armed conflict, such as biological, chemical and nuclear weapons; sexual slavery, enforced prostitution, forced pregnancy, enforced, sterilization, or any other form of sexual violence; and the conscription or enlistment of children under the age of 15 years into armed forces or groups participating in hostilities.

In 1997, two experts of the Subcommission on Prevention of Discrimination and Protection of Minorities presented reports on impunity, one in relation to civil and political rights, the other concerning economic, social and cultural rights. The reports propose a draft "set of principles for the promotion and protection of human rights through action to combat impunity". The principles refer to victims' legal rights as obligations of society, particularly the right to know, the right to justice and the right to reparations. If adopted by the General Assembly, these guiding principles would provided the strategic framework for the international campaign against impunity.

Towards an International Criminal Court

In 1945, at the Tribunal of Nuremberg, which judged the accused was criminals of Nazi Germany, the international community pledged that "never again" would it allow monstrous crimes against humanity or genocide to take place. For nearly half a century, the United Nations has recognised the need for a world court to prosecute and punish persons responsible for crimes of international concern, such as genocide, crimes against humanity, war crimes and the crime of aggression. In 1948, the United Nations General Assembly adopted the *Convention on the Prevention and Punishment of the Crime of Genocide,* one day before adopting the Universal Declaration of Human Rights. In 1949, a Diplomatic Conference for the Establishment of International Conventions for the Protection of Victims of War, held in Geneva from 21 April to 12 August, adopted four Conventions, which codified the humanitarian action of soldiers in times of war. The four *Geneva Conventions*, outlined the humane treatment of wounded, sick or surrounding combatants, prisoners and civilians, and banned the wilful taking and killing of hostages. By 1951, these international treaties against genocide, war crimes and crimes against humanity had entered into force, establishing a body of law known as *International Humanitarian Law*. The United Nations directed the International Law Commission to draft a statute for an International Criminal Court *(see below)*. But for a long time disagreement among member States on the jurisdiction of such a court hindered any decisive development towards its creation.

The atrocities that occurred in the former Yugoslavia and Rwanda were widely seen as failures of the international community to intervene in time to prevent serious human rights violations. However, Yugoslavia and Rwanda are not unique as conflict areas where massive violations of human rights and international humanitarian law occurred. In recent decades, there have been many instances of crimes against humanity community in war for which no individuals have held accountable. In Cambodia in the 1970s, for example, the Khmer Rouge killed over 1 million people. In many countries around the world, massacres of civilians, including countless women and children, continue in this day.

International Criminal Tribunal for the Former Yugoslavia

In 1993, faced with widespread atrocities committed under the policy of "ethnic cleansing" during the Yugoslavia conflict between the Muslim, Serb and Crotian communities, the United Nations responded by setting up an international tribunal to bring the perpetrators of the crimes to justice. In May 1993, the Security Council, acting under Chapter VII of the United Nations Charter, created the *International Tribunal for the Prosecution of Persons Responsible for Serious Violations of International Humanitarian Law Committed in the Territory of the Former Yugoslavia since (1991)* (ICTY). The Tribunal highlighted the need for a permanent International Criminal Court to deal with such violations quickly and effectively.

The Tribunal, which has its seat at The Hague, the Netherlands, was given the broadest mandate of any international investigative body since the Nurmberg trials. Its statute defines the Tribunal's authority to prosecute individuals responsible for four groups of offences; grave breaches of the Geneva Conventions of 1949; violations of the laws or customs of war; genocide; and crimes against humanity. Moreover, because the Tribunal was established under Chapter VII of the United Nations Charter, the Security Council can use sanctions and other measures to enforce the Tribunal's decisions.

Article 28: Right to Social Order Assuring Human Rights

To date, 60 individuals have been publicly indicated, and 28 of the accused apprehended. Five trials are ongoing before the Tribunal and two verdicts have been handed down. One individual was found guilty of crimes against humanity and sentenced to 20 years' imprisonment. In other case, the accused pleaded guilty to war crimes and was sentenced to five years' imprisonment.

The Tribunal has primacy over national jurisdictions and can issue an international arrest warrant if national authorities are unwilling to cooperate or fail to serve the initial indictment of the accused individual. The Tribunal then notifies the Security Council to enforce the warrant. By the middle of 1998, eight international arrest warrants had been issued. The attempts by the Tribunal to arrest indicated persons currently living in the Federal Republic of Yugoslavia have been generally without success. The Government has consistently refused to meet its international obligations to hand over those indicated for war crimes and crimes against humanity.

Article 29: Responsibility to Community Essential to Free and Full Development of the Individual

International Criminal Tribunal for Rwanda

In Rwanda, civil strife and internal violence led to genocide on a vast scale. From April to July 1994, a systematically planned genocide by extremist Hutu militia claimed the lives of between 500,000 and 1 million persons. The main victims of this carnage were members of the Tutsi minority and moderate Hutus. The civil war forced hundreds of thousands of Rwandans to flee to neighbouring countries. By mid-July, more than 2 million Rwandan refugees were living in camps in Burundi, Tanzania and Zaire. Many thousands more had been displaced internally within the territory of Rwanda.

In November 1994, the Security Council created the *International Criminal Tribunal for the Prosecution of Persons Responsible for Genocide and Other Serious Violations of International Humanitarian Law Committed in the Territory of Rwanda* (ICTR). The Tribunal also prosecutors Rwandan citizens responsible for genocide, crimes against humanity and war crimes committed in the territory of neighbouring States between 1 January 1994 and 31 December 1994.

While the Hague Tribunal consists of two chambers and an appeals chamber, the International Criminal Tribunal of Rwanda, which has its seat in Arusha, Tanzania, recently added a third chamber to accelerate the procedural process. The Chief Prosecutor, based in The Hague, serves for both Tribunals.

The International Criminal Tribunal for Rwanda issued its first indictment in November 1995. By 1998, three trials had commenced. As of August 1998, 35 indicted individuals were in custory in Austria.

One of the most dramatic cases so far before the Tribunal has been the trial of Rwandan ex-Prime Minister Jean Kambanda. In his long-delayed, first appearance before the Tribunal on 1 May 1998, Kambanda pleaded guilty to the crime of genocide. This is the first time in history that an accused individual publicly confessed to the crime of genocide. The former Prime Minister was subsequently sentenced to life in prison, also the first-ever conviction of an individual for the crime of genocide.

In the related trial, the former of the Rwandan District of Taba, Jean-Pierre, Akayesu, was convicted on 2 September 1998 of genocide against Tutsi citizens, as well as for the crimes of rape, torture and other inhumane acts and subsequently sentenced to life imprisonment.

Establishment the International Criminal Court

The *International Criminal Court* (ICC) was finally created at the United Nations Diplomatic Conference of Plenipotentiaries on the Establishment of an International Criminal Court, held in Rome from 15 June to 17 July 1998. Delegations from 160 countries, 17 intergovernmental organisations, 14 United Nations specialised agencies and funds and 124 NGOs participated in the five-week landmark Conference. The Rome Statute of the International Criminal Court was adopted by a vote of 120 in favour to 7 against, with 21 abstentions. The treaty establishing the Court needs to be ratified by at least 60 States before entering into force.

The establishment of the Court makes it clear that the international community no longer tolerates violations of human rights without assigning responsibility. Unlike the ad hoc Tribunals, the Court provides a comprehensive mechanism for punishing perpetrators of genocide and other crimes against humanity. The assistance that at least some perpetrators of war crimes, crimes against humanity or genocide may be brought to justice acts as a significant deterrent, and in itself may provide incentives to end conflicts.

The ICC forges a missing link in the international legal order, for the *International Court of Justice (ICJ)* at The Hague handles only cases between States. The ICC will act on the principle of individual responsibility, applied equally and without exception to any individual throughout a governmental hierarchy or military chain of command. The appropriate punishment would apply to heads of State and commanding officers, as well as to low-ranking soldiers in the field or militia recruits. Especially in situations of internal violence, in countries where there is no legitimate Government, ensuring accountability at the international level is crucial.

The Court, comprising the Presidency, a Trial Division, a Trial Division, a Pre-Trial Division, an Appeals Division, the Office of the Prosecutor and the Registry, will be located at The Hague in the Netherlands, but may convene elsewhere if necessary. The Assembly of States parties elects the Court's Prosecutor and 18 Judges, for terms limited to nine years, with no two judges of the same nationality. The judges, in turn, elect the President. The Assembly of States parties will define the precise nature of the Court's relationship with the United Nations at a later stage. The maximum penalty the Court can impose is life imprisonment.

The International Criminal Court will complement national criminal courts, which should normally try alleged criminals within their jurisdiction. The Court is needed only when national institutions have collapsed due to conflict (as in Rwanda) or when a State is unwilling to try its own nationals (as in the former Yugoslavia). The Prosecutor has the power to investigate and bring to justice individuals who commit genocide, crimes against humanity, war crimes and the crime of aggression, once its definition has been finalised.

Article 30: Freedom from State or Other Interference in Any of the Above Rights

Since the Nuremberg Tribunal of 1945, the crime of aggression has been recognised as the supreme international offence, a crime against peace which often incites the most serious mass human rights violations, including genocide, war crimes and crimes against humanity. The statute of the International Criminal Court provides for criminal responsibility for the crime of aggression, which is generally understood to composite planning, preparing, ordering, initiating or carrying out an armed attack or waging a war aggression, in violation of international treaties. In such a scenario, only individual in positions of leadership who order or actively participate in such acts of aggression could incur in responsibility. However, there is still no consensus on a definition or legal precedent for individual criminal responsibility for acts of aggression, as opposed to wars of aggression. The crime of aggression will only be part of the Court's jurisdiction after a definition—sufficiently precise and clear to meet the high level of specify required of criminal law—has been determined.

Some of the international crimes discussed but not included in the Rome Statute were the illicit traffic in narcotic drugs and substances, terrorism, and crimes against United Nations and associated personnel. As there is no unified international legal system for addressing the crimes of drug trafficking and terrorism, delegates agreed that these crimes could be more effectively investigated and prosecuted by national authorities under existing international cooperation agreements rather than by the International Criminal Court. This was also the rationale for not including crimes against United Nations personnel, which have been on the rise in recent years. Since 1992, almost 300 civilians have lost their lives in the service of the United Nations. Military peacekeeping personnel are also often the targets of assault, kidnapping and murder. This alarming situation prompted the General Assembly to adopt, in 1994, the Convention on the Safety of United Nations and Associated Personnel, which affairs individual criminal responsibility for attacks against United Nations personnel.

Annex—1

UNITED NATIONS LANDMARKS IN HUMAN RIGHTS: A BRIEF CHRONOLOGY

26 June 1945	Signing of the *Charter of the United Nations* and the *Statute of the International Court of Justice*, in San Francisco.
21 June 1946	The Economic and Social Council (ECOSOC) established the *Commission on Human Rights* and the *Commission on the Status of Women*.
9 December 1948	The General Assembly adopts the *Convention on the Prevention and Punishment of the Crimes of Genocide* (entered into force 1931).
10 December 1948	The General Assembly adopts the *Universal Declaration of Human Rights*.
12 August 1949	The Diplomatic Conference for the Establishment of International Conventions for the Protection of Victim of War adopts four *Geneva Conventions*, relating to the Amelioration of the Condition of Wounded and Sick Members of Armed Forces in the Field and at Sea, the Treatment of Prisoners of War and the Protection of Civilians in Wartime (into force 1950).
20 December 1952	The General Assembly adopts the *Convention on the Political Rights of Women* (into force 1954).
1 August 1956	ECOSOC calls for periodic reports (every three years) on human rights and studies of specific

rights or groups of rights. This resolution represent the first call for reports from Members States, and was a precursor to the reporting requirements contained in the many subsequent human rights covenants.

20 November 1959 The General Assembly adopts the *Declaration of the Rights of the Child (see also 20 November 1989).*

21 December 1965 The General Assembly adopts the *International Convention on the Elimination of All Forms of Racial Discrimination* (into force 1969). This Convention provides for the establishment of the Committee on the Elimination of Racial Discrimination.

16 December 1966 The General Assembly adopts the *International Covenant on Economic, Social and Cultural Rights* (into force 3 January 1976) and the *International Covenant on Civil and Political Rights* with an *Optional Protocol* (into force 23 March 1976). This Convention provides for the establishment of the Human Rights Committee *(see also 28 May 1985).*

6 June 1967 ECOSOC adopts *resolution 1235 (XLII),* authorising the Commission on Human Rights and the Subcommission on Prevention of Discrimination and Protection of Minorities to examine information relevant to gross violations of human rights and fundamental freedoms.

7 November 1967 The General Assembly adopts the *Declaration on the Elimination of Discrimination against Women.*

13 May 1968 The International Conference on Human Rights adopts the *Proclamation of Tehran.*

26 November 1968 The General Assembly adopts the *Convention on the Non-Applicability of Statutory Limitations to War Crimes against Humanity* (into force 1970).

11 November 1969 The General Assembly adopts the *Declaration on Social Progress and Development.*

30 November 1973 The General Assembly adopts the *International Convention on the Suppression and Punishment of the Crime of Apartheid* (into force 1976).

9 December 1975 The General Assembly adopts the *Declaration on the Protection of All Persons from Being Subjected to Torture and Other Cruel, Inhuman or Degrading Treatment or Punishment.*

23 March 1976	With entry into force of the *International Covenant on Civil and Political Rights* and the *International Covenant on Economic, Social and Cultural Rights,* 10 years after being originally opened for signature *(see 16 December 1966)*, the *International Bill of Human Rights* becomes a reality *(see also 10 December 1948)*.
18 December 1979	The General Assembly adopts the *Convention on the Elimination of all Forms of Discrimination against Women* (into force 1981). The Convention provides for the establishment of the Committee on the Elimination of Discrimination against Women.
25 November 1981	The General Assembly adopts the *Declaration on the Elimination of All Forms of Intolerance and of Discrimination Based on Religion or Belief.*
10 December 1984	The General Assembly adopts of *Convention against Torture and Other Cruel, Inhuman or Degrading Treatment or Punishment* (into force 1987). The Convention provides for the establishment of the Committee against Torture.
28 May 1985	ECOSOC establishes the *Committee on Economic, Social and Cultural Rights,* responsible for monitoring the implementation of the *International Covenant on Economic, Social and Cultural Rights.*
4 December 1986	The General Assembly adopts the *Declaration on the Right to Development.*
9 December 1988	The General Assembly adopts the *Body of Principles for the Protection of All Persons under Any Form of Detention or Imprisonment.*
24 May 1989	ECOSOC adopts *Principles on the Effective Prevention and Investigation of Extralegal, Arbitrary and Summary Executions.*
20 November 1989	The General Assembly adopts the *Convention on the Rights of the Child* (into force 1990). The Convention provides for the establishment of the Committee on the Rights of the Child.
18 December 1990	The General Assembly adopts the *International Covenant on the Protection of the Rights of All Migrant Workers and Members of Their Families.*

18 December 1992	The General Assembly adopts the *Declaration on the Rights of Persons Belonging to National or Ethnic, Religious and Linguistic Minorities.*
25 May 1993	The Security Council adopts resolution 827 (1993), establishing an *International Criminal Tribunal for the Prosecution of Persons Responsible for Serious Violations of International Humanitarian Law Committed in the Territory of the Former Yugoslavia since 1991*, with its seat at The Hague in the Netherlands.
25 June 1993	The World Conference on Human Rights adopts the *Vienna Declaration and Programme of Action.*
20 December 1993	The General Assembly adopts resolution 48/41, establishing the post of *United Nations High Commissioner for Human Rights.*
5 April 1994	Mr. José Ayala Lasso of Ecuador assumes the post of first *United Nations High Commissioner for Human Rights.*
8 November 1994	The Security Council adopts resolution 955 (1994), establishing an *International Criminal Tribunal for the Prosecution of Persons Responsible for Genocide and Other Serious Crimes against Humanitarian Law Committed in Rwanda during 1994*, with its seat in Arusha, Tanzania.
23 December 1994	The General Assembly proclaims the *United Nations Decade for Human Rights Education (1995 2004).*
12 September 1997	Ms. Mary Robinson of Ireland becomes the second *United Nations High Commissioner for Human Rights.*
17 July 1998	The Diplomatic Conference of Plenipotentiaries adopts the *Rome Statute of the International Criminal Court*, establishing the International Criminal Court, with its seat at The Hague.

Annex—2

THE UNIVERSAL DECLARATION OF HUMAN RIGHTS: A SYNOPSIS

This abbreviated version of the 30 Articles of the Universal Declaration of Human Rights provides an overview of the principles rights and freedoms that are very person's birthright.

The first two articles are fundamental principles underlying all human rights, Articles 3 to 21 comprise civil and political rights. Articles 22 to 27 refer to economic, social and cultural rights. The last three articles provides a framework of solidarity safeguarding the universal enjoyment of all human rights.

Article 1	*Right to freedom and equality in dignity and rights*
Article 2	*Freedom from discrimination*
Article 3	*Right to life, liberty and security of person*
Article 4	*Freedom from slavery and servitude*
Article 5	*Freedom from torture or degrading treatment*
Article 6	*Right to recognition as a person before the law*
Article 7	*Right to equal consideration before the law*
Article 8	*Right to remedy through a component tribunal*
Article 9	*Freedom from arbitrary arrest or exile*
Article 10	*Right to a fair trial or public hearing*
Article 11	*Right to be considered innocent until proven guilty*
Article 12	*Freedom from interference with privacy, including home, family and correspondence*

Article 13	*Right to freedom of movement and residence in one's own country and to leave and return at will*
Article 14	*Right to asylum*
Article 15	*Right to a nationality and freedom to change it*
Article 16	*Right to marriage and protection of family*
Article 17	*Right to own property*
Article 18	*Freedom of belief and religion*
Article 19	*Freedom of opinion and information*
Article 20	*Right to peaceful assembly and association*
Article 21	*Right to participate in government and in free elections and to equal access to public service*
Article 22	*Right to social security*
Article 23	*Right to work and fair pay for work*
Article 24	*Right to rest and leisure*
Article 25	*Right to adequate standard of living for health and well-being*
Article 26	*Right to education*
Article 27	*Right to participate in the cultural life of the community*
Article 28	*Right to social order assuring human rights*
Article 29	*Responsibility to community essential to free and full development of the individual*
Article 30	*Freedom from State or other interference in any of the above rights*

Annex—3

INTERNATIONAL HUMAN RIGHTS INSTRUMENTS

There are over 60 international human rights instruments today, and some are listed below. The core human rights treaties, which have established treaty bodies to monitor their implementation, are marked with an asterisk. Also listed is the year of adoption of a treaty and, where applicable, the year it entered into force and the current status of ratifications, as of August 1998.

Charter of the United Nations (1945)

International Bill of Human Rights

Universal Declaration of Human Rights (1948)

International Covenant on Economic, Social and Cultural Rights (adopted 1996, entry into force 1976, 137 ratifications)*

International Covenant on Civil and Political Rights (adopted 1966, entry into force 1976, 140 ratifications)*

First Optional Protocol to the International Covenant on Civil and Political Rights, allowing individuals to submit complaints to the Human Rights Committee (adopted 1966, entry into force 1976, 92 ratifications)

Second Optional Protocol to the International Covenant on Civil and Political Rights, aimed at the abolition of the death penalty (adopted 1989, entry into force 1991, 33 ratifications)

Prevention of Discrimination

Declaration on the Elimination of All Forms of Racial Discrimination (1963)

International Convention on the Elimination of All forms of Racial Discrimination (1965, 1969, 150)*

International Convention on the Suppression and Punishment of the Crime of Apartheid (1973, 1976, 101)

Declaration on the Elimination of All Forms of Intolerance and of Discrimination Based on Religion or Belief (1981)

Declaration on the Rights of Persons Belonging to National or Ethnic, Religious and Linguistic Minorities (1992)

ILO Convention concerning Employment and Occupation Discrimination (1958, 1960)

UNESCO Convention against Discrimination in Education (1960)

UNESCO Declaration on Race and Racial Prejudice (1978)

Human Rights of Women

Convention on the Political Rights of Women (1952, 1954, 110)

Declaration on the Elimination of All Forms of Discrimination against Women (1967)

Declaration on the Protection of Women and Children in Emergency and Armed Conflict (1974)

Convention on the Elimination of All Forms of Discrimination against Women, (1979, 1981, 161)*

Declaration on the Elimination of Violence against Women (1993)

Right of the Child

Declaration on the Rights of the Child (1959)

Declaration on the Protection of Women and Children in Emergency and Armed Conflict (1974)

Declaration on Social and Legal Principles relating to the Protection and Welfare of Children, with Special Reference to Foster Placement and Adoption Nationally and Internationally (1986)

Convention on the Rights of the Child (1989, 1990, 191)*

Human Rights in the Administration of Justice

Declaration on the Protection of All Persons from Being Subjected to Torture and Other Cruel, Inhuman or Degrading Treatment on Punishment (1975)

Convention against Torture and Other Cruel, Inhuman or Degrading Treatment or Punishment (1984, 1987, 105)*

Basic Principles on the Independence of the Judiciary (1985)

Body of Principles for the Protection of All Persons under Any Form of Detention or Imprisonment (1988)

Principles on the Effective Prevention and Investigation of Extra-legal, Arbitrary and Summary Executions (1989)

Basic Principles for the Treatment of Prisoners (1990)

Declaration on the Protection of All Persons from Enforced Disappearances (1992)

Social Welfare, Progress and Development

Declaration on Social Progress and Development (1969)

Declaration on the Rights of Mentally Retarded Persons (1971)

Universal Declaration on the Eradication of Hunger and Malnutrition (1974)

Declaration on the Use of Scientific and Technological Progress in the Interests of Peace and for the Benefit of Mankind (1975)

Declaration on the Rights of Disabled Persons (1975)

Declaration on the Right of Peoples to Peace (1984)

Declaration on the Right to Development (1986)

International Convention on the Protection of the Rights of All Migrant Workers and Members of Their Families (1990)

Slavery, Servitude, Forced Labour and Similar Instruments and Practices

Slavery Convention (1926, 1927, 40)

Convention for the Suppression of the Traffic in Persons and of the Exploitation of the Prostitution of Others (1949, 1951, 72)

Protocol amending the Slavery Convention (1953, 1953, 59)

Supplementary Convention on the Abolition of Slavery, the Slave Trade, and Institutions and Practices Similar to Slavery (1956, 1957, 117)

War Crimes and Crimes Against Humanity, including Genocide

Convention on the Prevention and Punishment of the Crime of Genocide (1948, 1951, 125)

Convention on the Non-Applicability of Statutory Limitations to War Crimes and Crimes against Humanity (1968, 1970, 43)

Principles of international cooperation in the detection, arrest, extradition and punishment of persons guilty of war crimes and crimes and crimes against humanity (1973)

Humanitarian Law

Geneva Convention for the Amelioration of the Condition of the Wounded and Sick in Armed Forces in the Field (1949, 1950)

Geneva Convention for the Amelioration of the Condition of Wounded, Sick and Shipwrecked Members of Armed Forces at Sea (1949, 1950)

Geneva Convention relative to the Treatment of Prisoners of War (1949, 1950)

Geneva Convention relative to the Protection of Civilian Persons in Time of War (1949, 1950)

Protocol Additional to the Geneva Conventions of 12 August 1949, and relating to the Protection of Victims of International Armed Conflicts (Protocol I) (1977, 1979)

Protocol Additional to the Geneva Conventions of 12 August 1949, and relating to the Protocol of Victims of Non-International Armed Conflicts (Protocol II) (1977, 1978)

Nationality, Statelessness, Asylum and Refugees

Convention relating to the Status of Refugees (1951, 1954, 132)

Convention relating to the Status of Stateless Persons (1954, 1960, 44)

Convention on the Nationality of Married Women (1957, 1958, 66)

Protocol relating to the Status of Refugees (1966, 1967, 132)

Declaration on Territorial Asylum (1967)

Declaration on the Human Rights of Individuals Who Are Not Nationals of the Country in Which They Live (1985)

Right to Self-determination

Declaration on the Granting of Independence to Colonial Countries and Peoples (1960)

Freedom of Association

ILO Convention on Freedom of Association and Protection of the Right to Organise (1948, 1950)

ILO Convention on the Right to Organise and Collective Bargaining (1949, 1951)

Employment

ILO Convention concerning the Promotion of Collective Bargaining (1981, 1983)

ILO Convention concerning Employment Promotion and Protection against Unemployment (1988, 1991)

ILO Convention concerning Indigenous and Tribal Peoples in Independent Countries (1989, 1991)

Marriage, Family and Youth

Convention on Consent to Marriage, Minimum Age for Marriage and Registration of Marriages (1962, 1964, 47)

Right to Enjoy Culture, International Cultural Development and Cooperation

Declaration of the Principles of International Cultural Co-operation (1966)

Annex—4

UNITED NATIONS HUMAN RIGHTS MONITORING MECHANISMS

At the heart of the United Nations monitoring system are the two types of human rights monitoring mechanisms. The so-called conventional mechanisms refer to the specific committees formally established through the principal international human rights treaties. These "treaty bodies" monitor the implementation of the individual conventions by the State parties.

Over the years, the United Nations has also developed an independent an ad hoc system of fact-finding outside the treaty framework, which is referred to as extra-conventional mechanisms or "special procedures". Independent experts report in their personal capacity as special rapporteurs or as members of working groups.

Treaty Bodies (Conventional Mechanisms)

Treaty bodies have been set up for the six core United Nations human rights treaties to monitor States parties' efforts to implement the provisions of the international instruments.

The *Human Rights Committee* (HRC) monitors the implementation of the International Covenant on Civil and Political Rights. Composed of 18 independent experts of recognised competence in the field of human rights, the Committee was established when the Covenant entered into force in 1976. The First Optional Protocol, which entered into force together with the Covenant, authorises the Committee to consider also allegations from individuals concerning violations of their civil and political rights. The Committee is also concerned with the Second Optional Protocol on the Abolition of the Death Penalty.

The *Committee on Economic, Social and Cultural Rights* (CESCR) monitors the International Covenant on Economic, Social and Cultural Rights. Composed of 18 internationally recognised independent experts in the relevant fields, the Committee was established by the Economic and Social Council in 1985, nine years after the Covenant entered into force. Unlike the other communities, whose members are elected by the States parties to the respective convention and report to the General Assembly, the members of the Committee on Economic, Social and Cultural Rights are elected by ECOSOC, to which they report.

The *Committee on the Elimination of Racial Discrimination* (CERD) monitors the implementation of the International Convention on the Elimination of All Forms of Racial Discrimination. Composed of 18 independent experts, the Committee began its work when the Convention entered into force in 1969 and is the oldest treaty body.

The *Committee on the Elimination of Discrimination against Women* (CEDAW), composed of 23 independent experts, has monitored the Convention on the Elimination of All Forms of Discrimination against Women since 1981.

The *Committee against Torture* (CAT) monitors the Convention against Torture and Other Cruel, Inhuman or Degrading Treatment or Punishment. Composed of 10 independent experts, the Committee was established in 1987.

The *Committee on the Rights of the Child* (CRC), composed on 10 independent experts, has monitored the Convention on the Rights of the Child since 1991.

Special Procedures of the Commission on Human Rights (Extra-conventional Mechanisms)

The ad hoc nature of the special procedures of the Commission on Human Rights allows for a more flexible response to serious human rights violations than the treaty bodies. Experts entrusted with special human rights mandates act in their personal capacity and are variously designated as Special Rapporteur, Representative, Independent Expert or, when several experts share a mandate, Working Group. They examine, monitor and publicly report to the Commission either on human rights situations in specific countries and territories or on global phenomena that cause serious human rights violations worldwide. Certain special mandates are also entrusted to the Secretary-General or his Special Rapporteurs. While never originally conceived as a system, the nearly 50 country and thematic mechanisms that have been established thus for clearly constitute and function as an effective system of human rights protection.

Contrary Mechanisms

Currently, some 20 mandates monitor the human rights situation in specific countries, including Afghanistan, Burundi, Cambodia, the Democratic Republic of the Congo (formerly Zaire), Equatorial Guinea, Haiti, the Islamic Republic of Iran, Iraq, Myanmar, Nigeria, Rwanda, Somalia, Sudan and the former Yugoslavia.

The General Assembly was established a Special Committee to Investigate Israeli Practices Affecting the Human Rights of the Palestinian People and Other Arabs of the Occupied Territories.

Thematic Mechanisms

The General Assembly has established a Special Representative of the Secretary-General for Children in Armed Conflict.

The Commission on Human Rights has established a Special Representative of the Secretary-General on Internally Displaced Persons and has created a number of important thematic mandates on:

Arbitrary detention

Contemporary forms of racism, racial discrimination, xenophobia, and related intolerance

Effect of foreign debt on the full enjoyment of economic, social and cultural rights

Effects of illicit dumping to toxic wastes and dangerous products on the enjoyment of human rights

Enforced or involuntary disappearance

Extrajudicial, summary or arbitrary executions

Freedom of opinion and expression

Human rights and extreme poverty

Independence of judges and lawyers

Religious intolerance

Right to development

Right to education

Sale of children, child prostitution and child pronography

Structural adjustment policies

Torture

Use of mercenaries and the right of peoples to self-determination

Violence against women

The Subcommission on Prevention of Discrimination and Protection of Minorities has also established a number of thematic mechanisms.

There are Working Groups on:

Communication (the 1503 Procedure reviewing individual complaints)

Contemporary forms of slavery

Indigenous populations

Minorities

The Subcommission has also appointed Special Rapporteurs and Independent Experts to conduct studies, including:

Impunity concerning economic, social and cultural rights

Impunity concerning civil and political rights

Human rights dimension of population transfer

Human rights and income distribution

Traditional practices affecting the health of women and the girl child

Systematic rape and sexual slavery during armed conflict

Treaties, agreements and other arrangements between States and indigenous populations

Human rights and states of emergency

Privatisation of prisons

Freedom of movement

Human rights and terrorism

Human rights and scientific progress

Thematic mandates are also entrusted to the Secretary-General, at the level of either the Commission on Human Rights or the Subcommission, including:

Human rights in the context of HIV/AIDS

Human rights and forensic science

Human rights and mass exoduses

Human rights and terrorism

Rape and abuse of women in the areas of armed conflict in the former Yugoslavia

Reprisals against persons cooperating with United Nations human rights bodies